To the memory of

John L. Crockatt (1920–2022)

DOWN TO THE SEAS AGAIN

Coles was told by an old-timer that Cohoe *was 'unfit to go outside the Solent' and was just a 'toy yacht'.*

DOWN TO THE SEAS AGAIN

The post-war renaissance of voyaging under sail

RICHARD CROCKATT

Illustrated by
CLAUDIA MYATT

Lodestar Books

Published 2025 by
Lodestar Books
71 Boveney Road, London, SE23 3NL, United Kingdom

lodestarbooks.com

A CIP catalogue record for this book
is available from the British Library

ISBN 978-1-907206-66-5

Typeset by Lodestar Books in Adobe Jenson Pro and Gill Sans MT

Printed in Wales by Gomer Press

All papers used by Lodestar Books are sourced responsibly

MIX
Paper | Supporting
responsible forestry
FSC
www.fsc.org
FSC® C114687

CONTENTS

INTRODUCTION

This book is about the generation of small boat sailors in Britain whose main achievements took place between 1945 and the mid 1960s. These included circumnavigations of the world as well as Atlantic crossings, and a variety of distances and destinations between. Some voyages were full of drama, others were simply (or perhaps not so simply) supremely competent feats of seamanship.

All in one way or another pushed boundaries, even if few records were broken or indeed aimed at. In most cases the voyages were carried out without the glare of media attention, but to devotees of small boat sailing the names of the crews and boats still resonate powerfully: Eric and Susan Hiscock (*Wanderer III*), Peter and Anne Pye (*Moonraker*), Adlard Coles (*Cohoe*), Edward Allcard (*Temptress* and *Sea Wanderer*), Humphrey Barton (*Vertue XXXV*), Stanley Smith, Colin Smith, and Charles Violet (*Nova Espero*), George and Isabel Millar (*Truant, Serica, Amokura*), Ann Davison (*Felicity Ann*), Patrick Ellam and Colin Mudie (*Sopranino*), Miles and Beryl Smeeton (*Tzu Hang*), John Guzzwell (*Trekka*).

The experiences of these sailors conjure up a particular moment in the history of small boat voyaging. Most were born in the first two decades of the twentieth century and learned their sailing between the wars. Though several served in the Navy or related services, the war brought them a sudden enforced abstinence from pleasure sailing which stoked an appetite for a new start once the war was over.

Adlard Coles was one of the first yachtsmen afloat again. Having gained permission from the Admiralty to launch as soon as hostilities in Europe were over in order to prepare a new edition of his book *Creeks and Harbours of the Solent*, he observed the Portsmouth celebrations of VE Day at a distance from the comfort of his yacht at anchor across the Solent in Wootton Creek. This moment was the prelude to two intensive decades of ocean racing and cruising for Coles, besides the founding of the publishing company which bears his name and remains a leader in the nautical field.

Eric Hiscock was as eager as Coles to resume sailing but bemoaned the fact that when the war ended his boat, *Wanderer II*, required an extensive refit. In the summer of 1946 he jumped at the offer to go cruising with a friend, Roger Pinckney, 'who had organised things better'. Within a few years the Hiscocks had commissioned a new boat, *Wanderer III*, and embarked on the first of their circumnavigations and a lifetime of ocean cruising. George Millar was another who couldn't wait to put the war behind him. After war service, featuring escape from German captivity and service behind enemy lines with the French resistance, George Millar left England in the early summer of 1946 with his wife Isabel and sailed via the French inland waterways to the Mediterranean and on to Greece. It was the first of a series of extensive cruises in European waters over the next two decades. That same summer Peter and Anne Pye cruised to southwest Ireland and to Spain and Denmark the following years, preludes to their two decades of ocean sailing. The Smith brothers spoke for a generation when they described *Nova Espero*, built by their own hands in 1948, as 'the realization of years of wartime dreaming'.

There is a striking clustering of voyages at the turn of the 1940s and 50s. The press of voyages in such a short space of time suggests there was something in the postwar air, compounded of a hunger for new opportunities and a desire to escape the fallout of war, including rationing and austerity. It could be described as the nautical equivalent of the postwar baby boom – an urge to put the past behind them and build new futures. In at least one case the thing to be escaped was the new Labour government in Britain. Dr Peter Pye had no wish to become an employee of the National Health Service and settled in 1948 for a life of voyaging in *Moonraker*. Edward Allcard had no obvious political agenda but regularly fulminated against bureaucracy and red tape. He dedicated the account of his second Atlantic Crossing, *Temptress Returns*, to 'that elusive thing THE FREEDOM OF THE INDIVIDUAL'. Ann Davison and her husband Frank had spent the war trying to restore an old fishing trawler with a view to sailing the world and were determined after the war to 'clear out... to somewhere where private enterprise was not regarded as a crime'. At the other end of the political spectrum, the Smith brothers, having spent the war in the RAF, espoused a communitarian ethic and aimed to establish a peace colony in Canada. In the event, they built *Nova Espero* and did a double Atlantic crossing, but when other life plans intervened the peace colony idea fell away.

Try as they might to escape the past, however, these voyagers encountered the aftermath of war at every turn. The straitened conditions of the time help to account for the sometimes primitive and shoestring, but undeniably uplifting, character of these early postwar adventures. Boatbuilding was hamstrung by a lack of decent timber and other materials such as lead for keels. While some new products such as plywood and new types of glue became available, high prices were always a problem. The big picture was of disruption to the economy caused by war, rationing of a wide range of products and materials, and limited household incomes which meant a delay in the resumption of normal patterns of demand and supply.*

It took drive and determination to fit out a small boat for cruising in such circumstances. As one of the first yachtsmen afloat after the war Adlard Coles was in a particularly good position to observe its effects. Night sailing was still forbidden, there were numerous restricted areas, and rationing was in force, which meant that Coles was dependent in his early cruises on his wife sending ration coupons and sometimes food parcels by post to selected ports for him to pick up. He records that in the summer months after VE day troop ships and hospital ships were common sights on the south coast. A full year after the end of the war, anchored off the Dorset coast and rowing ashore to go for a walk, he found notices reading 'Keep off – Danger. Mines.' The water close to the shore was strewn with litter: 'bottles, tins, ammunition cases, wires, all sorts of strange objects.'

Nor could the effects of war be escaped by 'going foreign': rather the reverse. On a cruise to the Channel Islands and Northern France in autumn 1946 Adlard Coles records the devastation inflicted by the Germans on lighthouses in France and the widespread damage on the Channel Islands. On the tiny island of Alderney 'the German fortifications remained and in some parts the land mines had not been cleared and there were still notices in German to be seen.' He was sur-

* These conditions are well described in Nicholas Gray, *Hillyard: The Man, His Boats, and Their Sailors*, Lodestar Books, 2021, pp.100-1.

prised to find how many buildings had been damaged, 'many apparently wantonly'. Eric Hiscock describes his first postwar visit to Brest, where there was still great difficulty in persuading people to inhabit the new town built to replace the bombed-out prewar centre. In Italy during his Mediterranean cruise in 1952, in search of someone who could speak English, Charles Violet encountered a former prisoner of war who had been interned in Britain and Canada and whose motley accent reflected the influence of his stay in both places.

Perhaps the fullest picture of the war's aftermath comes from the first two voyages of the Millars, undertaken in 1946 and 1950. They encountered the human and physical costs of the war at every turn in their wanderings through France and the Mediterranean. Their knowledge of languages and compulsive socialising with a variety of people gave them unrivalled access to the social life of the countries they passed through – unrivalled at least among British sailors of their generation.

The wider background to these postwar ventures was the struggle in Britain and elsewhere to reestablish some sort of normality in conditions which were often grim yet contained seeds of hope and aspiration. It is tempting to think that the British public experienced the end of the war as a dramatic moment but in all probability, as one historian put it, 'most people were neither depressed nor ecstatic'. In that respect the mood in the summer and autumn of 1945 reflected the spirit in which the war had been fought all along, which was one of grim determination to complete a task which had been forced on them. Sheer relief, a sense of satisfaction in a job done, and a desire to move on were uppermost. The result of the election in July 1945 spoke volumes about the mixture of feelings in the nation at large on achieving victory. Instead of Churchill being retained in power, in what seemed to many a brutal and unaccountable turn of events, the wartime hero was cast aside in favour of the personally colourless Labour party leader, Clement Attlee. Yet the programme of his party spoke to the pent-up frustrations and aspirations of millions of voters who believed the sacrifices of war demanded something better for the future.

There was also, despite (or perhaps because of) the onset of the atomic age, a strain of idealism which manifested itself in schemes for international peace and cooperation. The establishment of the United Nations Organization was the most prominent and wide-ranging of these but the Smith brothers' plan for a peace colony, albeit still-born, showed that the same impulse could assume more local and radical forms. The onset of the Cold War and in particular the advent of the nuclear era soon buried much of this idealism under clouds of suspicion and fear.

While it was rare for the postwar voyagers to register the impact of wider political events directly, there are exceptions which are of interest to the historian of this period. Peter Pye (like nearly all his fellow voyagers) was generally vague about years and dates but sometimes in passing he recorded events in the wider world which enable the historian to get an accurate fix and establish a timeline of a voyage. Among his sailing contemporaries George Millar was unusually politically aware and conveyed the atmosphere of certain key conflicts of the postwar period in his cruising narratives, notably the Greek Civil War in the late 1940s and France's long and bloody conflict over Algeria in the 1950s and early 1960s. In general, however, political events in the wider world were a distant backdrop for this generation of sailors, as indeed they probably are for most bluewater sailors, whose perspectives tend to be determined by the fluid medium of the oceans rather than the boundaries of nation states.

* * *

From a longer perspective this decade and a half marked the swansong of centuries-old maritime traditions. Boats were still made of wood, navigation was by compass and sextant, many boats were engineless, speed was measured by trailing log and depth by lead-line. Radios were limited in range, if indeed they were carried, and safety equipment was primitive by comparison with now. Independence and self-sufficiency were a minimum requirement, a given, not a matter of bravado. Of course, these conditions did not end in 1960; they continued through the 1960s until, during the 1970s, fibreglass and electronic navigation were well on the way to replacing traditional materials and methods. However, an important change was already beginning to make itself felt by the beginning of the 1960s which can be broadly defined by the word 'publicity'. A growing preoccupation with records and racing coupled with media coverage and sponsorship, whether of individual sailors or races, brought a new element into small boat voyaging.

From this point of view the 1960s are a transitional decade. The heroic achievements of Francis Chichester, Alec Rose, and Robin Knox-Johnston, which in distance covered surpassed that of many of the figures described in this book, represent continuity with the past in that they too sailed in wooden boats and navigated in the traditional way; but the global voyages of this trio also look forward to the new era of publicity. Symbolic of this is Francis Chichester's 1962 east-west Atlantic 'race' in which, sailing against the clock rather than other boats, he sought successfully to improve on his winning time in the 1960 single-handed transatlantic race. In the 1962 crossing he carried a radio transmitter/receiver with the express purpose of communicating with the *Guardian* newspaper which reported daily on his progress. For his epoch-making 1966-67 circumnavigation in *Gipsy Moth IV* along the route of the old tea clippers the same arrangements were made, with the addition of reports to the *Sunday Times*. There is a direct line from this to the webcam of today relaying conditions aboard minute by minute in real time. Two years later it was the *Sunday Times* which sponsored the first single-handed non-stop round-the-world race which saw Robin Knox-Johnston triumphant in *Suhaili*. The era of the large-scale sponsored sailing event was born.

The issue is not the relative merit of the 1950s voyages over those that came later. As is always the case, the achievements of one generation rest in part on those who came before or, as Isaac Newton famously put it, 'I have been able to see so far because I have stood on the shoulders of giants.' In preparing *Suhaili* for the rigours of the Southern Ocean Knox-Johnston consulted, among other authorities, Eric Hiscock's *Cruising under Sail*. The Hiscocks had no ambition to be the first or fastest. By the time of the great circumnavigations of the late 1960s Hiscock and his wife had already completed two leisurely circuits of the world besides other long-distance cruises. Chichester most certainly did seek to break records. His goal in 1966-7 was to challenge the speed record of the clipper ships in which he succeeded beyond expectation, completing his circumnavigation with only one stop, another historic achievement. His 14,000 miles from Britain to Australia was the longest continuous solo passage to date. Knox-Johnston likewise set his sights on new and unprecedented goals. The Golden Globe single-handed race of 1968-9, which Knox-Johnston won as the sole finisher, was designed to capitalise on the ambitions of sailors from several countries to be the first to sail non-stop round the world. Alec Rose's circumnavigation, which took place between the Chichester and Knox-Johnston voyages, harked back to the earlier style, though he gained much, including a knighthood, from the growing public interest in such voyaging.

The new element in these and comparable voyages lay partly in the aims that (with the exception of Rose) were avowedly competitive, and partly in the surrounding culture. By the mid-1960s long-distance sailing in small boats was news. It was one of the frontiers of achievement still open to adventurers and there was a ready public appetite for the dramas which surrounded such feats. The intensity which could be aroused by the ambition to succeed in this field was clearly visible in the fate of Donald Crowhurst who, going far beyond his and his boat's capacities, entered the 1968 Golden Globe race and was lost at sea, after falsifying his daily positions to appear much further on than he really was. Ten years earlier it is doubtful whether the public would have cared enough to generate such inflated and potentially dangerous ambition in individual sailors.

The postwar voyages evoke different emotions and associations. There was indeed media coverage of some, generally when they were complete or nearing completion; exceptionally, however, Eric Hiscock records that his departure from the Isle of Wight in late summer 1952 on a voyage around the world was announced on the BBC six o'clock news. The Hiscocks made a film of their second circumnavigation (1959-62) at the behest of, and with film stock provided by, the BBC. This reflected the interest aroused by their first and also the spread of television in households across the UK during the 1950s, but the approach was low key. The Hiscocks never achieved – and certainly did not seek – the level of public recognition accorded to Chichester, Rose or Knox-Johnston, least of all knighthoods.

The nomadic wanderings of Miles and Beryl Smeeton from the mid 1950s to the late 1960s still challenge belief in the range and in the heroic level of the exploits they undertook but, like many of the voyagers covered in this book, their reputations were barely noticed by the general public. In part this was because they deliberately kept their plans quiet. John Guzzwell took the same approach, which partly explains why his achievement as the first Briton to sail solo around the world has rarely been adequately acknowledged. Exceptionally, there was intense interest in Ann Davison's 'Atlantic epic' since she was a woman and would be the first to make the crossing solo, though she herself disavowed concern with this aspect of the voyage: 'it did not interest me in the least'. Edward Allcard gripped the attention of the world's media when on the last leg of his return across the Atlantic in 1951 he discovered a stowaway aboard, a highly attractive young woman who had stolen on board at the Azores and sailed with him to Casablanca. Newspapers vied with each other in imagining any number of scenarios. Ever the gentleman, however, and unconcerned with fame, Allcard continued his voyaging as before, mostly out of the limelight. His appearance on the BBC's *Desert Island Discs* in 1955 gave him a moment in the sun but scarcely influenced the course of his life.

For the most part media attention in the 1950s was sporadic. The Smith brothers' experience on their arrival home after their crossing from New York to Yarmouth, Isle of Wight in 1949 was not untypical: intense local interest but, as far as wider coverage was concerned, famous for a day. The experience was more or less repeated two years later when Stanley Smith and Charles Violet reached New York after *Nova Espero*'s second crossing.

Communication with home when under way, such as it was, came down to hailing passing ships and asking them to 'report us to Lloyds of London', a common practice among vessels crossing the oceans. It was not unusual for yachts to establish their positions from passing steamers if they had been unable to take sun sights for several days. Needless to say, such contacts were chance occurrences and could not be relied on for day to day navigation or communication. For extensive periods these voyagers made do with dead reckoning. For practical purposes they were on their own once they left the land.

Sponsorship or endorsement from manufacturers of equipment was of marginal significance. In 1951 Stanley Smith and Charles Violet sailed the diminutive *Nova Espero* from Yarmouth, Isle of Wight, to New York, carrying with them some goods with the aim of promoting British industry in the year of the Festival of Britain, but the expected payoff failed to materialize when they reached their destination, at least as far as financial return was concerned. The voyages described in this book were essentially private ventures. All the skippers published accounts of them in article and book form but newspaper reports were generally one-off items, not the result of prearranged tie-ins or sponsorship.

* * *

For all the common ground between these voyagers – which comes down to a love of the sea, seamanship and a spirit of adventure – there is clearly no such thing as a fixed nautical type. Even on the seamanship side there is great variation. The Smeetons set off across the Atlantic before they knew much about offshore sailing but proved to be remarkably resourceful in a crisis. Much the same is true of the Millars. Ann Davison confessed that 'the fact that I knew nothing about boats, very little about sailing, and was terrified of the sea was no deterrent to a full-scale production of a dream'. She may have been exaggerating but not by a huge amount; in the event she went on to complete a memorable passage. As it happens, like Francis Chichester she was an experienced pilot long before she took up sailing, which indicated native resourcefulness as well as an ability to master technical skills.

At the other extreme, Eric Hiscock had an encyclopaedic knowledge of all aspects of sailing, rigging, and managing a voyage in a way which optimized the available resources, and he clearly enjoyed the cruising life. His books became stock manuals for a generation of sailors. Most were published by the august Oxford University Press and contained a huge amount of detail, including numerous photographs (mostly his own), and drawings. If there was a cruising 'establishment' in the 1950s and 1960s, Eric Hiscock was its key representative by virtue not only of his cruising achievements but of his ability to explain what it was all about.

Edward Allcard wore his knowledge rather more lightly but possessed extensive sailing experience, including a solo return voyage to Norway just before the war when he was still in his twenties. He was trained as a naval architect and, in common with Humphrey Barton, was also a marine surveyor. Both made extensive use of their skills in modifying, re-rigging, and in Allcard's case rebuilding, various craft, and both owed their survival at moments of crisis to their expertise. The Smith brothers came from a nautical family which included a boatbuilder and a lifeboat coxswain, so it was perhaps inevitable that they should build their own boat and take naturally to adventuring. John Guzzwell came from a line of fishermen and seamen, sailed with his family to South Africa at a young age, and devoured the literature of the sea from his teenage years. Once the idea of a long ocean voyage took hold of him he was single-minded in addressing the practical challenges, which started with building his own boat.

So far as personality type is concerned there were dreamers, pragmatists, driven individuals, no-nonsense military types, or various combinations of these. Some lived highly organised lives at sea while others were more relaxed. Even risk-taking, which lies at the heart of adventuring, was not uniformly expressed. The Hiscocks look positively staid beside the Smiths, the Smeetons, Edward Allcard, or Humphrey Barton who seem on occasion close to the edge. Adlard Coles was as competent an organizer and manager as Hiscock but had a driving dare-devil streak. The irrepressible Smeetons seem larger than life, like something out of a *Boy's Own* adventure annual. So far as extent of voyaging is concerned the Millars could hardly compete with the other voyagers but their aristocratic, edgy personalities lend a unique quality to their adventuring. Patrick Ellam and Colin Mudie were inveterate adventurers but also the ultimate technicians who calculated everything down to the last 't', completing an almost faultless Atlantic crossing in what many regarded as the most unlikely of craft. Peter and Anne Pye, along with Ellam and Mudie, had the distinction, Humphrey Barton once remarked, of having enjoyed almost every moment of their sailing. Their voyages were conducted without disasters, breakages, or untoward incidents. John Guzzwell possessed an enviable combination of technical skill in all facets of seamanship, calmness under pressure, and sheer enjoyment of life. Ann Davison was acutely aware of being a woman in a largely man's world, but held to a very simple philosophy which enabled her to disregard any stereotypes or restrictions on her ambitions. 'The only way to live', she wrote, 'is to have a dream green and growing in your life; anything else is just existing and a waste of breath.'

Individualists they may have been but they had in common certain stereotypically British traits of reserve and a tendency to understatement. Flights of rhetoric and colourful descriptive prose which feature in the writings in particular of Edward Allcard, Peter Pye, and Miles Smeeton did not extend, by and large, to self-examination. We learn a lot about their approach to voyaging but less about their inner feelings, doubts and fears. Where these are alluded to, as for example in the case of Ann Davison, we are never quite sure how to take them. Descriptions of how she came over in person, which generally convey the impression of a steady, self-contained character, do not always tally with the more fragile image she projects of herself in her books. Eric Hiscock confessed to a dread of bad weather but one could always be sure that such fears would be firmly put in their place when the chips were down. The same applied to Humphrey Barton. Above all what these sailors shared was a reluctance to make a fuss about feelings, fears, or anything else. Hiscock's dedication of *Cruising Under Sail* can stand as a motto for a generation: 'To Roger A. P. Pinckney, one-time Commodore of the Royal Cruising Club, *who taught me and many others how to cruise without fuss*.' (Italics in the original.)

These postwar voyagers also showed a cooperative spirit. Most were closely aware of the others' doings, and some life-long friendships were formed. Eric Hiscock sailed with Adlard Coles regularly just after the war when his own boat was still refitting, and he also helped Coles with the editing of *The Yachtsman* magazine. The Hiscocks and the Pyes encountered each other several times during *Wanderer III*'s first circumnavigation between 1952 and 1955. The Pyes also became close friends of the Smeetons. In *The Sea is for Sailing*, Peter Pye's account of *Moonraker*'s second ocean voyage, Pye recalls a chance meeting with Miles Smeeton in Fambridge, Essex at a time when the Smeetons had not yet taken up ocean sailing, but were looking for a boat to sail back to British Columbia where they had settled after the war. They found *Tzu Hang* in Dover but before they set off, Smeeton said to Pye: 'why don't you come out to British Columbia and spend the winter with us?' which they accordingly did. Chance also brought the Smeetons into contact with John Guzzwell in San Francisco while they were on passage to New Zealand and Guzzwell was in the early stages of a planned circumnavigation. They quickly became friends. *Tzu Hang* and *Trekka* sailed virtually in company across the Pacific to New Zealand, island hopping along the way. Guzzwell then mothballed his boat in New Zealand and joined them as crew on *Tzu Hang* for the fateful first attempt to round Cape Horn, after which he resumed his solo circumnavigation in *Trekka*.

On their return from their visit to the Smeetons in British Columbia, having heard and read so much about Ann Davison, the Pyes made a point of visiting her in Florida, where she was living after the Atlantic crossing, and were hugely impressed by her. Long before that Atlantic voyage Davison had received a letter from Humphrey Barton in response to the publication of her book *Last Voyage*, an account of her and her husband's experiences on a seventy-foot fishing trawler which was wrecked in the channel, with the death of her husband. Once she had conceived the idea of an ocean voyage, she wrote to Barton for advice which he gladly offered. He helped her find a boat and advised on the preparation of *Felicity Ann* for her Atlantic crossing.

Barton also intersected with Edward Allcard in a number of ways, not least because he had previously owned two of Allcard's boats. They met in New York in 1950 following their east-west crossings of the Atlantic, and again twenty years later in Freeman's Bay, Antigua, and became good friends. Eric Hiscock wrote the introduction to Smith and Violet's account of their 1951 Atlantic crossing, *The Wind Calls the Tune*, expressing deep admiration for that pair whose character and approach were so different from Hiscock's own. Kevin O'Riordan, Humphrey Barton's crew on *Vertue XXXV*'s 1950 Atlantic adventure, wrote to Miles Smeeton before he and his wife embarked on their first long passage that 'you will be perfectly all right provided that you have a buoyant boat, plenty of water, and don't mind being alone for weeks and weeks.' It seemed, Smeeton reflected, that 'all three conditions were fulfilled.' Even the Millars, who generally moved in different circles, took advantage of the experience of fellow British yachtsmen, not least Adlard Coles who advised them about anchorages in northern France.

In short, there was something like a community of voyagers who learned from each other as well as seeking and enjoying each other's company. The same applies today with the important difference that the community was so much smaller then. This too lends the period a distinctive character.

* * *

And what of their boats? They were as varied as the characters who sailed in them, though there are some interesting connections and contrasts. All were under thirty-six feet with the exception of the Smeetons' ketch-rigged *Tzu Hang* which was forty-six feet on deck, and all three of the Millars' boats which were around fifty feet. Of their designers the name which crops up more than once is Jack Laurent Giles, founder in 1927 of Laurent Giles naval architects of Lymington, which is still a flourishing concern. Whenever Laurent Giles is mentioned the Vertue class come to mind, combining classic lines – beautiful sheer, moderate beam, long deep keel – with sea-keeping ability and performance. Laurent Giles produced numerous boats of this type from the 1930s through the 1960s in various sizes from the twenty-five foot Vertue itself, to the forty-six foot *Dyarchy* (1938), the Hiscocks' *Wanderer III* (1951), and Humphrey Barton's 35 ft *Rose Rambler* (1962). It is sometimes said that the Bristol Channel pilot cutter is the basis for these designs, but the crucial difference lies in the moderately cutaway forefoot in the Laurent Giles underwater profile, which makes them much handier in stays than the straight-stemmed pilot cutter, as well as lighter in displacement.

Humphrey Barton had a hand in the publicizing of the Vertue when he made his famous east to west Atlantic crossing in 1950 in *Vertue XXXV* by the northern route, but he had already made extensive cruises in the late 1930s in earlier versions of the design. From 1936 he was employed at Laurent Giles as a marine surveyor and had a particularly close knowledge of the firm's designs, of which he was to own two more. He probably did more than any individual to make them famous. His only rival in this regard might be Eric Hiscock whose twenty-four foot *Wanderer II*, launched in 1938, was a Laurent Giles design very similar to a Vertue, though gaff rigged and a foot shorter. In her he cruised the British isles extensively as well as making a passage with his wife to the Azores. The thirty-foot *Wanderer III*, which was essentially an extended Vertue, sailed into the history books with the Hiscocks as a result of their two circumnavigations in the 1950s, and became the basis of the Wanderer class of boats.

Laurent Giles also, however, drew some revolutionary designs drawing on aircraft construction techniques, including the fifty-five foot *Gulvain* which featured reverse sheer and an aluminium hull. With Humphrey Barton as skipper she was first home in the 1950 transatlantic race and had several other notable wins. The flat-sheered, light-displacement *Myth of Malham* won the Fastnet races of 1947 and 1949. It was with such designs in mind that Patrick Ellam approached Jack Giles in late 1949 with a request that he draw a small, light-displacement craft which would be capable of taking him across the Atlantic. Ellam had been experimenting for months with ultra-light displacement dinghies in passages across the English channel with a view to testing his theory that a very small boat of the size and weight of a dinghy could be made safe in any weather and undertake ocean voyages. The result was the diminutive, reverse-sheered *Sopranino* which not only took Ellam and Mudie across the Atlantic but became the model for the Junior Offshore Group (JOG) concept of racing yachts. Inspired by the example of *Sopranino*, John Guzzwell chose Laurent Giles as designer for *Trekka*, another reverse sheer craft of only twenty-one feet. Guzzwell built her himself and went on to complete a solo circumnavigation several years before Chichester's more famous voyage.

An idea of the standing of Jack Giles can be gained from an incidental comment by Peter Pye, whose *Moonraker* was at the opposite extreme of design and build. She was a twenty-nine-foot Polperro fishing boat, rigged as a gaff cutter, straight-stemmed, beamy, with high bulwarks, and deep of draught. Pye described her as a ship that 'looks like a box and sails like a witch, built in the year 1896 by the eye of a craftsman, in a shape that might bring tears to the eyes of Jack Giles but would please those of Captain Joshua Slocum.'

For the rest, the postwar voyagers' boats are a mélange of styles and builds. Edward Allcard's *Temptress* and *Sea Wanderer*, respectively a yawl and a ketch, were fairly heavy displacement craft built in the early twentieth century, both of which he modified extensively for voyaging. The Millars started out in 1946 with a heavy displacement Looe lugger, moved then to a pencil thin Robert Clark designed cruiser-racer, and from there to the beautiful fifty-foot Fred Shepherd designed yawl *Amokura* which is still in commission today.

The Smeetons' bermudan-rigged ketch *Tzu Hang* was forty-six feet and had been heavily built of teak in Hong Kong. She became their home for over twenty years. The Hiscocks and Pyes were also liveaboards for extended periods but were evidently content with more confined quarters. After the war Adlard Coles initially favoured relatively light displacement double-enders of Scandinavian Tumlare design for his first two postwar boats –*Zara* and *Cohoe I* – before turning in the 1950s to the designer Charles Nicholson for *Cohoe II, III* and *IV*. By this stage Coles was a dedicated ocean racer and his changes of boat after the war were dictated by this priority. However, he had always been a serial boat-owner, observing in an article for *Yachting World* in 1959 that he had owned ten boats since starting out sailing in the 1920s. Others such as the Pyes and the Smeetons remained devoted to one boat for their entire sailing lives.

At the small end of the scale, the Smith brothers shared the conviction of Patrick Ellam that small was not only beautiful but functional for extensive voyaging, though their concept was different. *Nova Espero*, which was designed and built by the brothers themselves, was of similar size to *Sopranino* but more conventional in lines and with greater displacement, and carried a gunter rig. John Guzzwell's *Trekka* was similar in conception to *Sopranino* but was a bermudan-rigged yawl and rather more heavily built, for the rigours of a proposed circumnavigation. Ann Davison's canoe-sterned bermudan sloop *Felicity Ann*, at twenty-three feet overall, was not much bigger than *Nova Espero* or *Sopranino* but looked considerably more substantial with her greater freeboard and sizeable coach-roof. She was a small yacht rather than an overgrown dinghy. If you take out *Tzu Hang* and the three boats owned by the Millars, the other boats whose most famous voyages took place in the 1940s and 1950s together average out at around twenty-six feet.

* * *

It would clearly have been possible to add other British names to the list offered here, to say nothing of sailors from other countries, especially France, Sweden, Belgium, the United States, New Zealand and Australia. However, this is not a comprehensive history but, as will be clear from the remarks below, a choice made on the basis of close personal interest. It seemed best to focus on those sailors whose voyages and writings I knew well and could narrate with enthusiasm and perhaps even understanding.

In line with this priority, considerable attention is given in the following chapters to the early sailing careers of my subjects, frequently overlooked in accounts of their major exploits. Often they are of interest in themselves, sometimes they illuminate the major achievements, and in many cases both. Crucially, they show the learning processes, the mistakes, false starts and minor triumphs that often precede great achievement. Eric Hiscock's accounts of his interwar cruising, most of all a single-handed passage from the Solent to the western isles of Scotland and back, are full of challenging and instructive moments which he conveys with a freshness not always matched in his later writings. Humphrey Barton's dinghy adventures in the 1920s were not only indicative of a can-do approach to sailing which bore fruit later in cruising and ocean racing, but deserve to be better known on their own terms. The same applies to Adlard Coles, Edward Allcard and Patrick Ellam, who all made the most of dinghies before moving on to cruising yachts. The shipwreck that led to the tragic death of Ann Davison's husband casts a sombre yet revealing light on her Atlantic crossing, to say nothing of her earlier experience as a pilot. The Smeetons' early years, which were full of adventures that had nothing to do with sailing, explain much about their achievements as voyagers on the seas, and the same can be said of the Millars.

By the same token, we cannot ignore the later careers of these voyagers. Why did some become virtually institutions – one thinks of the Yarmouth, Isle of Wight lifeboat being named after Eric and Susan Hiscock – while others slipped out of the limelight? In fact, many continued sailing well into old age and undertook passages which exceeded the achievements of the voyages which initially made their names. Over a decade after the exploit which brought Edward Allcard to public attention – being the first to cross Atlantic solo in both directions – he made an epic year-long passage from Buenos Aires to Valparaiso in Chile, spending six months in and around Cape Horn which included a rare westabout (i.e., the 'wrong way') solo rounding of the Horn. He then continued to roam the world's oceans, now married and in a much larger craft, and gave up sailing and living aboard only in his early 90s. The Smeetons also rounded Cape Horn westabout in the 1960s, many years after their more famous earlier attempts to round the Horn which resulted in two dismastings. Humphrey Barton continued to live aboard his *Rose Rambler,* in which he made eighteen Atlantic crossings, until he physically no longer could. And so it goes on. While the primary focus of what follows remains the immediate postwar years, the indomitable voyaging spirit lived on in these sailors' later exploits.

* * *

Besides the intrinsic interest of the voyages and voyagers described here, my account is motivated by a more personal interest. As their books came off the presses during the 1950s most appeared on my father's shelves. I was too young to read them until the late 1950s and even then I believe I looked at them mainly for the photos and drawings, which were and still are powerfully evocative of time and place. Then through my mid to late teens and many more times in later years I read and re-read them with the result that they have become part of my mental furniture. My own sailing experiences, which began in dinghies in 1953 and extended later to cruising, never remotely matched theirs in scope but were enough to give me an inkling of the challenges they faced.

Some stray encounters over the years have made that generation of sailors more real to me than might otherwise have been the case. It was my good fortune to sail in *Rose Rambler,* Humphrey Barton's last boat, which after his death came into the ownership of someone I knew. She was a Laurent Giles design of thirty-five feet and a wonderfully capable cruising boat, which I was able to confirm on an east coast passage from Lowestoft up to northern Scotland. At some point in the early 2000s I was at Upson's boatyard at Aldeburgh and caught a glimpse through a half-open shed door of a shape I recognized instantly – the massive bow section of Peter and Anne Pye's *Moonraker*. She was clearly in the yard for restoration. I spent a good hour poking around the shed, re-imagining her as the ocean voyager she had been. At around the same time at Pin Mill in Suffolk I came across an example of the Siani class that was based on the Smiths' *Nova Espero*. Cabinless, as was her original design, quite slender, and with very low freeboard, she looked like an estuary dayboat, not the crosser of oceans she became in the Smiths' hands. These and other moments brought vividly to life the accounts I had read in the books by these voyagers.

This book is the product not only of nostalgia – to be sure there is something of that – but of what we can learn from this generation of sailors and what their experiences tell us about the human spirit. For those, like this author, who retain an attachment to tradition in sailing and seamanship yet have also embraced modern navigation methods, and admire the skills of contemporary ocean racers as well as cruisers, the postwar generation remains talismanic. This book is unashamedly a celebration as much as a history of their achievements.

Chapter 1

ADVENTURERS ON THE QUIET

Eric and Susan Hiscock: *Wanderer I-V*

One morning in early May 1938 Eric Hiscock was in the Irish Sea on passage to Douglas, Isle of Man, when a gale blew up from the direction of the harbour. He was only a mile off but it was touch and go whether he would make it. He double-reefed the mainsail, bringing the gaff jaws only a few feet above the boom, but with such a short luff it was impossible to stay her round. He could make to windward only by wearing round at the end of each tack (bearing away, gybing and bringing her up on the wind on the other tack). It took him three hours to beat the one mile into the harbour. He learned later that the lifeboat lookout had been watching his progress, ready to come to his aid if necessary.

Hiscock had spent the previous winter planning a cruise to Scotland. Inspired by the adventures of John Buchan's Richard Hannay, Hiscock planned to sail from his home port of Yarmouth, Isle of Wight to the wild and remote Loch Scavaig in Skye, location of key scenes in *Mr Standfast*. He was thirty years old, single, already an experienced cruising sailor, an established contributor to the yachting press, and author of a cruising guide to the south west of Ireland. His boat was the twenty-four-foot engineless gaff-rigged cutter *Wanderer II*, designed in 1937 by Laurent Giles with lines very similar to those of the slightly bigger Vertue whose first incarnation, *Andrillot*, was already under construction. Hiscock could not afford the bigger boat, so Giles drew a smaller version to suit his pocket. He had four months' cruising time ahead of him. He could just as well work on the book he was writing on board as ashore. Thus began a pattern as cruising sailor and author which carried him through till the end of his life in 1986.

This scene presents a sharp contrast with the usual image of Eric Hiscock. Firstly, on this 1938 voyage he was single-handed, while in all his best-known cruises he was accompanied by Susan whom he married in 1941. They had met in the early 1930s when she was only seventeen and already a keen sailor. Characteristically Hiscock did not dwell on personal matters, so there is little detail about their route from first meeting to marriage. However, he did note in passing in an account of a cruise to Brittany in 1939 that he had put in to La Trinité near the Gulf of Morbihan 'to pick up a friend who had come out to join me for a day or two'. A footnote reveals that the friend was 'Susan Sclater, and we got married two years later'. They evidently made a perfect team – both highly independent individuals who cooperated effortlessly. Hiscock made a point throughout his writings of praising her skills and fortitude, but the key to their success lay surely in their total compatibility. They never had children, were perfectly fulfilled in the life they had chosen, and if they argued or disagreed, managed to keep discord firmly in its place. Meanwhile, however, on this Scottish venture in 1938 he was evidently as comfortable sailing solo as he was later with Susan. Whether from choice or necessity he could be totally self-sufficient, and on this cruise to Scotland such a temperament was certainly required.

Secondly, the idea of the voyage being inspired by a scene in a John Buchan novel, with its intimation of romance and adventure, seems out of keeping with the sober, undemonstrative character Hiscock projects in most of his writings. We do not generally associate the Hiscocks' voyages with struggle or adversity. They seem models of planning and execution. In fact, he insisted somewhat primly that 'a successful voyage is a planned voyage' rather than a matter of wandering about 'wherever the winds chanced to blow us, which is contrary to our principles'. In his account of their first circumnavigation (1952-5), Hiscock reported an interview with an Australian journalist:

> With shorthand pads at the ready and pencils poised, they started shooting questions at us. 'What was your most desperate situation?' We said we were sorry but there really had not been any.... 'But surely you must have had some excitements? A leak. A fire?' Again we shook our heads. 'Didn't any of your sails split?' We tried to explain that such things do not usually happen during properly conducted cruises or aboard well-found sailing yachts. But the reporters were losing interest in us rapidly by then and soon took themselves ashore.

Eric Hiscock was not without a sense of irony and fun. He knew what he was doing, which was deflecting attention away from what he felt were inessentials and above all recoiling from sensationalism and publicity. But the pose was not entirely manufactured. The Hiscocks were indeed meticulously organised individuals who seemed successfully to have ironed out any wrinkles which life, weather, and mischance might present. Adlard Coles said of Eric that 'his achievements... are due to his perfectionism, a characteristic he shares with Susan over anything they undertake'. This applies as much to maintenance as to boat-handling, navigation, victualling and the rest. While Wanderer II was in build Hiscock noted that 'because I like to know that beneath its parcelling and serving every splice has at least four tucks, I undertook the rigging myself. I believe there were 90 splices all told.' It was this approach and these skills which made his instructional books *Cruising under Sail* and *Voyaging under Sail* so popular, a status which they continue to enjoy.

Yet the picture of Hiscock's solo struggle to reach Douglas harbour also contains a vital truth about his life and character. While he declared on more than one occasion that he dreaded bad weather and even that he was 'timid by nature', neither he nor Susan ever shied away from a challenge which might test them to the full. They voyaged in the spirit of Arthur Ransome's words carved in *Wanderer III*'s companionway: 'Grab a chance and you won't be sorry for a might-have-been.' It is time to look behind the managerial image of the Hiscocks and bring out the adventuring side of their sailing lives.

* * *

Hiscock was born in 1908 and brought up in Southampton.* Sailing was the dominant theme of his life from an early age. He sailed dinghies at Bembridge on the Isle of Wight where the family spent every summer. At boarding school in Bromsgrove near Birmingham he was unable to take part in ball games because of poor eyesight and put his energies into sailing and rowing. In his teens he was already subscribing to yachting magazines. At University College, Southampton

* Thanks are due to Eric Hiscock's niece Janice Aslin for information about his early life.

he coached the rowing eight. The desire to own his own boat was a wholly natural progression from these early steps.

Hiscock records the seemingly odd fact that he was able to buy his first boat as a result of the bankruptcy of a company called Waste Products Ltd in which his father had invested some of Eric's money. With the onset of the depression his father refunded Eric the money which enabled him to go sailing. He never looked back. In the 1930s he laid the foundation of his subsequent career as the doyen of British cruising yachtsmen, sailing whenever and wherever he could, writing regularly for the yachting press, editing magazines and annuals, besides producing numerous books which were indeed his livelihood. While he was listed as sole author of his numerous publications, from the time he and Susan were married he never failed to acknowledge her contribution to the production of his books and articles or indeed to their lifetime of cruising. Theirs was a joint enterprise. Uniquely among the sailors covered in this book, Eric and Susan Hiscock received MBEs for services to yachting, which recognised their special place among the postwar voyagers. It is worth noting that his books were published by Oxford University Press rather than a specialist yachting publisher, which ensured that his writings reached a wider public than those of most other cruising sailors.

Hiscock's first boat, bought in his twenties, was, he conceded, 'a poor thing, as yachts go' but he did not know that when he bought her for the sum of fifty pounds. She was an eighteen-foot sloop 'too fine forward to balance her very heavy quarters, and to make matters worse her mast was too near the bow', giving her a monstrous amount of weather helm. However, with all her faults, she was the test bed for his sailing life. He named her *Wanderer*, thinking this was an original choice, till a painter he had hired to scribe the name on her transom pointed to a neighbouring motor-boat in bad repair and said 'What, another of 'em?' Hiscock later discovered a dozen Wanderers listed in Lloyds Register. Unabashed he stuck with *Wanderer* for this and all his subsequent boats so that the name *Wanderer* is irrevocably associated with Eric Hiscock. He gave her a long bowsprit and turned her into a cutter which solved the steering problem. He rebuilt the interior and transformed her into a proper cruising vessel. Basing himself in the Beaulieu River he ranged in *Wanderer* along the south coast as far as

Cornwall, making many mistakes but generally reaching his goals and laying the foundations of his career as cruising sailor and author.

While mostly solo in his own boat, Hiscock showed a gift for friendship with other sailors, who evidently appreciated his skills and welcomed him as crew. Notable among these was Roger Pinckney, later Commodore of the Royal Cruising Club, in whose Bristol Channel pilot cutter, *Dyarchy*, Hiscock cruised all over northern Europe during the 1930s, as he did later in her successor, also named *Dyarchy*, which Pinckney had built to a Laurent Giles design in 1938. Another regular berth was in *Tern II*, a gaff-rigged yawl formerly owned by Claud Worth, prominent yachtsman of the late Victorian and Edwardian era, which boasted the unusual addition of a square sail. Hiscock's accounts of passages with its skipper Clive Wright are among the liveliest of his pre-war writings, not least his description of the ripping of the mainsail to shreds in a Channel gale, which throws an interesting light on his reply to the Australian journalist many years later, referred to earlier, about whether any such disasters had happened on their circumnavigation. Hiscock's sang-froid came not from having been able to evade difficulties either by luck or design, but from having met such challenges and overcome them.

Meanwhile, by the end of the 1930s Hiscock's own *Wanderer II* already had several substantial cruises under her belt, notably to the Channel Islands and the southwest of Ireland, to be followed by the Scottish cruise already referred to. Hiscock still lived ashore but he was totally committed to the cruising life. His account of these early cruises in *Wandering Under Sail* (1939 and later editions) contains his most sparkling writing and offers a glimpse of the boyish adventurer lurking within the super-competent sailor. On his maiden cruise to the Channel Islands in *Wanderer II* in 1937 he relates that in order to get properly awake after an interrupted night at sea he 'stripped off the layers of clothing which had accumulated during the night and went over the stern to tow along on the end of the mainsheet'.

Never one to take the easy path, Hiscock opted to dispense with an engine, which meant that he was often reliant on a twelve-foot 'sweep' to get him out of trouble. On one occasion on this same cruise he sculled for five hours to reach St Peter Port in Guernsey. Acknowledging that an engine would have made things simpler entering and leaving ports, he believed that it would have led to the 'ruination of such seamanship as I may have acquired'. 'Besides,' he added, the technique of engineless cruising under sail 'is very different from, and much more interesting' than power-assisted cruising. (Having said that, when it came to building the thirty-foot *Wanderer III* in the early 1950s the Hiscocks chose to install an engine, albeit a 4hp Stuart Turner two-stroke unit with no reverse gear which at best gave 3 knots in flat water. Hiscock could still hardly bring himself to turn his back on the purity of sail).

Then came the war. His progress was curious in two respects: firstly, this apostle of engineless sailing served in the RNVR for two years as an engineer, a job he fell into, he reports, on the strength of once having owned a motor-bike; secondly, after two years' active service he was told after a routine medical examination that his poor eyesight rendered him unfit for service. Hiscock protested to the surgeon-commander that the navy had hitherto acknowledged the need for people with particular skills even if they fell short of perfect physical requirements, that he was currently serving as chief engineer in a submarine chaser, besides which prior to the war he had cruised over 20,000 miles in small vessels, was a competent navigator, knew the coasts on both sides of the Channel intimately, and had written books of sailing directions about them. 'I don't believe a word of it...' said the surgeon, adding that 'I consider you are a danger in the service, and I shall do all I can to have you discharged.' Appeals and protests by Hiscock were in vain. Surgeon-commanders apparently had the last word.

There followed an interlude during which he worked in a pulpboard mill close to the farm where Susan, now his wife, worked. In a short but vivid book about his wartime experiences, *I Left the Navy* (1945), Hiscock recounts his experiences of factory work on the night shift, rebuilding an old cottage in which he and Susan would spend their early married life, then moving on to farm work. During this period he acquired an astonishing range of skills, including plastering, concrete-laying, carpentry, bee-keeping, and operating a combine-harvester and other machines, in addition to growing vegetables and flowers. He showed the same resourcefulness and attention to detail in these land activities as he did in sailing. At the same time he accepted an offer of the editorship of a yachting magazine, which he did not name but was in fact *The Yachtsman*.

Then at last he was back in naval service. Susan had noticed his restlessness and knew he was pining for the sea. Sensing his mood, she quoted Masefield to him 'A wind's in the heart of me, a fire's in my heels,/ I am tired of brick and stone and rumbling wagon-wheels…' – but ever the practical individual she also pointed to a headline in the *Daily Telegraph*: 'Can you man a boat?' An organization called the Admiralty Ferry Service was looking for personnel to move small craft from port to port around the coast. It was composed mainly of yachtsmen who were considered for one reason or another unfit for service in the regular navy. He applied and was accepted. Hiscock thus found himself in the same job as Humphrey Barton, the redoubtable small boat voyager and surveyor at Laurent Giles, and with whom he was well acquainted. The last chapter of Hiscock's wartime memoir contains a stirring account of a passage from Lowestoft to Plymouth in a ninety-foot MFV in which he was chief engineer, including a vivid description of a spell he took at the wheel as they struggled through mountainous waves in the teeth of a Channel gale. 'This is the life', he reflected, 'which I have been missing for so long'. He was not the only postwar voyager whose wartime service gave him a depth of maritime experience far beyond that of the average yachtsman.

* * *

In 1950, with several years of cruising in British and French waters behind them, the Hiscocks planned an 'experimental ocean voyage' in *Wanderer II* 'with the idea in our minds that one day we might go voyaging far afield to see something of the world'. They chose the Azores which at 1200 miles WSW of the Lizard would constitute a good test of their abilities and those of their vessel. And so it proved to be. An early gale on the outward passage blowing from the direction of their intended course forced them to divert to the Scilly Isles. After two hundred and six miles sailing since they had left Falmouth they had made good just sixty-two towards their destination. They experienced two further bouts of heavy weather on the voyage out during which they went through all methods of coping: running before the wind under only staysail, running under bare poles, heaving to, lying to. Just as striking as their management of heavy weather was the challenge posed by absence of wind. At crucial moments they had to resort to the sweep. Just short of La Coruña in northern Spain the wind died and they were forced to scull for a couple of hours. Sheer weariness induced them to anchor outside the harbour but within a short time a sea breeze set, in putting them on a lee shore. They made the harbour under sail but were faced with another hour's sculling in the sheltered waters before they reached an anchorage.

It is a feature of Hiscock's writing about sailing that he moved seamlessly between telling a story and showing how it's done, an approach which he applied as much to dietary and culinary matters as to nautical skills. On the return from the Azores their supply of bananas was ripening so rapidly that 'we had to eat fourteen a day to keep pace with them'. When they ran out of salad dressing 'Susan made some with the olive oil from the tinned sardines, the vinegar from the pickled onions, and sugar, mustard and pepper'. On their first circumnavigation Susan experimented with baking bread, recording an initial disaster in which a sudden gust of wind through the main hatch picked up the bag of flour and deposited it all over the cabin. Nothing daunted, Susan cleaned up and produced a hot, crusty ring loaf. Thereafter on longer passages she baked two or three times a week.

When, in the wake of the Azores voyage in *Wanderer II*, they decided to have a larger boat built and embark on a circumnavigation, they had already developed to a high level the mentality of liveaboards. The thirty-foot *Wanderer III*, another Laurent Giles design, carried, in addition to all the necessaries of life, equipment for developing and printing the photographs to illustrate the articles which would pay for the venture. Hiscock was already an accomplished photographer, as is evident from the many journal articles, books, and annuals he had published in the years before setting off in *Wanderer III*. On their second circumnavigation (1959-1962) they added filming to their repertoire with film stock and camera, plus some training, provided by the BBC, who commissioned a visual record of the voyage. The resulting documentary, first broadcast in 1963, offers wonderful footage of their lives at sea and on shore, and brings out even more starkly than the books the distance in accents and attitudes between their time and ours.

The Hiscocks' first circumnavigation, which took place between 1952 and 1955, made their name as bluewater sailors. Hiscock set out their goals with characteristic modesty: 'For a long time Susan and I, who are both well used to the handling of small sailing craft, had wanted to make a long voyage. This was chiefly for the satisfaction of achieving something by our own unaided efforts and by the practice of such skill as we might have acquired; but we also wished to see a little of the world, which we could not afford to do in any other way, and to gather copy and photographs for the books and articles which are our livelihood.'

This voyage, described in *Around the World in Wanderer III* (1956), took them across the Atlantic via the Canary Islands to Barbados, from where they island-hopped through the Windward and Leeward Islands before taking the Panama Canal into the Pacific and on to New Zealand via the Marquesas Islands, Tahiti, Samoa, and Fiji. Restrained in temperament and highly organized as he was, Hiscock's account conveys a vivid sense of freedom and openness to experience both at sea and ashore. In the Caribbean they revelled in a thrash to windward during which 'we drove Wanderer as hard as we could and she responded gamely, forcing her way steadily out to windward and never letting the steep seas stop her, but she hammered them hard so that fountains of spray shot out of each side of her rounded buoyant bows every time she smashed into one'. Whenever they were inclined to grumble about the heat or a gale or any other discomfort, they would remind themselves that they were free of the fate of 'thousands of pale-faced office workers who were at that moment fighting to get back to their homes in the suburbs'. On the 4000-mile, forty-day passage across the Pacific from Panama to the Marquesas islands Hiscock celebrated the ocean as 'a vast, colourful desert, something so great and indifferent that our tiny vessel, with straining sails and hissing wake which was obliterated after she had passed, seemed indeed a puny thing, allowed to continue safely on her way on sufferance'.

On the more strictly nautical front, Hiscock offered an unusually clear and detailed description of the process of taking a sun sight with a sextant, while marvelling at the magic of being able to find one's position on the surface of a featureless ocean by taking observation

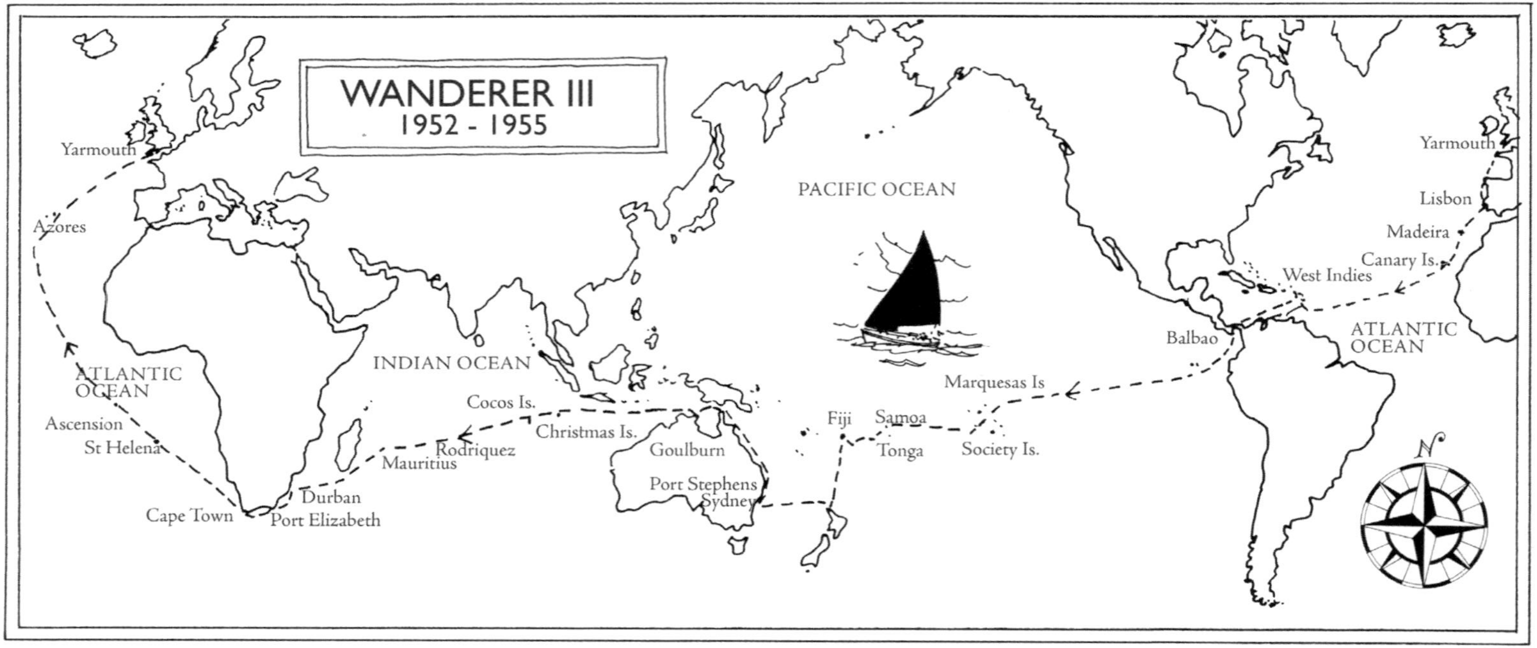
WANDERER III
1952 - 1955
Yarmouth
Azores
ATLANTIC OCEAN
Ascension
St Helena
Cape Town
Port Elizabeth
Durban
Mauritius
Rodriquez
INDIAN OCEAN
Cocos Is.
Christmas Is.
Goulburn
Port Stephens
Sydney
PACIFIC OCEAN
Fiji
Samoa
Tonga
Society Is.
Marquesas Is
Balbao
West Indies
Canary Is.
Madeira
Lisbon
Yarmouth
ATLANTIC OCEAN

of distant objects in the universe. Coupled with his account of the routines of the day on passage, their watch system, sail changes, and all the business of keeping the boat moving towards its destination, Hiscock vividly communicates a sense of what life aboard a small vessel is like on a long passage.

Encounters ashore, especially with Americans, produced notes of humour arising from cultural differences which also feature in many other accounts by British voyagers, not least Peter and Anne Pye whom the Hiscocks encountered several times in the Atlantic phase of this voyage. An American official in the Canal zone, taking details of boat and crew, asked Eric his age, to which he replied forty-four. 'And Mrs Hiscock's thirty-nine,' said the official. 'However did you know?' asked Eric. 'Without looking up from his writing the official replied: "no dame is ever more than thirty-nine."' At the other end of the canal they were invited to a 'brawl' at the American Legion Club which turned out to be a fancy dress party. Having no costumes to hand, the Hiscocks made do with draping two tattered blue ensigns round their waists, only to be greeted with stony silence when they entered the room. A 'tough looking customer in ragged shorts' approached them and explained the problem: '"See here you folks. I'd have you know there's a British yacht in port and", pointing to the blue ensign on which we were sitting, "that's no way to treat their flag."' Explanations were duly forthcoming and they enjoyed the party and got aboard late.

Behind the surface of the Hiscocks' seemingly strait-laced manners lay an openness to experience without which indeed the life they had chosen would have been impossible. Eric showed a particular susceptibility to sensual experience which he was not shy about expressing. In Tahiti he was intrigued by the permissive sexual mores of the Tahitians, who, he said, had not yet been persuaded by missionary teachers that indiscriminate sexual intercourse and bearing children out of wedlock was sinful. He was no less impressed by the freedom with which the Tahitians danced, in contrast to the Europeans who, once they had had plenty to drink, generally looked 'dissipated and ill at ease.' On the Pacific island of Bora Bora the Hiscocks attended a party organized by the crew of a visiting British yacht. Among the party-goers were some islanders who had participated in an inter-island dancing competition. Eric was entranced by the hula dance of a young woman in the moonlight which he described with almost poetic intensity:'...as she performed the swift but graceful movements of the dance in ever-increasing tempo, the firelight shone in rippling waves on her skirt.'

From the Pacific Islands their voyage took them to the North Island of New Zealand, on to Sydney and then north along the length of the eastern coast of Australia, following Cook's log of the same passage made nearly 200 years before. On passage across the Indian Ocean towards the Cape of Good Hope they met with a fifteen-day gale between the Cocos islands and Mauritius, during which their tiny seventy-five square-foot trysail was set the entire time. Off the southern coast of Madagascar they experienced a squall which Eric estimated at eighty knots. He bore away, not attempting to hand the trysail which he knew would be ripped to shreds if allowed to flap. He recalled that 'Wanderer tore through the black night faster than I have ever known before... Dimly I could see the bow-wave rising high each side of her as from a speed-boat.'

The rest of the circumnavigation was completed in seamanlike fashion without great dramas for which, Eric concluded, 'we were grateful to Providence for bringing us safely home'. He considered *Wanderer*'s most hazardous journey to have been her subsequent trip through the streets of London on a ten-ton trailer to the second National Boat Show at Olympia where she was to be displayed as an example of British workmanship. This too she survived in good order, leaving many onlookers, Eric believed, judging from the far-away look in their eyes, 'dreaming of wide oceans... and imagining themselves far away in boats of their own'. Meanwhile, the Hiscocks held to Arthur Ransome's injunction to 'grab a chance and you won't be sorry for a might-have-been' – words which were carved in *Wanderer*'s companionway. A second circumnavigation was in the offing.

In the interlude between the two circumnavigations Hiscock reflected in the *Yachting World* Annual for 1957 on his ideal boat in the light of their experience in *Wanderer III*. Greater beam to give her increased initial stability and easier motion was high on the list. That would mean higher Thames tonnage and hence greater cost, which was what had dictated the her dimensions. But would greater beam

Hiscock celebrated the ocean as 'a vast, colourful desert'.

mean a sacrifice in performance, especially to windward? Hiscock noted that the Pyes' twenty-nine foot *Moonraker* was a foot wider in the beam than *Wanderer* and carried a gaff cutter rig but achieved the same average daily runs as *Wanderer* over long distances. Hiscock therefore opted for the gaff rig for his ideal boat, downwind ability compensating for any limitations to windward. Perhaps most striking was his admission that he had been wrong to choose an engine of a mere four horsepower for *Wanderer III* – it proved useless on the very occasions when it was most needed, such as entering a channel which was too narrow to beat through, or making good distance in anything but a flat calm. His ideal boat would have a diesel engine of generous capacity.

In the event, the Hiscocks stuck with *Wanderer III* for their second circumnavigation largely because they could not afford to commission a new boat. When ten years later the opportunity arose to build new, their choice bore only a distant relation to the ideal boat sketched out in 1957 except that the commitment to a substantial engine remained. Meanwhile he reflected that, given her size, *Wanderer III* satisfied their current needs, besides which 'to us she is a personality and we understand her'.

The second voyage initially took a similar route as the first (to the Pacific via the Panama Canal and to the North Island of New Zealand) and was conducted with the same skill and aplomb. This time, however, after leaving New Zealand they headed for Papua New Guinea and the Torres Strait, with only a brief but, as we shall see, incident-filled stop on the northern tip of Australia. The big difference in the second voyage was the decision to come home via the Suez Canal rather than via the Cape of Good Hope.

Comparison of the written account of the second circumnavigation with the film (both entitled *Beyond the West Horizon*) shows interesting omissions in the latter. The book devotes a whole chapter to the stranding of *Wanderer III* on Coker Island off the coast of northern Australia which almost brought their voyage to an end. After resigning themselves to losing the boat, they made it ashore and encountered a carpenter who mustered a band of locals, including a whole school class of Aboriginals and their teachers, who helped the Hiscocks recover their floating home, enabling them to continue the

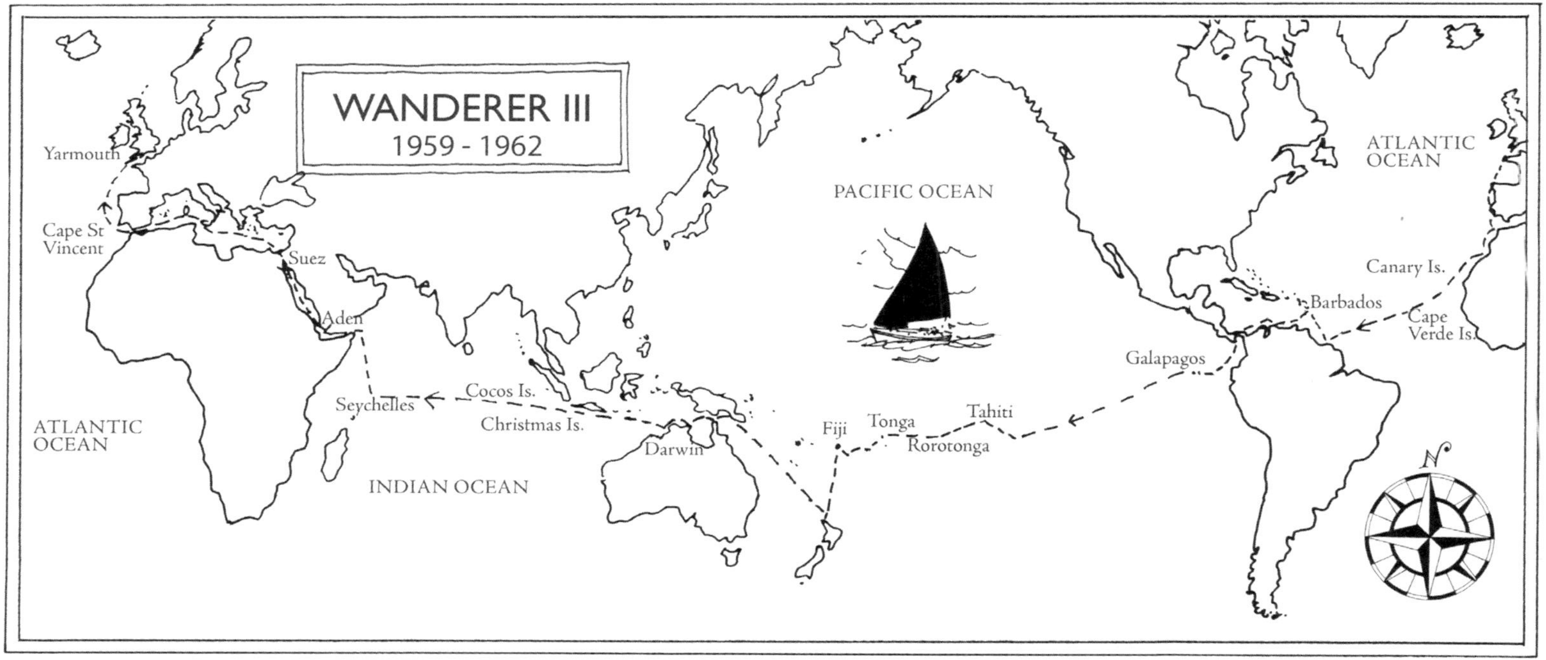
WANDERER III
1959 - 1962
Yarmouth
Cape St Vincent
Suez
Aden
Seychelles
Cocos Is.
Christmas Is.
Darwin
ATLANTIC OCEAN
INDIAN OCEAN
PACIFIC OCEAN
Fiji
Tonga
Rorotonga
Tahiti
Galapagos
Barbados
Canary Is.
Cape Verde Is.
ATLANTIC OCEAN
N

voyage. It is a dramatic and touching sequence of events, nothing of which appears in their film of the voyage. Also omitted from the film was mention of Eric's broken rib in a severe gale on passage to Fiji and a boil on Susan's hand which went septic and required daily hospital treatment when they eventually reached Fiji. Both Hiscocks were allergic to anything that smacked of sensationalism, with the result that the full story of their achievements rarely reached beyond the yachting world.

* * *

In the late 1960s the Hiscocks commissioned a new yacht, the steel-hulled fifty-foot bermudan ketch *Wanderer IV*. She displaced twenty tons compared to *Wanderer III*'s eight and had a sixty horsepower engine. Except for the commitment to a sizeable engine she bore little relation to the ideal boat Hiscock had sketched out ten years earlier, confirming the experience of many boat owners that 'the ideal boat' is a changeable and elusive concept. Nevertheless, over a period of twelve years the Hiscocks cruised 77,000 miles in her, completing a third circumnavigation in 1976.

With the purchase of *Wanderer IV*, they finally sold their house in Yarmouth, Isle of Wight and opted to base themselves in Whangarei in New Zealand's North Island. Hiscock's accounts of these voyages have many of the same qualities as his earlier ones but the bigger, more sophisticated boat brought with it bigger and more complex problems. In the grumpy first chapter of *Sou'West in Wanderer IV* which describes the building of their new craft, Hiscock recounts a succession of glitches in the electrical systems, problems with the rudder, and many other design problems connected with the accommodation, to say nothing of poor relations with the builder. He even doubted that he had chosen the right rig for the boat. It is a sad falling off from their experience with *Wanderer III*.

Nevertheless, the Hiscocks stuck to their task. They made their peace with the boat's foibles and undertook some of their most adventurous cruises, including a year in California and a circumnavigation of the South Island of New Zealand where they spent several weeks in the remote and demanding waters of Fjordland. Hiscock's susceptibility to attractive young women makes an intriguing re-appearance here. He describes an encounter on a Pacific Island with an all but naked young woman who climbs aboard their boat in the middle of the night with a flimsy story about escaping from her cruel father. Hiscock eventually drops her ashore but reflects that other options could have been open to him such as offering her clothes and a cup of coffee or a berth for the night or accepting 'her final suggestion'. 'As we neared the shore', he recalled, 'she leant towards me, smelling nicely of frangipani, and putting a hand on my knee said in best Mae West style: "You come with me?"

Well what would you have done?'

* * *

It is no surprise that with their advancing age, rising demands of maintenance, and persistent problems with the steel hull, the Hiscocks should think about a new boat. They moved on to a wooden 40-foot cutter, constructed of triple-skinned diagonal strips of the tropical hardwood kauri. *Wanderer V* was launched at Whangarei in 1981. Her maiden voyage round the Western Pacific took them once again to Fiji, New Caledonia, Sydney and back to New Zealand. Now in his mid-70s, in the final chapter of what was to be his last book, *Two Yachts, Two Voyages* (1984), Hiscock reflected ruefully on the changed cruising scene, characterised, in his view, by excessive reliance on technology, over-crowded anchorages, and a loss of traditional skills. He tried hard not to come over as mere curmudgeon but there is no disguising his alienation from the world of mass cruising. His is the perhaps predictable lament of one who learned his skills the hard way at a time when deep-water cruising was a minority undertaking. It speaks volumes about the Hiscocks' uncompromising mode of cruising that they never owned a radio transmitter. Independence for the Hiscocks really did mean self-reliance, not some airy idea of freedom from the constraints of the shore.

Eric died in 1986 at Whangarei. Three years later Susan moved back to Yarmouth, Isle of Wight, where she resumed sailing the West Wight Scow class she had learned in some sixty years before. Wanting to attend a meeting of the Royal Cruising Club across the Solent in Beaulieu, she decided to sail over in her Scow *Shrimp*, a solo adventure which perfectly displays the casual offbeat courage of this septuagenarian voyager. In a fresh southwesterly breeze she found herself on a dead run off the entrance to the Beaulieu River where she 'gybed and brought the wind on to the beam to tear into the river'. After the meeting she opted not to stay for the evening party so as to ensure a daylight passage back to Yarmouth. Leaving Beaulieu she fetched across the Solent to Gurnard Bay, but with contrary wind and tide she could make no way towards Yarmouth and was forced to anchor and wait for the ebb. She got out her sandwiches and 'watched with some irritation the effortless way a couple of sailboards swooped around, oblivious of the tide'. The sun set at eight and it was fully dark by the time by the time the tide turned in her favour. A bright moon helped illuminate the last few miles to Yarmouth. Rounding the pier, she recalled, 'the harbour's FULL notice was up and I needed an oar to help me through the crowd of yachts'. She finally stepped ashore at midnight. 'It has been a good day,' she observed, 'with the night passage a spicy bonus.'

A few years later, with the help of a legacy from Susan's will, the Yarmouth RNLI station launched a new lifeboat, the *Eric and Susan Hiscock (Wanderer)*. One can be sure that, for all the modesty they characteristically displayed about their achievements, this was a tribute they both would have been glad to accept.

Chapter 2

A HAPPY SHIP

Moonraker and the Pyes

With her distinctive red mainsail and the antiquated charm of her lines, *Moonraker* must be granted at least equal billing with the crew in the Pyes' cruising story. *Red Mains'l* indeed was the title of the book which described her first ocean voyage – a double Atlantic crossing – and launched Peter Pye as a bluewater voyager and author beyond the pages of specialist yachting publications.* The tie between boat and crew was peculiarly close. Peter Pye regularly referred to her as 'Moonie', relying over the years on her strengths and managing her foibles as one would a cherished family pet. Dr Pye, a west London GP, and his wife Anne bought *Moonraker* in the early 1930s and their affinity with the boat was such that they never toyed with the idea of exchanging her for another. He once wrote that he suspected Moonie was 'extremely jealous' and 'if she thought we were going to sell her, she'd drown us'. Their cruising life lasted over thirty years and ended only with Peter's death in 1966 at the age of sixty-four following a tragic surgical accident.

Moonraker was a twenty-nine foot Polperro fishing vessel, originally rigged as a yawl and built in Looe in the 1890s by the famous boatbuilding family of Ferris. The Pyes' first encounter with her was not promising. While on holiday in Polperro in the early 1930s they asked a fisherman if any boats were for sale 'and he pointed to one, lying like an ugly duckling apart from her more attractive sisters.' She was short and stocky and paint was peeling from her bulwarks, but she did have a lovely sheer and they liked the run of the hull aft which suggested she might have a good turn of speed despite her chunky look. It was Anne who saw the possibilities in her and the offered price of £25 was hugely tempting. With money Anne

* Dr Pye's given names were Edmund Arthur and until the mid-1950s his publications appeared under the name E .A. Pye. However, he was seemingly always known as Peter and from 1957 onwards this was the name under which he wrote.

had saved up they would have enough to convert her into what they wanted, assuming she was sound. Close inspection showed that she was sturdily built, dry as a bone and free of rot, a judgement that was confirmed by a boatbuilder friend who said that if the Pyes didn't buy her he would.

The next few days were spent clearing out decades of accumulated grime and gear, including a rusty old single-cylinder Kelvin engine which was quickly disposed of. Then came the refit which was undertaken by the friend who had surveyed the boat. Everything was designed for simplicity: lanyards rather than rigging screws, paraffin lamps rather than electricity, a gimballed primus stove in a new galley by the companionway so that food could be passed up to the helm. They built a smaller self-draining cockpit and installed a new 6hp engine which gave her three and a half knots on flat water. She was to be re-rigged as a gaff cutter with a substantial sail area of 650 square feet with her three lower sails and topsail.

During the 1930s, as Pye recalled, 'we learned to sail our ship', making many modifications to improve her cruising potential, including an extra ton of ballast, heavier shroud plates, larger-gauge anchor chain, and additional storage space for charts. Then came the war and *Moonraker* lay in Fambridge, Essex for the duration, leaving them wondering whether they would ever sail again. In common with many others whose cruising experience long pre-dated the war, the coming of peace brought the urge to resume the old sailing life but also to embrace something new. In the Pyes' case this meant opting to drop their old lives and take to the oceans.

It was not an instant decision. The first seed of the idea was sown long before the war. A surgeon colleague had lent Dr Pye a book called *Two Hundred Pound Millionaire* by Weston Martyr which told the story of a doctor who found he could live on a small boat for 200 pounds a year. It was this – and some savings Anne had squirrelled away unbeknownst to her husband – which had led them to buy *Moonraker* in the first place. Now, in the wake of the war and after annual cruises which had taken them to Ireland, Denmark and Spain, Dr Pye was confronted with two very different medical conditions. One was the return of duodenal pain which was evidently related to stress, and the other was the looming prospect of 'State Medicine' which Pye regarded as 'too depressing.' It is often forgotten how many in the medical profession opposed the establishment of the NHS, not least the British Medical Association (BMA) itself, and a large proportion of the older doctors. Peter Pye was in mid-career at this point. Once into his new cruising life he reflected on how happy he was not to be in the NHS, 'for the hand of the state has tightened its grip on the doctor's throat, paralysing the good he can do'. Medicine as an art, he said, 'was lost'; it was all science now and 'I was never good at sums.' Dr Pye was definitely old school.

It takes an effort of imagination on the part of the twenty-first century cruising sailor to grasp the experience of the postwar generation. When the Pyes set out for south-west Ireland in the summer of 1946 in their fifty-year-old gaff-rigged former fishing boat, rationing was still in force amid a general climate of austerity. In the absence of marinas, hour-by-hour weather forecasts, satellite navigation, and the myriad safety systems to which the present generation has become accustomed, *Moonraker* and her crew had no choice but to take what came. On this occasion, leaving from the Helford River bound for the Scilly Isles, they were forced to put into Newlyn in the face of strong westerlies and with a seasick crew of two friends they had invited for the passage to Ireland. Coincidentally they encountered the Hiscocks who were similarly bound for Scilly, a moment which was captured on camera by Pye in a fine shot of *Wanderer II*. Next morning *Moonraker* set off again for Scilly with similar results, except that this time on returning to Newlyn the invited couple promptly departed. Having concluded well before this that at least one extra crew member was required for passages, the Pyes were lucky to be able to recruit an experienced replacement at short notice. From that point on the cruise proceeded more or less as planned, featuring a rich mix of frustrating windless periods and wild squalls necessitating numerous sail changes before they made their landfall at the Old Head of Kinsale after two days and nights sailing.

There was nothing seemingly remarkable about their subsequent cruise along the coast as far as the Kenmare River, which marked its furthest extent, and the return via Bantry Bay and Baltimore, except that Peter Pye's account exudes that combination of surface calm and underlying drama which is characteristic of all his writings about their passage-making. There were challenges enough on this trip which others would have made a meal of in the telling, but which the Pyes dealt with in an efficient and understated manner. The tiny harbour of Cleanderry with its twenty-five-foot-wide entrance was negotiated with ease. Rock-strewn narrows and tidal gates were taken in their stride; sail changes came thick and fast to suit conditions and the engine was used only when the wind failed altogether. The Pyes maintained impressive command of their vessel in often testing conditions without ever compromising their urge to explore the most difficult and out of the way destinations. They were also open to the romance of Ireland, as is apparent in this wistful reflection on their departure for England. 'This morning we were sad, for tonight we must leave this delightful country, untouched by war, where there is a gaiety of spirit and a contentment in the simple pleasures of life which exists no longer in the towns and cities of England.'

This cruise to Ireland, like their trip to northern Spain the following year, was perfect preparation for the Atlantic crossing. Peter's first use of the sextant was on the return from Ireland and inevitably much more practice was gained on the cruise to Spain. Though proclaiming an aversion to maths, it is clear from his prize-winning account of the Spanish cruise, published in the Royal Cruising Club journal for 1947, that he became a highly competent ocean navigator who rarely missed a landfall, and that he was cool and calm enough to make good any mistakes without fear or fuss.

The truth is that Pye and his wife were made of stern stuff behind their relaxed demeanour. He was small in stature and gentle by nature but possessed natural authority as a seaman. One of his crew members later wrote of him that 'his seamanship was of the instinctive rather than intellectual type – and his instinct was unfailing'. A photo of 'the skipper' in *Red Mains'l* shows him standing in the cockpit, hands in pockets, wearing what look like old, crudely belted grey canvas ducks, a dark shirt with an open collar, a broad smile on a big open face, made bigger by the receding hairline, and humorous creases round the eyes and upper cheeks. He has the look of a man comfortable in his skin, full of good humour, unconcerned with appearances and ready for anything. A photo of Anne, 'the mate', shows her somewhat more smartly attired in shorts and a buttoned shirt, intently focused on taking a sextant sight, perfectly balanced on the heaving deck amid ocean rollers.

Peter was definitely skipper but Anne was essential to the project. She was the organized one who attended to details. Peter was not shy about conveying his devotion to Anne. He records laconically on the opening page of *Red Mains'l* that 'to this day I cannot think why she married me, nor can she. I suppose it is really because she never gives up on anything once she has started it. We had a practice, a small house, a smaller car, and a large overdraft and we were happy as the day is long; we still are.' Mutual trust and respect were integral to the success of their voyaging. Their occasional disagreements were quickly addressed and disposed of. Peter makes frequent references to her sailing skills, particularly in helming downwind. For her part, Anne's devotion to Peter and to *Moonraker* was manifest from the start in her unwavering desire to go voyaging despite suffering horribly from seasickness at the outset of each passage. The Pyes must go down with the Hiscocks and the Smeetons as among the most successful sailing partnerships of their own or indeed any time.

* * *

The stage was set for the first Atlantic voyage which began in Fowey on 22 June 1949. Content as they were together, out of concern for safety and comfort the Pyes generally took on extra crew for long passages. Cruising was supposed to be fun, not a test of endurance, Pye said. It says a good deal about their relaxed approach to voyaging in such a small vessel that they generally made happy choices. For the Atlantic crossing they were to be joined in Vigo, Spain by Christopher Ellis, an experienced sailor who had been in bomb disposal during the war. He had written to them offering himself as crew but could only join them in August. For the first leg to Vigo they recruited a young man called John Harwood, a friend of Peter's cousin whom they had never met. He was a dinghy sailor with no offshore experience and proved to be a capable helmsman but 'blissfully ignorant' of the strain on mast and gear in a hard blow and lumpy seas. On the first night out, with Peter and Anne below and John on watch, Peter was aware of the boat careering through a stormy night and labouring under too much sail. John was indignant when Peter called for a reef but changed his tune when *Moonraker* proved to be drier, more comfortable and faster under reduced sail. An incident which could easily have blown up into something unpleasant was quickly and effectively dealt with. It is not without reason that experienced blue water sailors say that voyages most often fail because of crew problems.

Once beyond Ushant they set a course for north-west Spain. The wind eased, the swell went down and Peter waxed lyrical on his ten-till-one watch about the beauty of the night. After being relieved by Anne he fell asleep straight away but soon had the sense of being at anchor in Fowey harbour with its 'square, stone keep guarding the Polruan shore'. In the moonlight Anne was at the helm intent on steering. 'Anne do come down to bed; there's no need to sit out there now that the anchor's down.' He heard her voice as if from a great distance saying 'we're not at Fowey, we're crossing the Bay of Biscay'. He sat down beside her and the scenes of Fowey harbour melted away. It was now three o'clock. He had been sleep-walking.

In Muros, their second port in Spain, at anchor just outside the small harbour, they woke to the sound of the anchor dragging following a wind shift which was now blowing them on to the wall. A delicate manoeuvre ensued which involved letting out more chain to re-bed the anchor and then making sail with a triple-reefed main and small jib with a view to sailing the anchor out. Timing was of the essence. 'If we got the mainsail set while the anchor still held, then we had a chance; without it there was none.' The three of them, still in their pyjamas, were soon soaked to the skin but managed to set the sails and tack her off the lee shore. In the event 'she beat off that shore like a thorough-bred, and after two tacks I dared to look astern to where the wall was fast receding'. Once the anchor was out, with Anne at the helm, Peter and John hauled in the rest of the chain and the anchor. They sailed her round to a neighbouring bay protected from the worst of the wind which blew hard for three days.

At Vigo John found a berth on a boat returning to England while Christopher joined *Moonraker* bringing with him 'an immense canvas hold-all, a suitcase, a duffle-coat, a pair of leather-soled thigh boots and a drawing-board' – shades of Carruthers joining *Dulcibella* in *The Riddle of the Sands*. Fortunately, Christopher's transition was less bumpy than Carruthers' and he soon proved himself an able and inventive member of the crew, coming up with ways of sail handling, especially of the spinnaker, which Peter had not thought of.

The first Atlantic crossing from Madeira to Barbados occupies a single chapter of a mere twelve pages in Pye's account, and the return from Bermuda to the Azores only ten. It is a pattern repeated in his books about their later voyages. The challenges of long passages are almost taken for granted while attention is focussed on coastal and island hops and also on shore time. Not that the longer passages are without incident or interest. On the night before the crossing, as he went to sleep, Peter reviewed all the warnings he had received about their upcoming voyage. Would it be a test of endurance rather than the pleasure they hoped it would be? Would their 'puny boat' with its iron fastenings and antiquated rig stay the course? Would the crew get on each others' nerves?

In the event, the passage proceeded with a rich mixture of enjoyment and the inevitable stresses posed by wind and weather, plus occasional irritations such as eye infections, sickness, and headaches, all of which Dr Pye was able to treat with expedition. Christopher proved to be a highly compatible crew and entered fully into the spirit of the venture, even to the extent of winning a banana-eating competition prompted by all the bananas taken on board at Madeira ripening at once. He ate seventeen at a sitting. On a more serious note, Christopher voiced a common reaction among those who crewed on *Moonraker* when he wrote that Peter's special quality was being able to make everyone he came in contact with feel special. Both Peter and Anne, he wrote, 'made me feel like an only son'.

Once in the north-east trades, after struggling to prevent a gybe, they lowered the main sail and set twin spinnakers. They also managed to arrange a Heath Robinson system of self-steering. Nothing, however, seemingly could stop the wild rolling under just the twin headsails until they found that setting the trysail and sheeting it down the centre-line of the boat had the instantaneous effect of steadying the motion to a tolerable level. In mid-Atlantic they coincided with the British yacht *Debonair* which had left Falmouth the same day the Pyes had left Fowey. 'Are you the Pyes?' came the cry from the Fisks who were bound for New Zealand with their two young children.

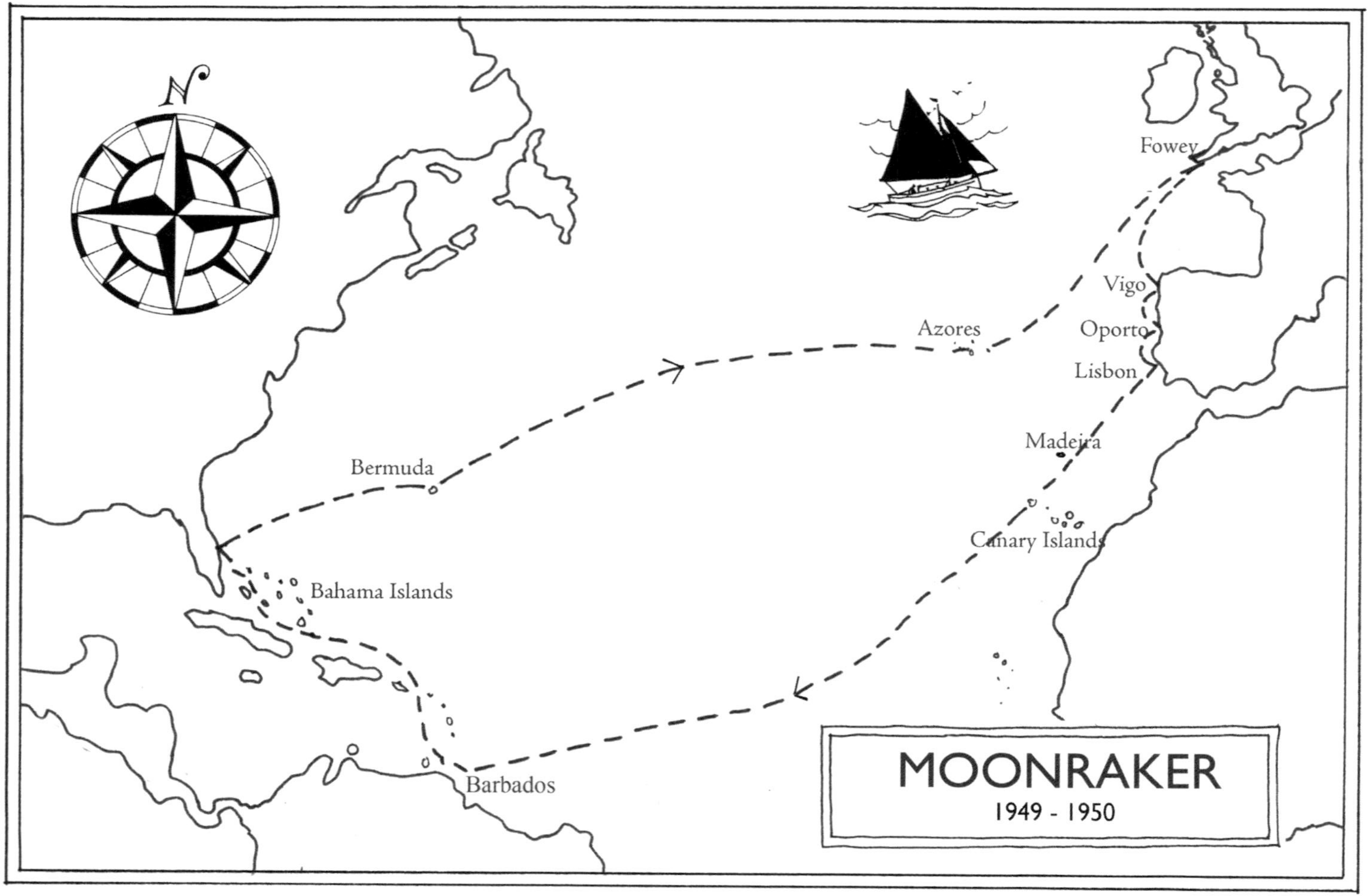
N
Fowey
Vigo
Oporto
Lisbon
Azores
Madeira
Canary Islands
Bermuda
Bahama Islands
Barbados
MOONRAKER
1949 - 1950

They talked across the water and took photographs of each other, a contact which was to be renewed in the Caribbean.

The only emergency they experienced on this crossing was a near case of man overboard. Peter was on the foredeck adjusting the trim of the sails and had put a turn of the sheet round a pin without securing it with a knot: 'the port spinnaker lifted a moment, filled with a bang and whipped the sheet off the pin. Instinctively I hung on for a second and was whisked off my feet into the air. I grabbed the forestay and let the sheet run through my hand, but the fright took my breath away.'

Landfall was duly made at Barbados after thirty days at sea. There ensued six months of island hopping through the Caribbean and on to Florida. For the most part it was a sequence of happy visits and encounters with island residents and other sailors, punctuated by the occasional drama, such as a grounding on a submerged reef on the approach to the harbour of the tiny island of Eleuthera in the Bahamas. This resulted from a momentary lapse of attention on Peter's part, and could have been disastrous but for the appearance of two powerful motor-boats which combined to pull *Moonraker* off the reef in time to prevent her being left high and dry on the falling tide. For a moment, while she was in peril, Peter reflected that 'I never knew till then how much I loved our ship.' Their rescuers would not accept any salvage fee for their trouble. *Moonraker* was indeed a lucky as well as a happy ship.

If there was another cloud on the horizon during this phase of their cruise it was news of the return of a Labour government in the general election of 1950, albeit with a reduced majority. On balance, Peter reflected, the result was 'fairly satisfactory' as the government's small majority would 'slow 'em down a bit.' The Fisks of *Debonair*, with whom they were sharing an anchorage at Antigua, would accept no such consolation and were glad to have decided on a move to New Zealand. Anne for her part was impatient with any criticism of Britain, 'even if it were only aimed at the Labour Party' and doubted whether the Fisks would escape red tape by going to New Zealand. They would have to find an uninhabited atoll in the south seas to achieve that.

American prosperity offered a striking contrast to the grim austerity of postwar Britain. Meeting more and more Americans as they moved northward in the Caribbean, the Pyes' imaginations were already excited by their 'vitality and the way they search after new things'. Florida confirmed their impressions of American openness and generosity while also revealing the cultural gulf between the two nations. Was it true, Peter was asked after giving a talk at the Kiwanis Club (a charitable organization devoted to helping children), that England was 'a communist state'? And was war likely to break out this year [presumably with the Soviet Union]? On the first question Peter said that he 'put their worst fears to rest', while to the second he responded that 'the sea protects you Americans but it seems to act like a sounding box; I've heard more about war in the last fortnight than I have in four years in England.' Evidently, the Pyes' political instincts chimed with those of many Americans but their British compound of pragmatism and studied detachment from controversy, remained inescapable.

Among the many characters and boats they encountered in the Caribbean was the American yacht designer and Commodore of the Cruising Club of America, Rod Stephens, who invited them aboard *Revonoc*, a forty-five foot ocean racer designed by the company of which he was a partner – Sparkman and Stephens. They became good friends and Stephens later supplied the foreword to *Red Mains'l*. Stephens was highly complimentary about the Pyes' sailing skills when they were given the chance to helm *Revonoc*. Of Peter he wrote that it is often assumed that a sailor will be either a cruising or a racing type but 'in this instance it was apparent to all that both skills had been combined to an extreme degree in one person'. Of Anne he said that 'the surprise came when she relieved her husband at the helm and in due course left us wondering which of our visitors was the more responsible for their cutter having sailed so far so successfully'.

Following *Moonraker*'s arrival at Barbados there were several crew changes. When Christopher left at Grenada they tried out two new crew – Hugh and Bob – with a view to taking one of them along on the return Atlantic passage. The choice fell on Bob, though not without some friction between Peter and Anne over her making the offer to him before consulting Peter. As it was, the arrangement worked well. For the passage from Bermuda to Fowey they added a fourth crew member on the grounds that Peter had had a recurrence of pain from a duodenal ulcer. Mike was a young man with little sailing experience and was highly susceptible to seasickness, but he too earned his place in the ship, becoming a competent and willing crew member. Nevertheless, four adults sharing the space on a twenty-nine foot boat for an extended period is a challenge under any circumstances. That it worked for an Atlantic crossing is nothing short of a marvel.

The return took them to Bermuda then Flores in the Azores and back to Fowey which they reached on 26 July 1950, thirteen months after their departure. The sting in the tail was stormy weather for most of the passage between the Azores and Fowey. It might be thought that this would cast a pall over the previous year of travel to exotic destinations, but for Peter Pye the opposite was the case. He reflected that 'long after tropic islands and coral beaches had faded from my memory, I should remember the thrill of this homeward passage, best of all these last twelve days from Flores'. Returning home was not just the end of the voyage but a reconnection with his roots. In this respect the Pyes differed from their fellow bluewater vagabonds, the Hiscocks, Smeetons, and Allcards, who, when not voyaging, made their homes outside the UK.

* * *

The most important outcome of this first voyage was a determination to keep going. Two years after their return to England the Pyes embarked on a three-year cruise. It resulted from an invitation to spend the winter of 1953-4 in British Columbia with Miles and Beryl Smeeton, later famous bluewater sailors but then only just about to embark on the sailing life. The Pyes and the Smeetons first met in February1951 on the foreshore at Fambridge in Essex while the Smeetons were looking for a boat to sail back to British Columbia. They got into conversation and soon became friends. Ten days after this encounter the Smeetons found the forty-five foot ketch *Tzu Hang* in Dover harbour and bought her. Though beginners at offshore cruising, they were never lacking in self-confidence. They cut their teeth on a hair-raising night crossing of the Thames estuary to deliver the boat to Essex where they planned a refit. Over the next few months they often sailed in company with *Moonraker*. The Smeetons' biographer remarks that 'on these occasions the Smeetons – or Miles, at least –

were at great pains to camouflage their ignorance, while every move that Peter and Anne made displayed the effortless confidence of their twenty-year partnership'. The upshot was the plan for Peter and Anne to sail to the Smeetons' home in British Columbia, which became the subject of Peter's second book, *The Sea is for Sailing* (1957).

Leaving Fowey in July 1952, they took a year to reach the Smeetons' home at Musgrave Landing at the southern end of Vancouver Island, sailing via the Panama Canal, the Galapagos Islands, the Marquesas Islands and Tahiti, then north to Hawaii. In distance covered and variety of conditions it far exceeded their first voyage and cemented their reputation as highly accomplished ocean sailors in what many people regarded as the most unsuitable of craft. Time and again they would be greeted by disbelief when they said they had sailed her from England, though it did not take long for the initiated to appreciate the Pyes' mastery of their boat and the cruising life.

After spending the winter of 1953-4 with the Smeetons they sailed north via the Queen Charlotte Islands to the waters of Southern Alaska before returning south down the American coast with stops at San Francisco, Santa Barbara and San Diego. As before, their response to America was a mixture of pleasure at the welcome they invariably received and fascination at the profound differences between America and Britain. 'Your country glitters and you forget, being used to all these brassy lights, that our eyes are not accustomed to it, or perhaps you have never realized, that English are so very different.' Peter Pye presents, if not exactly a stiff upper lip, a native reserve which, he says, makes the English visitor 'unable to swallow America when you push it down his throat'. From their last American port of San Diego they cruised the length of the Mexican coast where they experienced both 'the magic of Mexico' and the rigours of the Gulf of Tehuantepec which, Peter noted, had the same reputation as the Portland Race in the English Channel – a place to be treated with extreme respect. In line with the pilot book warnings they were met with a vicious night-time gale which gave Anne a miserable bout of seasickness and produced dangerous confusion on deck, resulting in a smashed riding-light glass and the skipper's blood on the deck. Picking up the pieces, they negotiated the coasts of the central American republics, arriving at Panama in January 1955. Sailing north from the Canal

'long after tropic islands and coral beaches had faded from my memory, I should remember the thrill of this homeward passage...'

through the Caribbean, after stops in Florida and Charleston, South Carolina they headed for Bermuda and England. They dropped anchor in Fowey in July 1955.

* * *

When not on lengthy ocean voyages, the Pyes made annual cruises to destinations in northern European waters, some of which they wrote up for the yachting press. One European venture which merited a whole book was their cruise to Finland in 1959. A Captain Eino Koivistoinen in the port city of Kotka near the border with the Soviet Union had heard through a mutual acquaintance that the Pyes were interested in sailing to Finland and wrote offering to show them 'not only the beauty of our countryside but how our people live.' He sounded so simpatico that Peter was eager to meet him but Anne put the seal on the decision by telling him that she had let their cottage in Essex for six months, so they had no choice but to leave.

The resulting cruise showed all the Pye trademarks of resourcefulness in piloting their boat through new and tricky waters, curiosity about people and places, and a knack for describing their adventures. Peter was the primary author but his account, as in all his writings, is liberally sprinkled with extracts from Anne's journal which enliven the text and create a sense of immediacy. In *A Sail in a Forest* (1961), Peter is more than ever the travel writer, conveying enthusiasm for Finland and the Finnish, not least for the strength of their resolve in the face of the Russian bear on their border. The Russian threat had a long history but was still very much alive. Peter records being menaced by four Russian patrol boats when *Moonraker* strayed near the twelve mile limit off the Finnish coast. When they arrived at their destination of Kotka several days later than expected, their host, Captain Koivistoinen, said he feared they might have fallen into the hands of the Russians.

There are plenty of lighter moments. Peter analyses their first sauna experience from a medical point of view while also celebrating its morale-boosting effects. They make a trip by air to Lapland with friends, explore Helsinki, and visit an English woman whose husband was a close friend of Sibelius. Everywhere, though, they are reminded of the devastation caused by the Russian attack on Finland in the

'Winter War' of 1939, not least the annexation of part of Karelia, a region which lay at the heart of Finnish patriotism and many years before had been the subject of Sibelius' most famous piece of music, the Karelia Suite.

So absorbing were the sights and culture of Finland and so practised were they at sailing *Moonraker* that the nautical dimension often slips into the background. It does not disappear, however. On one particularly tricky passage on the island-strewn coast east of Helsinki they found themselves beating to windward in a narrow channel in the teeth of a rising gale. Looking up from the chart, Anne said: 'if you want to go on you must do the pilotage yourself. I will have nothing to do with the wrecking of the vessel.' Peter was reminded of an earlier occasion cruising in the Friesian Islands when Anne's anger at his determination to go on in the face of danger had saved them and *Moonraker* from potential disaster. Anne had accused him of being 'frightened of being afraid'. On both occasions Peter evidently accepted the charge and heeded her warning. Of such stuff are strong marriages made.

* * *

Peter and Anne had plenty more sailing in them. A summer cruise to the Hebrides in 1960 via the Caledonian canal and a trip to Scandinavia the following year ('to see that we did not get on each other's nerves') were followed in the spring of 1962 by their departure for Brazil. A friend had once described Rio de Janeiro as the most beautiful harbour in the world, and the idea, once planted, grew 'as an oak does from an acorn'. The result was a fourteen-month voyage which Peter described as the most enjoyable they had ever made. Leaving Fowey in April, they reached Recife in August and Rio De Janeiro in October where once again Peter showed that his political antennae were in good working order, noting that the world was on the brink of nuclear war in the Cuban missile crisis.

Wherever they stopped, their capacity for friendship also showed to good effect, not least because Peter's medical expertise was regularly in demand. Their reliance on friends was never more apparent, however, than in a serious medical emergency experienced by Peter. While at anchor in Ilha Grande, some miles south of Rio, he slipped

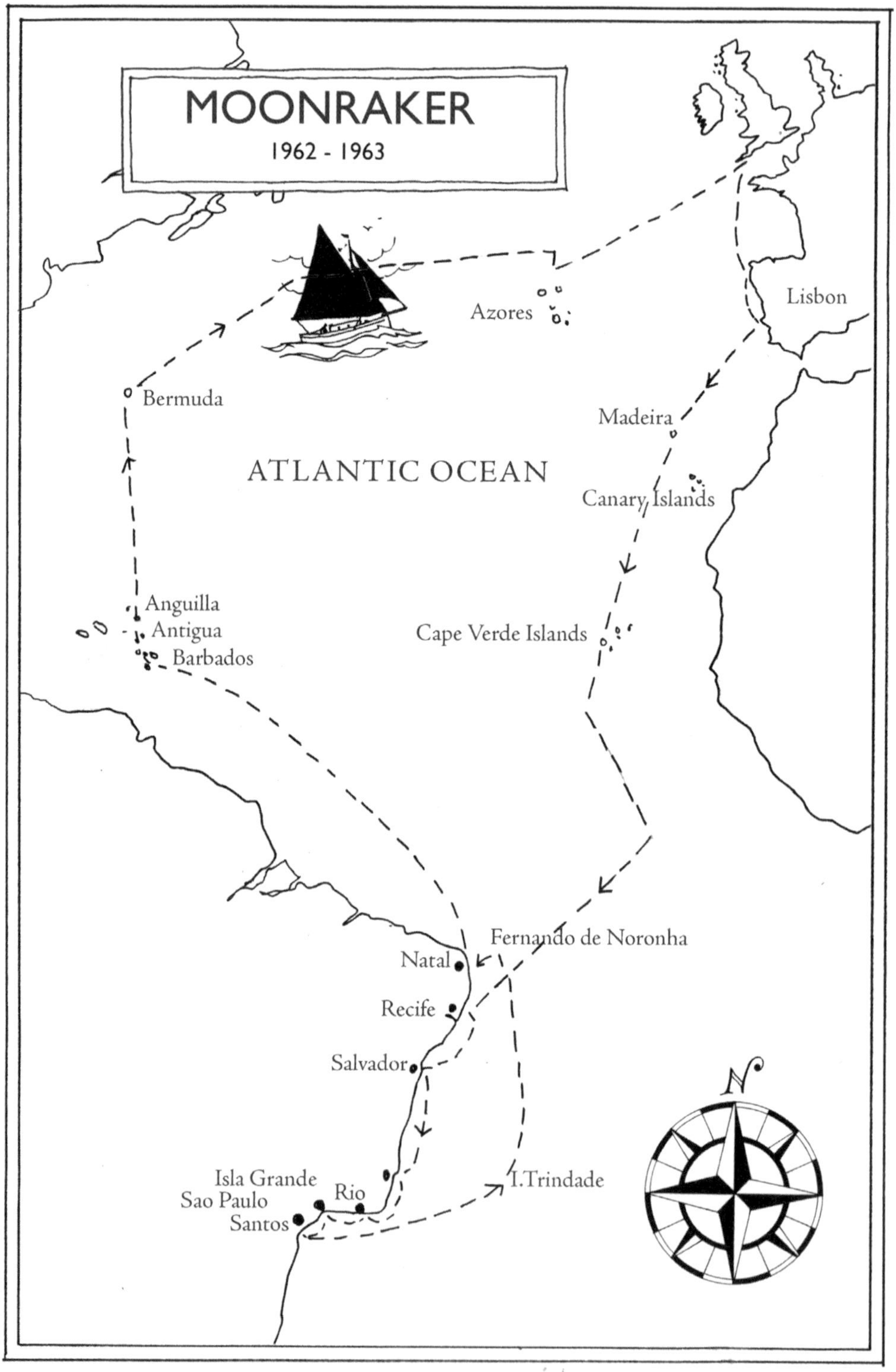
MOONRAKER
1962 - 1963
Azores
Lisbon
Bermuda
Madeira
ATLANTIC OCEAN
Canary Islands
Anguilla
Antigua
Barbados
Cape Verde Islands
Fernando de Noronha
Natal
Recife
Salvador
Isla Grande
Sao Paulo
Santos
Rio
I.Trindade
N

and fell awkwardly on his side in the cockpit. Initially it appeared to be only cracked ribs but his conditioned worsened, his breathing became poor, and both lungs were clearly suffering from infection. It was pneumonia. When he was well enough to leave the hospital, some friends lent them a flat where they stayed until he had recovered.

It was two months since he had set foot on *Moonraker* when they took passage to Santos, about one hundred and thirty miles south of Rio, the most southerly point of their voyage. They had intended to sail to Tristan da Cunha, a remote island over two thousand miles southeast of Rio, before heading for home but Peter was in no condition to extend their voyage to such a degree. Getting home would be difficult enough, though as always the Pyes never shirked a challenge. They opted to make a wide sweep out into the Atlantic almost as far as the Ilha Trindade before turning north to the island of Fernando de Noronha and from there back to the Brazilian coast for a brief stop at Natal before sailing north for home. In truth Peter and Anne were in dispute about this part of the voyage: he wishing to indulge his 'obsession' with remote islands and she wanting to return to Brazil. So they did both.

The remainder of the voyage took them to the now familiar waters of the Caribbean and from there to Bermuda and across the Atlantic to home waters. Peter remarked in his log of the voyage, published in the Royal Cruising Club journal, that despite some moments he would prefer to forget this had been the most enjoyable of all their voyages. He gave credit to Brazil from which, he said 'the materialistic West could learn a great deal', but also to their crew Jock McLeod, a highlander from Skye who was also an experienced sailor and fellow member of the Royal Cruising Club of which Peter Pye was now Vice-Commodore. Once again it was a happy ship, perhaps their happiest of all.

This venture nevertheless took its toll. Age compounded Peter's health problems; he was now over sixty years old. Photos of him on board during their last voyage show him thin and drawn. His stomach ulcer continued to cause trouble to which was added a double strangulated hernia. In 1966 they made a short cruise to the Mediterranean during which Peter experienced serious pain and, adding to their misery, Anne broke her wrist. On their return to England they stopped at Plymouth where he underwent surgery for the hernia but tragically died on the operating table after a mis-labelled cylinder delivered the wrong gas. His account of the Brazil voyage, *Back Door To Brazil,* was completed by Anne after his death but not published until twenty years later along with his three other books in an Omnibus Edition (1986). On Peter's death Anne returned to Mizzen Cottage in Southminster, Essex where she led a quiet life and died in 1983.

As for *Moonraker,* she spent several years in Exeter Maritime Museum before being sold to a friend of Anne's and restored at a boatyard in Maylandsea, Essex. She then moved with a new owner to Denmark, where there is a report of her being seen in 2003. She next surfaced (which this author can confirm) at Upson's yard in Aldeburgh in the 2010s where she was undergoing what amounted to a total rebuild of the hull. From there she was transported to the West country for finishing, reportedly now under new ownership. Many will applaud the restoration of this unique vessel with her rich and well-recorded history but it will be remarkable if she is ever sailed so far and with such commitment as was shown by the Pyes in their three and a half decades with *Moonraker.*

Chapter 3

A SAILING LIFE

Adlard Coles: *Cohoe I-IV*

Among mid-twentieth-century yachtsmen Adlard Coles is something of an enigma. His name is everywhere, not only by virtue of his formidable record as a cruising and a racing sailor but because the company he founded after the war, Adlard Coles Nautical, became a leading publisher in the field.* Coles also acquired and edited *The Yachtsman* for over ten years and wrote fifteen books in his own right, including sailing guides to the south coast and northern France, accounts of his own cruises and races, and not least a compelling autobiography, *Sailing Years* (1981).

Despite the range of his activity and the amount he wrote, he gives away very little of himself in his writings. He rarely engaged in private reflection. The result is that, even more than with the other voyagers portrayed in this book, it is hard to know what made him tick beyond an unquenchable desire to sail and supreme competence at doing it. This may owe something to the circumstances of his early life. Later in his life and writings counter-currents would become visible but his first steps in life encouraged self-containment and restraint.

Born in 1901, he lost his parents when he was six years old and was brought up by his grandparents. They were kindly people and 'spared no effort to make me happy' but, he reflected, 'I received a Victorian upbringing.' He recalls a visit to a London club to see a distant cousin who was a General and being told off when they got home because he had not addressed the General as 'sir'.

During his early teens he developed Bright's disease and was given only six months to live by a leading specialist. While recovering he was sent to Weymouth to live with an uncle who was also a doctor. It was a decisive move for his future. Living in a house overlooking Weymouth Bay he was able to watch the yacht racing from his bed-

---

* Janet Spinlove has disentangled the complex history of Coles's highly successful publishing ventures in *The Marine Quarterly*, 35 (Autumn 2019), 101-4.

room window. 'In the summer of 1914 I saw and knew by sight all the big yachts which were racing in Weymouth Bay.' He also bought *The Yachtsman* for twopence each week, little knowing that one day he would be proprietor of the magazine. He then moved to a public school in Surrey where there was a compulsory morning swim in an open-air swimming pool which in winter sometimes had a thin film of ice over it. In retrospect he believed that this, and the cold bath and regular exercises insisted on by his grandmother when he was at home, was a good training for ocean racing.

Adlard Coles gained an interest in the sea during his time at Weymouth but began sailing at the relatively late age of nineteen while he was a student at Cambridge University in the wake of the First World War. However, he took to it with such speed and determination that by his mid-20s he already had extensive cruises behind him and had published two books. His training ground was Chichester Harbour where during one summer vacation his university friend Basil Rowe, 'a highly experienced and hard-sailing friend,' took him out 'every day regardless of weather and gave me the best possible initiation.' From then on he seized every opportunity to get out on the water. While still a student, he hired a dinghy for two weeks' single-handed sailing at Plymouth. On another occasion he gained an introduction to the owner of a Brixham sailing trawler who was regarded as one of the best skippers of his day. 'Skipper Batho allowed me to take as full a part in the work as my inexperience allowed and when ashore I stayed with him and his wife and son.' Coles was evidently not short either of ambition or a work ethic.

At twenty-one, having come into a small amount of money, he bought his first boat, a small centre-board double-ender called *Jessica*, in which he cruised the Solent area and as far west as Poole. She was not, he recalled, a very good boat, being very tender 'and little more than a day boat', but he was proud of her and lived aboard for long periods in the most spartan conditions. Indeed throughout his sailing life Coles seems to have been almost oblivious to discomfort. Jessica was soon replaced by 'an elderly twenty-two-foot cutter called *Lapwing*' but his third boat, the twenty-six-foot gaff-rigged *Annette*, was his first proper yacht and he soon began to make plans for extensive cruising.

Annette had been designed for racing in the Le Havre estuary and with long overhangs, a waterline length of only nineteen feet, and huge sail area she was hardly ideal for cruising. However, she had an immense beam of nine feet two inches which made her relatively roomy below. To prepare her for her new life he had Moody's yard in Bursledon make various alterations. Two feet came off the boom and the gaff, the large cockpit was mostly decked in, leaving only a canvas bucket for the helmsman's feet, and new sails were made.

Meanwhile he still had a degree to finish and a career to plan. It is an indication of his single-mindedness that he chose his profession entirely to fit in with his intention to sail. He opted, perhaps surprisingly, for accountancy but it proved to give him not only the freedom and independence he craved but the skills which enabled him after the war to run a successful publishing business.

Before entering articles, however, there was sailing to be done. Fired by a reading of *The Riddle of the Sands* and E F Knight's *Falcon on the Baltic,* he set off for the Baltic with two companions soon after graduation. One was a First World War veteran with one eye and a gammy leg who was nevertheless able to steer and possessed the priceless talent of being able to produce a meal under any conditions. The other (like Arthur Davies's companion in *The Riddle of the Sands*) was a student friend who could speak German. This was not the only parallel with Erskine Childers's famous book. Coles proved equally adept at negotiating the notoriously difficult waters of the Friesian Islands. In one instance they ran aground on the top of a mud bank on an ebb tide. His solution was to take the dinghy out into the channel with the chart, sounding line and binoculars to find the nearest deep water and survey the surrounding area. With this information in hand, on returning to the boat they 'proceeded to dig a channel with the sculls and bucket through the soft mud to the deeper water'. When, long after dark, the tide rose and filled their little channel, they moved out to the main channel, anchored, and retired for the night.

Coles's account of this cruise, *In Broken Water* (1924), was a notably confident debut. He proved equal to the challenges faced by a small engineless boat which included gales in open water as well as creek-crawling and negotiating the Dutch and German canals. Life in harbour could be challenging too. They experienced an attempted robbery in the German port of Cuxhaven where homeless boys and tramps lived in a de-commissioned lightship. It was a time of economic collapse in Germany where 'revolution was expected at every moment, riots and robberies were an everyday occurrence.' A private yacht with presumably rich Englishmen on it was an obvious target. The patter of feet was heard on the deck in the small hours but Coles's effort to catch them was foiled. 'I got hold of one, intending to give him a ducking, but he was slippery as an eel, and I slipped on the deck, which was wet with early morning dew – so he got away.' This is another reminder of a scene in *The Riddle of the Sands* in which Carruthers is asleep down below on his own and hears the sound of feet on the deck. His efforts to seize the intruder also fail, though he is left with one of the intruder's boots in his hand.

Coles writes no-nonsense prose but is a careful observer of his surroundings and has a wry sense of the dramatic. One evening on Norderney, returning from a cabaret show to the harbour they found no *Annette*. She had evidently been stolen. After a night spent trying to locate her, including vain attempts to rouse the local police, they received a report that she had been found aground in the tidal harbour of Norddeich on the mainland opposite Norderney. A 'fast motorboat' was hired to take up the pursuit. By morning the village had turned out in force to help with the search. 'Our striking force', Coles noted, 'consisted of the chief of police, a sergeant and two young constables, all armed with big revolvers. Next in command now appeared to be the pianist of the local cabaret, who strutted about in a brightly coloured sweater.' Last but not least was a crew of 'mahogany-faced fisherman with their kindly faces set in grim determination to help these poor Englishmen'. Altogether, Coles concluded, 'we made a fine assault party, the only pity being that Gilbert and Sullivan were not present to witness it'. In the event, the fast motorboat, which turned out to be an old fishing boat, ran aground before reaching Norddeich harbour, leaving the posse high and dry for the next few hours. *Annette* was recovered later largely undamaged but was in a mess below, and the culprits escaped. 'We undoubtedly provided Norderney with great entertainment', Coles observed.

Two years later Coles continued his association with authors of nautical works when he travelled to Riga to buy *Racundra*, the thirty-foot gaff ketch then owned by Arthur Ransome, with the intention of sailing her back to England. Interestingly, Coles never named Arthur Ransome but referred only to 'the original owner'. (As yet Ransome was known primarily as a journalist, most recently as the *Manchester Guardian* correspondent in Russia. The first of his children's nautical adventure books did not appear till 1930.) Part of the arrangement with Ransome was that the name *Racundra* should not appear in any publication resulting from Coles' return trip to England in order not to create any confusion with Ransome's own book *Racundra's First Cruise*. In the event, Coles renamed the boat *Annette II* and the association of Ransome with Coles's acquisition did not become public knowledge for more than thirty years.

The book that resulted from this cruise, *Close-Hauled* (1926), was every bit as dramatic and fluently written as his first one. It is particularly notable for its account of a southerly gale on the return across the North Sea which is reprinted as chapter I of his *Heavy Weather Sailing* (first edition 1967) which became the authoritative work on this subject. The gale hit when they were about thirty miles north east of the Sandettie light vessel, still fifty miles from their destination of Dover. But there was no hope of making progress in that direction. Their only option was to heave to, go below, and hope the wind did not shift into the west or north-west which would put them in dangerously shallow waters. 'The position was romantic in the extreme: hove-to in the night of an equinoctial gale, surrounded at a distance of about twenty miles, except to the north, by a broken circle of shoals. We were absolutely in the hands of chance.' The wind pushed them north but they had no idea where they were till the Galloper lightship appeared about three miles to starboard. This was of only temporary use since they were being driven north at a pace and could see very little. Besides, Coles noted, 'I had never sailed before on the east coast, and my North Sea chart which covered the Thames mouth was of too small scale to be any use.'

At last after dawn the next day a town appeared on their port bow which proved to be Southwold, then as now one of the trickiest entries on the east coast. True the gale had moderated somewhat but on an ebb tide – Coles reckoned it was two hours after high water – with a narrow entry between wooden piers and big seas running, they were fortunate to make a safe entrance. Typically, even though dog-tired and desperate to reach port, Coles was not prepared to leave everything to chance. As they approached the mouth of the river, he sounded twice with the lead.

A notable feature of this account is that he was accompanied by his wife, whom he had married shortly before the start of the trip. His 'sailing wife', as Coles describes her, was evidently an able helmswoman and possessed of great stamina which included the ability to prepare food and hot drinks under the worst conditions. Mamie never raced but they enjoyed a lifetime's cruising together.

On return from the Baltic Coles settled down to accountancy, doing as much sailing as time would allow, but in-between whiles he started a publishing company, edited *The Yachtsman*, wrote books on finance and accountancy, and also designed board games with nautical themes, such as *Ship-a-Hoy* and *Flotilla*. He was clearly not a man to sit around and do nothing. Besides a good deal of dinghy racing, and cruising in Channel waters and northern France, two further extensive cruises were possible in Scandinavia during the 1930s. Somewhat ironically, given his apparently robust health and strenuous sailing ventures, he was ruled out of active service in the war because of diabetes and spent much of the war editing manuals on naval gunnery and seeing them through the press.

* * *

Thus far the name Adlard Coles was not associated with ocean racing but it was in this field that he excelled in the post-war years. From the first postwar ocean racing season of 1947 onwards he proved to be a relentless driver of a boat, whatever the conditions. Typically, he won the first ocean race he entered after the war, a 200-mile course from Southsea to Le Havre and back to Brixham. His was the only Royal Ocean Racing Club (RORC) Class III boat to finish in the near gale conditions and he beat all the others on corrected time. This included a few hours at anchor in Swanage Bay sitting out a foul tide. Out of twenty-eight entries sixteen retired. He also won the Plymouth–La Rochelle race in the same year, this time in predominantly light weather, plus the overall Class III points championship for the season. His boat was the thirty-two-foot *Cohoe* (see frontispiece) which he had bought the previous year, the first of a long line of boats with that name. She was an extended Scandinavian Tumlare design with a beam of only seven feet four inches, and her accommodation was so cramped that she never carried a crew larger than three. With her narrow beam and high aspect Bermudan rig, to windward she was virtually unbeatable against boats of her class, though Coles's success owed much to the strength of his crew, among whom was his son Ross who proved to be as determined and able as his father.

Coles was told by an old-timer that Cohoe was 'unfit to go outside the Solent' and was just a 'toy yacht'. Undaunted, he entered the Santander race the following year in what proved to be another heavy weather slog. Coles and another crew member, Geoff Budden, were washed overboard in the Bay of Biscay in storm force winds. Both remained precariously attached to the yacht's lifelines, while Coles's son Ross was off-watch down below, but providentially it was the time for a change of watch and Ross poked his head out of the companion way to find the cockpit empty. He was able to haul Geoff aboard and not a moment too soon since 'he had fallen in head foremost with his head towed under water by the speed of the boat.' Coles's own situation was less dire but he could not easily have extricated himself from the tangle he was in without a helping hand from his son. This race features in Chapter 5 of *Heavy Weather Sailing*.

These and other races in testing conditions were the perfect preparation for the dramatic events of 1950 which included two races: the Bermuda–Newport and the Transatlantic races. In preparation, *Cohoe* was shipped over to Bermuda but not before she had been altered by having her bow extended by three feet in order to meet the entry requirements for the Bermuda race which specified a minimum overall length of thirty-five feet. With her new aluminium extension supported by a network of 'stringers, strengthened by brackets, angle-pieces and vertical frames' *Cohoe* proved as ever to be a formidable competitor. She failed to win honours in the Bermuda race, being beaten to the line by the Royal Naval Sailing Association sloop *Samuel Pepys* by twenty-three seconds after 1200 miles of racing, but the real achievement of all the boats in this race was to have survived a tropical cyclone with winds estimated at near hurricane force for some of the fleet. By coincidence this was the same storm in which

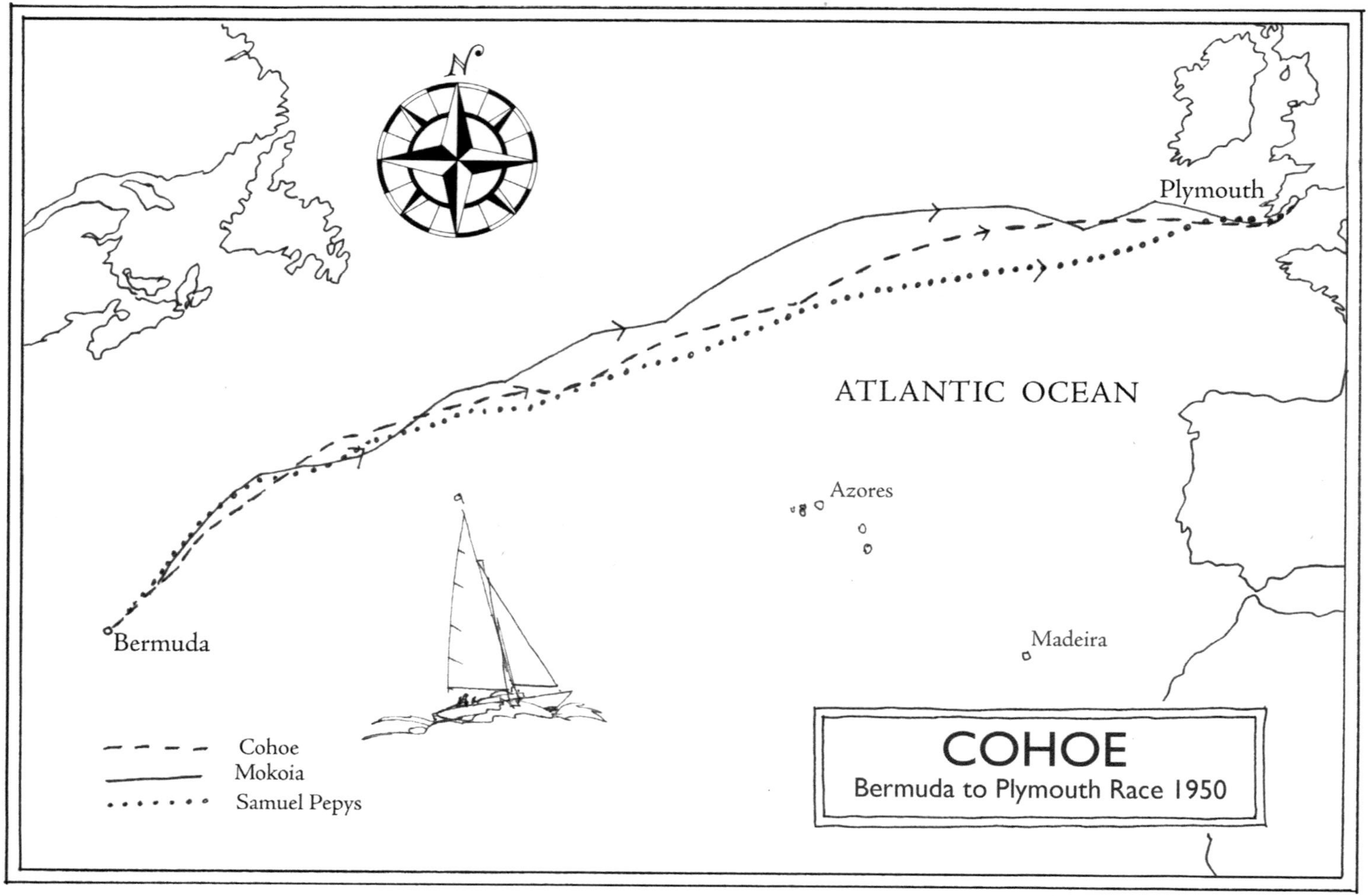
COHOE
Bermuda to Plymouth Race 1950
ATLANTIC OCEAN
Plymouth
Bermuda
Azores
Madeira
N
Cohoe
Mokoia
Samuel Pepys

Humphrey Barton experienced a knock-down and near catastrophe in *Vertue XXXV* as he neared the end of his marathon east to west crossing.*

A week after the finish of the Bermuda race *Cohoe*, minus her artificial bow section, was at the starting line for the transatlantic race from Bermuda to Plymouth along with *Samuel Pepys*, skippered by Erroll Bruce, the innovative Laurent Giles design *Gulvain*, skippered by the indomitable Humphrey Barton, who was still nursing cracked ribs from his transatlantic crossing in *Vertue XXXV*, and two other boats. Once again gales were a feature of this race and once again Coles proved both his nerve and his skill by piling on the sail when he felt it was necessary. At one stage he had been forced to heave to in order to prevent damage and get some rest, at the inevitable cost of vital race miles. 'By brutal driving', Coles observed, over a period of four days *Cohoe* regained those miles by dint of setting 'the heavy nylon spinnaker... by day and by night'. Cohoe won the race on corrected time in another display of the qualities which made Coles such a formidable offshore racer.

In 1952 Coles had a new ocean racer designed for him by Charles Nicholson and built by Souters of Cowes. *Cohoe II* was only three feet longer than *Cohoe I* but had close to double the internal volume and twice the displacement. She was well suited to the alternation of racing and cruising which was a pattern Coles maintained throughout these years. He relished the family cruises they made to Brittany in their first season with the boat and to Ireland the following year. The Brittany cruise started at Benodet and included fourteen different anchorages in fifteen nights while the Irish cruise, which lasted a month, began at Crosshaven and took them west to Dingle and the Blaskets, once again stopping at innumerable anchorages and exploring out of the way bays. Coles brought as much concentration to cruising as he did to racing, as is clear from the focus on detail in his cruising logs, the pleasure he took in exploration, and the number of cruising guides he wrote.

Meanwhile, however, in the 1950s racing absorbed much of his energy. In the 1953 RORC season, Coles won his class in the La Coruña

* See Chapter 5 for discussion of Humphrey Barton.

Coles brought as much concentration to cruising as he did to racing, as is clear from the focus on detail in his cruising logs, the pleasure he took in exploration, and the number of cruising guides he wrote.

race and then achieved an overall win in the Cowes to Cork race. In keeping with the pattern of many races in which Coles competed, this one took place in heavy weather and featured the retirement of eight out of the eleven starters, the only other boats to complete the course besides *Cohoe II* being two Class I boats.

Of the many other races which Coles entered, the most notable was the 1957 Fastnet which, until the disaster of 1979, was widely regarded as the toughest of all. The wind blew at gale or near gale force for the whole race. This time Coles was sailing a 'faster all-round boat', *Cohoe III*, built for him in 1956 to another Charles Nicolson design. She was the same overall length as *Cohoe II*, but had a transom rather than a counter stern, and was of much heavier displacement. She was specifically designed for heavy weather, with construction and gear all above average strength, which made her perfectly suited for the conditions of the 1957 Fastnet. Coles won his class and came sixth overall. It was a brutal beat against a south-westerly gale for much of the way along the south coast of England, and once again Coles sat out a foul tide, in this case in Dartmouth, where they were able to repair a broken cabin door and mast fittings which had worked loose. The wind moderated at Lands End but then went into the north-west and increased in strength as they crossed St George's Channel, making another beat towards the Fastnet Rock. Few boats completed the course without significant damage, including the overall winner, the American yawl *Carina*, which suffered several broken timbers at the bow when she fell off a wave. Once again, Coles's account of this race featured memorably in *Heavy Weather Sailing*.

Coles had ten more years of offshore racing, including the 1959 and 1961 Fastnets in both of which *Cohoe III* achieved fourth place overall. Ever restless and determined to push success to the maximum, he acquired a new boat for the 1963 Fastnet. *Cohoe IV* was an early example of a Nicholson 36 with a fibre-glass hull which proved to be fast and weatherly. True to form, Coles won Class III and came second overall, beating stiff competition from American and British Admirals Cup yachts. In 1966 he qualified for an old age pension which meant, he noted, that he had more time for sailing than ever. Reverting this season to *Cohoe III* he won Class III and came second overall in the Cowes-Dinard race. In a race to Spain later in the year they came close to being dismasted when a weld on the stainless steel bowsprit failed. They ran her off downwind and made repairs which enabled them to complete the race. Despite their low place in this race, *Cohoe III* still came third in Class III in the points championship. The following season was his last but he still managed respectable results in both the Fastnet race and the Class III points championship. At the end of the 1967 season when he gave up ocean racing Coles could look back on twenty years of being consistently among the most successful of British ocean racing skippers.

* * *

Given his record both in cruising and racing it is easy to see why Coles should be regarded as the authority on tactics in heavy weather. What stands out is not merely his resourcefulness and daring under extreme pressure but his endless curiosity about wind and weather, boat design, and sailing tactics in all conditions. Later editions of *Heavy Weather Sailing* include chapters by a variety of other authors on specialist topics. The fourth edition, for example, published in 1991 several years after Coles's death, includes a whole new section entitled 'Expert Advice' on every conceivable subject including yacht design for heavy weather, rig and spar considerations, multihull design, meteorology, stability of yachts in large waves, the design and use of drogues, preparation for heavy weather, clothing and perhaps inevitably also seasickness. It says much for Coles's standing in the yachting world and the quality of the foundation he laid in the first edition that *Heavy Weather Sailing* should have become the leading work in the field.

It would be a mistake to conclude this portrait without recalling that Coles remained a dedicated cruising sailor who did as much as anyone, through his example and publications, to promote the cruising life. Behind the hard-driving racing skipper lay a more private man who relished the simple pleasures of being on the water. *Sailing Days*, which describes a range of modest cruises undertaken in small boats during the 1930s, was published in 1944 as if in defiance of the gloom and stresses of the war. The book invited experienced sailors to recall their own best days afloat but also to encourage 'those who have been frightened by the idea that it is a rich man's sport'. In particular, Coles pointed to the chapters of the book which covered cruises he and his wife undertook in a fourteen foot Island class dinghy which, he noted, 'cost only about 50 pounds, inclusive of sails'. In this boat they sailed all over the Solent, 'exploring all its creeks and Harbours from Keyhaven to Wootton and spending three or four weeks in Langston and Chichester harbours'. This small book remains a matchless evocation of the simpler pleasures of sailing in small boats.

In *More Sailing Days* (1947), his first postwar book, Coles was eloquent about the pleasures of his return to sailing and the opportunities to revisit old cruising haunts. There is no more evocative picture of Coles's dedication to the cruising life than his account of how he spent VE day. Armed with special permission from the Admiralty to launch his yacht to prepare a new edition of *Creeks and Harbours of the Solent*, on 8 May 1945 he took the bus from Burlesdon to Itchenor where his Tumlare yacht *Zara* was lying at anchor. He crept out of Chichester Harbour with the aim of making for his mooring at Burlesdon on the Hamble but missed his tide and altered course to Wootton Creek on the Isle of Wight. It was dark by the time he dropped anchor. From his snug berth in Wootton Creek he watched the firework display across the water in celebration of VE day. Conveniently close but happily distant from the crowds, Coles recalls that as night fell he 'turned in, glad, after the six war years, to be sleeping once more in the cosy cabin of a little yacht'. With this recollection we gain a glimpse of stillness and inner contentment at the centre of Coles's often frenetic sailing life.

Chapter 4

EDWARD ALLCARD

The Single-Handed Phase: *Temptress* and *Sea Wanderer*

Edward Allcard was the epitome of the single-handed sailor – independent-minded, omni-competent, content with his own company and perhaps above all, blessed with extraordinary mental and physical stamina. He was born in 1914 into a family of means, educated at Eton, and trained as a naval architect. His Atlantic and South American voyages from the late 1940s through the early 1970s in *Temptress* and then *Sea Wanderer* place him in that special category of lone sailors whose exploits flow as much from character as from their skill as seamen.

Other than the necessary qualities sketched above, there is no formula for the character of the solo voyager, just varieties of individuality which the circumnavigators so admired by Allcard amply demonstrated. Unsurprisingly, Joshua Slocum was a constant reference point but so also were Alain Gerbault and Louis Bernicot, respectively the third and fifth solo circumnavigators, whose stirring voyages in the 1920s and 1930s are scarcely recalled today outside France. Allcard spoke French and translated Bernicot's *Voyage of the Anahita*. He also admired the Argentinian solo circumnavigator Vito Dumas, whose epic circumnavigation of the world took place during the Second World War and, perhaps for that reason, is less well known than it should be. Allcard memorably met Dumas in 1965 in a boatyard in Buenos Aires where *Sea Wanderer* was up on the hard. Allcard had been trying to contact him when Dumas turned up in the yard, pointed to himself and said in a husky voice 'Vito Dumas'. Allcard spoke Spanish and they had a good chat. The next day came news of Dumas' death. This encounter was of a piece with Allcard's vivid awareness of the sea-going tradition and of his own part in it, a perspective which lends depth and interest to his narratives.

Allcard's own individuality consisted of relishing 'the freedom and independence to do as I liked'. He dedicated his second book, *Temptress Returns*, to 'that elusive thing THE FREEDOM OF THE

INDIVIDUAL'. But his voyages were more than escapes from the shackles of civilization. In between them he engaged actively with the life ashore, frequently because he needed to earn money to keep his voyaging going. During his leisurely voyage in *Sea Wanderer* to South America via the Caribbean, which began in 1956 and lasted close to a decade, he stopped in Tangier for six months and set up a chartering business, in part for day sailing but often for longer trips. He did the same in the West Indies later in the voyage. He also got to know local fishermen and accompanied them on fishing trips. Since on passage he often relied on catching fish for fresh food, his curiosity about fish and fishing was of great practical use.

Like many other long distance sailors he wrote books to help finance his voyaging, but writing was evidently a pleasure rather than a chore. On his return voyage across the Atlantic he re-read his own recently published account of the outward voyage and confessed that 'perhaps egotistically, I thoroughly enjoyed it'. We can put this down to a boyish delight in his own powers as a writer rather than an urge for public recognition. For the most part he shunned publicity and went his own way, though on occasion he attracted a good deal of attention which, as we shall see, he was not shy in making use of for his own ends.

The impression he projects is of a gypsy of the sea. He carried very little cultural baggage – or at least none which got in the way of remaining open to experience. In fact by all accounts he was a gentlemanly and cultured individual whose books are full of colourful descriptions and reflections on any number of topics. Above all he was an acute observer of the life of the sea – the creatures in it, wind patterns, weather, waves, currents, in fact the totality of the ocean environment in which he seemed peculiarly at home. He ruminated on politics, social life, human nature and natural history, in all of which he expressed a folksy nature-based wisdom. He was against 'isms' (except 'individualism') and any unnatural systems of rule which encouraged regimentation of people into masses. He read widely when conditions permitted, above all nautical books by sailors like himself and plenty of older maritime history but also Darwin, Jack London, Gerald Durrell and others. Yet he also had the capacity to connect in a peculiarly direct way with people and places. He was notably free of crankiness, doubtless because the discipline of solo voyaging over decades, achieved without major accidents or disasters, demanded a continuous focus on practicality.

And then in his fifties this seemingly confirmed soloist, albeit one who had tried marriage briefly many years before, met and married a much younger woman with whom he spent the rest of his life. There had been earlier signs of him playing with the idea of a mate in all senses of the term but until Clare appeared, the call of freedom always won. Hardly missing a beat, he quickly took to having a permanent crew which soon included a daughter. For several more decades, now in a sixty-nine foot Baltic trading vessel called *Johanne Regina*, Edward and Clare roamed the seas, until in his nineties they settled in land-locked Andorra where he died in 2017 at the age of 102.*

* * *

Like most gypsies of the sea, Edward Allcard began young. He was taught to sail at the age of six by his father's boatman (a detail revealing much about his background) who later left him a fifteen foot sailing dinghy called *Dora*. At the age of fifteen Allcard sailed *Dora* down the Thames from Teddington to the sea, sleeping under an awning slung over the boom. He wrote a log of his adventures which still survives and shows a precocious facility for writing besides a questing and adventurous spirit. A short excerpt gives a flavour of his youthful prose and spirited personality:

> I cast off her painter and slowly paddled into the main stream of the Thames, half a mile above Teddington Lock. I hoisted the mainsail and unrolled the jib and swiftly glided downstream to the lock... I forked out my bob, and went through... In the brilliant sunlight the green banks of the Thames looked lovely until the tide went out. Well, then it was not so lovely.†

* An account of their meeting, married life and global travels together is contained in Clare Allcard's stirring memoir, *A Gypsy Life* (1994).

† Quoted in a blog by Jill Dickin Schinas, another intrepid sea wanderer, whose memories of Edward Allcard, published shortly after his death in 2017, I have drawn on for Edward's early life. See 'From 57 degrees to 57 degrees in '66,' at yachtmollymawk.com March 2017.

At school he was an oarsman, as his father had been, and there was little doubt that his life would be involved in some way with the sea. After school he took the unusual step for someone of his background of becoming an apprentice at a Clydeside ship-building yard, which gave him a practical grounding for the field of naval architecture which was his chosen profession. Meanwhile, his sailing ventures graduated to a solo voyage to Norway and back in the last months of peace before the Second World War. Unsuccessful in his effort to join the navy because of poor eyesight, he spent the wartime years designing and sometimes testing air-sea rescue craft.

* * *

The stage was set for Allcard's historic postwar voyages which made him the first to sail the Atlantic in both directions single-handed. Given this success it is worth recalling that his initial attempt ended in failure. Departing Penzance in November 1947 in a twenty-ton cutter, *Content,* he 'waltzed into a series of biting gales' in which critical pieces of gear broke, including the metal tiller jaws. For two days he had no means of steering and by the time he had effected a repair, the loose rudder had worked open a seam in the transom through which water was pouring. Struggling back to the Cornish shore after eight days at sea, he gave up on *Content* as unsuitable for single-handed voyaging.

In Dartmouth a few weeks later he came across *Temptress,* a thirty-four-foot double-ended yawl built in 1910, which proved a much better fit. Her ten foot beam on a waterline length of twenty-nine feet plus her ample freeboard made for 'a little ship which for her size is remarkably stiff, able, and dry.' She carried a gaff mainsail, a bermudan mizzen, and two headsails. Photos of her under sail show a workmanlike sea-going vessel with nothing designed for show, an approach which Allcard took with all the boats he owned. The truth was that he was sometimes inclined to go to sea before every single job had been done, relying on his knowledge and skill as a naval architect to catch up on details while under way. In the case of *Temptress* he conceded that 'it could not be said that the boat was properly fitted out', though he was keen to point out that the engine was in first class order and that the keel bolts had been recently replaced. By the summer of 1948 she was ready for sea, but not before a heart-stopping moment when she she started to sink on launching and was only saved by being beached. There was much shaking of heads among locals, many of whom never expected to see him again, but Allcard stuck doggedly to his plan of tackling 'the Great Atlantic'. On the evening of 27 August 1948, Allcard recalls, he looked astern to see the coast of Cornwall 'already a thin grey line' and dropping away fast. It would be three years before he returned.

These were momentous years in the annals of small boat voyaging on the Atlantic by British sailors. By the time of Allcard's return in the summer of 1951 Peter and Ann Pye had crossed and re-crossed the Atlantic in *Moonraker*, the Smith brothers and Charles Violet had done the same in the tiny *Nova Espero*, Humphrey Barton had made his epic east-west crossing in *Vertue XXXV*, and Miles and Beryl Smeeton were on passage from Fowey to British Columbia via the Panama Canal in *Tzu Hang*. In the summer of 1950 the first transatlantic race from west to east took place, which included Adlard Coles's *Cohoe*. In May of that year Eric and Susan Hiscock sailed their twenty-four-foot cutter *Wanderer II* to the Azores and back, a tryout for their three year circumnavigation in their next boat, *Wanderer III*, which began in July 1952. A month after Allcard's return to Britain in summer 1951, Patrick Ellam and Colin Mudie set off on their crossing to Barbados in the nineteen-foot *Sopranino*.

Most of these voyagers had particular destinations in view. In Allcard's case, beyond the general idea of an Atlantic voyage, his precise goal was unclear. If he had one in mind, you would not know it from the early chapters of his account of the voyage, *Single-handed Passage* (1950). He simply sailed off in the direction of the Bay of Biscay and wended his way to Gibraltar which he reached after six weeks' sailing. Actually the reader knows Allcard is bound for New York because there is a map on the inside cover of the book showing his course. Otherwise we are left in the dark, cruising along with the author, sharing the first days of fair winds to be followed by three days of a Biscay gale which Allcard describes with bumptious energy. 'At five-thirty', he writes, 'the weather really started to take its gloves off', while a few hours later, switching metaphors, 'in the rigging the wind was tuning up like a band of performers ready for the curtain'. During the worst of the storm he noted that it was nevertheless 'not difficult to boil water for Bovril and then make the inevitable bowl of porridge, into which I gave unenthusiastic digs with the spoon'. Allcard was rarely at a loss when it came to providing for his stomach, however difficult the conditions.

Once at Gibraltar, he toyed with sailing for South Africa and New Zealand but settled for 'New York or bust'. Now the reader knows for certain where Allcard is heading, but in keeping with his desire to keep boundaries to the minimum, there is no timetable. Freedom to change his mind according to conditions and circumstances was uppermost but the desire for privacy was another. Having on a previous occasion let it be known when he planned to leave he was mobbed by journalists; now he always tried to keep it secret. He stayed eight months in Gibraltar refitting, waiting for the hurricane season to pass before departing on a 4800-mile continuous passage to New York, following very closely the route Alain Gerbault had taken in 1923.

What Allcard conveys above all in his account of the voyage is intense engagement with the sensations, pleasurable and disagreeable, of this peculiarly arduous way of travelling the world. He describes being soaked by a wave while perching on the rail aft 'doing his business'. He observes with fascination the rich variety of wildlife, including taking a dip in the Caribbean amid a shoal of barracuda, not knowing their reputation. (Much later, in Antigua, he almost died from ciguatera poisoning.) He suffered a variety of injuries, any one of which could have proved fatal to his voyage had they been a little more serious. On this voyage as on others, a combination of luck and dogged determination invariably saw him through.

The need for running repairs was a constant drain on Allcard's energy, but rather than drag him down it unleashed his skills gained from professional training but also a never-daunted native ingenuity. One particular crisis arose in Bermudan waters when the mast band holding the throat halyard was torn out of position in a squall and twisted round almost to the point of biting into the shrouds. Mainsail and staysail were quickly lowered and for two days he sailed under 'the ridiculous rig of jib alone'. His plan was to leave repairs till he reached port but in the event the wind died away to a dead calm and he decided to seize the opportunity to undertake repairs at sea. The first challenge was to hoist himself up to the top of the thirty-foot mast in a bosun's chair, after which he was exhausted and running with sweat. Once he had reached the mast band the boat started rolling and he could do nothing for ten minutes. It took an hour and a quarter of careful work with spanner, bolts and washers to reattach the fitting in the correct position. It was as well he had completed the work at sea since by now he was in the horse latitudes, bereft of wind for three days and still far from port.

It was not always a story of hardship. In line with the pleasure he took in food, he took every opportunity offered by calm weather to cook up the best meals he could, including, as he approached the doldrums, a fine dining menu of soup à la Tendora, steamed giant fish steaks, potatoes, beans, pineapple rings with cream, followed by coffee, chocolate and liqueur brandy. 'Even if the cream was evaporated milk', he notes, 'and the brandy Spanish, the Ritz would have been hard put to supply such a repast'. And he always remained thin as a rake.

Meanwhile, the miles were logged amid the 'ever-changing conditions which can be expected by a sailor,' from flat calm in the horse latitudes when progress seemed to come to a halt to the welcome arrival of south-westerlies as he neared the coast of America. By this stage Allcard and *Temptress* were ready for anything the weather gods could throw at them. Crossing the Gulf Stream only four or five days from his destination he was visited by a vicious south-westerly gale of which, he notes '*Temptress* did not care a jot for heavy weather, but just continued scooting to the north at three or four knots on her own, helm lashed firmly and headsails sheeted hard in. I was superfluous.' She sailed three hundred miles without a hand at the tiller. He duly arrived in New York on 9 August 1949, eighty days out of Gibraltar.

* * *

For all Allcard's dislike of publicity, he exploited the fame which came his way in the United States to full advantage, as he recounted at the beginning of his next book which described the return Atlantic crossing. The fact is that he had arrived in the United States without a visa and had initially been DOB (Detained on Board). Threatened with a fine by the Immigration Department, Allcard made it clear that he was not to be cowed. In a partial backdown by the authorities he was told his case would be decided by the State Department in Washington, the outcome being that the visa requirement was waived and he would be permitted to stay thirty days. In fact he stayed a year. If the authorities had tried to boot him out after such an arduous voyage, he says, 'the newspapers would have descended on the story like flies on a dung heap'. Publicity had its advantages after all.

Allcard's return voyage across the Atlantic, which began in mid-August 1950, was notable for two things, the first being that because of various delays he set off in the hurricane season. There was much shaking of heads among the New York sailing fraternity and also from Humphrey Barton who had arrived there earlier in the year in *Vertue XXXV* after his own Atlantic crossing. Barton visited Allcard aboard *Temptress*, which, as it happened, he knew well, having sailed her to Spain and back in the late 1920s. When some years later Barton wrote a book about Atlantic adventurers, he called Allcard 'intrepid' but said most of the troubles experienced on this voyage were of his own making. These troubles included a fearsome succession of storms, including a knock-down which broke the mizzen mast and came close to ending his voyage there and then, broken ribs and toes, exhaustion and the loss of two and a half stone in weight. He was lucky to have survived, Barton concluded.

Coming from a hard-driving sailor and inveterate risk-taker, this judgement cannot easily be dismissed. Without doubt Allcard sometimes pushed his luck to the limit. Invariably, however, his resourcefulness and robust constitution enabled him to escape the worst, and above all he never gave up. At a point of near exhaustion approaching the Azores he recalls crying out 'I cannot go on. But I went on – there was nothing else to do. To stop was death. And I wanted to live.'

The second noteworthy feature of this voyage was that at Horta in the Azores he acquired a stowaway. A few hours after departing from Horta, he noticed a movement at the main hatch then 'a clutching hand, followed by a frightened white face half-hidden by straggling black hair.' He recognised her as Otilia Frayao, who had come on board *Temptress* for a trial sail in Horta. Twenty-three years old, she was bent on escaping the Azores and going to England where she hoped to study. There was never a chance of taking her back to Horta. They had a following wind and *Temptress* was poor to windward.

Once over the initial shock, Allcard grew to enjoy her company, even to the extent of wondering whether he should give up bachelorhood. The answer was no, but Otilia's youthful beauty certainly charmed him. She became competent at the helm, cooked, albeit with more enthusiasm than skill, and entertained him with long rambles in Portuguese, including her own poetry, to which he replied in an English as foreign to Otilia as Portuguese was to Edward. Bonding was achieved in part through efforts to teach each other their languages. Not least among the attractions of Allcard's account is that he spices it with extracts from Otilia's diary, which offer curious sidelights on Allcard. During yet another gale, she writes: 'I feel so wretched that I can't even cry. Allcard spends the days gazing at the sea through the portholes. As a heavier sea hits us, I hear him murmur "well done": then silence again.'

Otilia did get to England, but not with Allcard. She left the boat at Casablanca and made her way to England separately. They remained in contact, meeting for the last time in 2009 to celebrate Allcard's ninety-fifth birthday. Meanwhile, just as the first Atlantic crossing had made his name, if only briefly, beyond the sailing fraternity, this second more sensational story, along with the photos of Otilia which accompanied them, proved irresistible to a wider public.

* * *

The publicity surrounding the stowaway sensation changed nothing about the way Allcard lived his life. His most challenging voyages were yet to come, now in a new boat, the thirty-six-foot *Sea Wanderer*. Built in 1911 in the Baltic port of Lübeck for an Englishman who planned to sail round the world, she was shipped to New York in 1929 after her owner abandoned the idea of a circumnavigation. It was there in 1950, as Allcard was about to return across the Atlantic in *Temptress*, that he found her as a near wreck and bought her with a future venture in mind. She was stored ashore until, a few years later, he made her seaworthy enough to sail across to Britain. There she had a thorough refit at his favourite boatyard, Mashford's in Cornwall, in preparation for the role he had in mind which was to circumnavigate the world.

He moved the mizzen mast forward and reduced the height of the mainmast, turning her from a tall yawl into a more snugly rigged ketch. He chose the bermudan rig for the mainsail in the light of problems he had experienced with *Temptress*'s gaff rig. All the other modifications – installation of a big reliable diesel, a cabin stove which could burn wood or coal, a smaller cockpit and a new doghouse so that he could seek shelter within easy reach of the helm, bigger water tanks – were designed with severe conditions in mind and proved their worth in the coming years.

Besides the refit, there was the small matter of a name. She was called *Wanderer* when he bought her but Eric Hiscock, evidently claiming copyright in the name, asked him to change it. Allcard balked at first but then agreed, though with some irritation since his boat was several decades older than Hiscock's. Not one to make a fuss about inessentials, Allcard set off from Plymouth in November 1956 bound for the Caribbean, once again with a loose timetable. After another gale-ridden crossing of the Bay of Biscay and a stop in Gibraltar he reached Tangier where he set up a chartering business. After five months of mixed fortunes there, he departed for the Canaries. There he met a young man called Peter Tangvald who, like Allcard, planned a crossing to the Caribbean. 'Why not make it a race of it?' said Tangvald. The goal was to reach English Harbour in Antigua by Christmas, which was forty days away, the prize being one dollar.*

Tangvald's *Windflower* was longer and faster than *Sea Wanderer* but Allcard had self-steering gear which would allow him to get more rest. In the event, Tangvald won by two days. They took thirty-three and thirty-one days respectively in what Allcard claimed was the first east-west transatlantic race. Once again, Allcard's reason for going to the Caribbean was to charter in order to raise money for his real destination, which was the River Plate with the thought then of rounding Cape Horn.

* * *

It took four years before he was ready for the next stage of his long-term plan. In August 1961 he departed the Caribbean for a voyage to La Paloma near Montevideo, taking a route which on paper looks

* The astonishing story of Peter Tangvald and his son Thomas is well told by Nicholas Gray in 'Thomas Thor Tangvald,' *The Marine Quarterly*, 55 (Autumn 2024), 91-8.

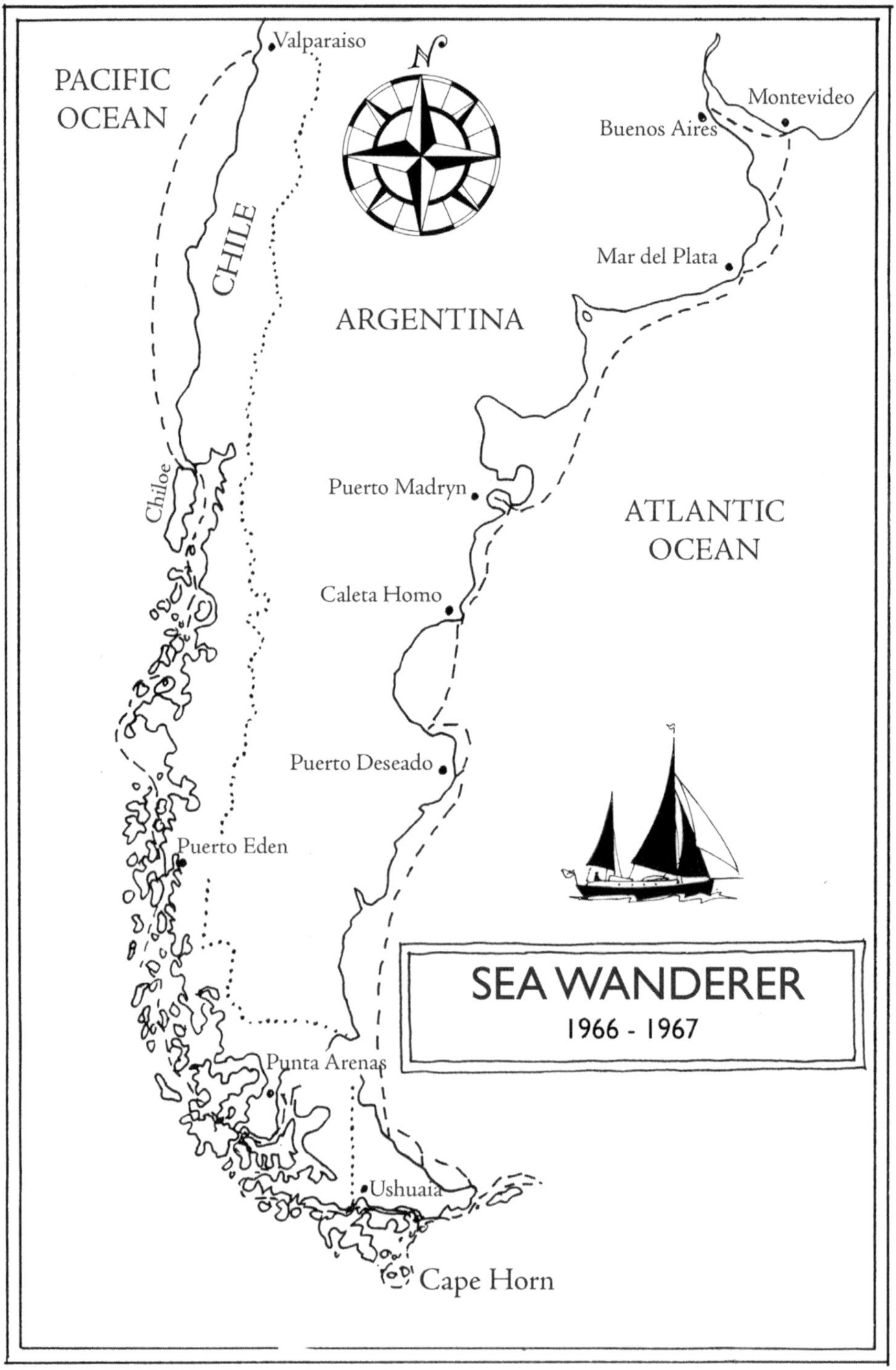
Valparaiso
PACIFIC
OCEAN
CHILE
N
Montevideo
Buenos Aires
Mar del Plata
ARGENTINA
Puerto Madryn
Chiloe
ATLANTIC
OCEAN
Caleta Homo
Puerto Deseado
Puerto Eden
SEA WANDERER
1966 - 1967
Punta Arenas
Ushuaia
Cape Horn

excessively circuitous but in actuality made best use of the winds and currents. 'Sailing in a small boat from the West Indies to the South Atlantic needs careful route planning', Allcard reflected in explaining why he took an initial course so far north and then southeast almost to the Cape Verde Islands. Only thus could he pick up the trade winds on the other side of the Atlantic which would take him south towards his destination of Montevideo. He devoted long hours to navigation, almost, he confesses, to the point of mania, and was fully conversant with the history of the great navigators going back to Magellan.

His account of this passage in *Voyage Alone* (1967) is vintage Allcard – colourful in the writing and brimming with energy, the product of a born story-teller. Clare Allcard, whom he met and married shortly after this voyage, testified to his attention to detail, particularly with reference to how it sounded. Throughout his life he evidently revelled in the act of writing. When writing his last book towards the end of his life he would ask her to read out passages and would add or cut words according to rhythm and sound.*

For another four years he lived in the River Plate area preparing himself and the boat for what arguably was his most impressive solo achievement – a year-long passage from Buenos Aires to Valparaiso in Chile via Cape Horn. Little was known about this voyage until his account was published the year before he died, *Solo Around Cape Horn* (2016). At the prompting of Clare he had begun the writing at the age of 92. It was in part a journey into history. He had in mind constantly the historic voyages of Magellan, Drake, Cavendish, Schouten (the first European to round the Horn, and the one who gave it its name), the ill-fated *Wager* of Anson's fleet in the 1750s, and Fitzroy's *Beagle*, and many others. He also had a rough plan to meet up with that modern legend, H W Tilman, who was due to be in the region.

Allcard spent the best part of six months in and around Tierra Del Fuego. Rounding the Horn itself was only one incident, if inevitably memorable, in an incident-packed exploration of the region. In the first place, like many before him, he found that getting to Cape Horn was anything but straightforward. He set off on the 1200-mile passage from Buenos Aires to Tierra Del Fuego in early January 1966.

* Thanks are due to Clare Allcard for this recollection.

The Roaring Forties lived up to their name. Near half-way to Tierra del Fuego he put in to Puerto Madryn in the Golfo Nuevo, which was large enough, Allcard noted, to be classed as an inland sea. Some enjoyable encounters ashore were followed by a succession of gales which defeated his efforts to leave. On the third attempt he managed to exit the gulf and recalled, as he was faced with a huge swell rolling up from the south, that this was where the single-handed Bernicot had been turned upside down. Allcard was forced to heave to but eventually concluded that there was no point in trying to make headway south. He turned back towards the Golfo Nuevo, lashing himself to the helmsman's seat to avoid being washed overboard. On the fourth attempt he finally made it and was rewarded with a north-easterly which put him on a dead run in the direction he wanted to go.

In the sheltered natural harbour of Caleta Horno a few hundred miles further south he made final preparations for the southern latitudes of the Horn itself. He ticked off a long list of jobs ranging from mucking out the bilges to fitting a fore-guy on the main boom, which taken individually were small but together were designed to plug any number of chinks in the boat's armour which fearsome conditions further south might expose. And by the time he reached the Cape Horn region he would be late in the season, well into the southern autumn.

Like many before him, Allcard found Le Maire Strait between Tierra Del Fuego and Staten Island as hard as anything he had experienced. His plan was to use Rio Grande on Terra Del Fuego some sixty miles northwest of the Strait as his jumping off point for passage down to the Horn. He reached Rio Grande in March 1966 and spent ten fraught days there fighting strong tides and almost perpetual gales. Seizing an opportune moment to leave, a few days later he entered the Bay of Good Success on the western side of Le Maire Strait in good weather. It was not to last. In his effort to complete his passage through the Strait and reach the Horn, he encountered four days of howling gales which pushed him north and east of Staten Island. Not least of his worries was the appearance of water up to the level of the floorboards in the cabin which he traced to a leak in the rudder trunk which had worked loose from the violent stresses of the previous twenty-four hours. He was forced to pump for his life.

He rounded the Horn in full sunshine and a moderate breeze carrying full sail.

After a long struggle and a change of wind direction he was able to turn round and find refuge at an anchorage in Puerto Cook on Staten Island's north coast. In quieter weather the leak subsided but it would need a full repair at the first opportunity.

His best option now was to return to the Bay of Good Success before making a new attempt to reach the Horn. Once there, he abandoned his original plan of sailing directly to the Horn and chose instead to head for Haberton in the Beagle Channel, home of the late Lucas Bridges, whose book *The Uttermost Part of the Earth* about his family settling there in the 1870s, making friends with the native population, and learning their language had inspired Allcard's plan to visit Tierra Del Fuego in the first place. He arrived at the Bridges' estancia in Haberton in early April to a warm welcome by the family.

Over the next few months, true to form, Allcard engaged with the local life as well as exploring the region for himself. He was no bird of passage ticking Cape Horn off on his wish list. In Puerto Williams in the Beagle Channel he made himself popular with the authorities at the Chilean Naval base by designing a cradle to enable them to slip a vessel that needed repair, in return for which they slipped *Sea Wanderer* who also needed attention. He also responded to a request from the commandante of the naval base to rescue a man who had been sent to an island sixty miles away to collect a consignment of dried beef and was now marooned since the base's patrol boat had been wrecked. Not long afterwards he spied an old whaleboat being rowed by some Yaghan Indians against a headwind. Finding they had thirteen more miles to go he offered to give them a tow which they gladly accepted. Weeks later, on being recognised by a Yaghan Indian he was invited to a wigwam and offered a cup of tea. Meanwhile, the extended Bridges family offered him daily hospitality and warm friendship; Haberton became like a second home.

Allcard's capacity to explore the most remote and inhospitable spots of the region, not least Cape Horn itself, relied greatly on his skill and confidence in the use of ground tackle. Rather than sail directly around the Horn into the teeth of the prevailing westerlies, Allcard ventured out from the eastern end of the Beagle Channel and threaded his way through the Cape Horn archipelago, anchoring twice in remote bays en route to the Horn itself. He was lucky. He rounded the Horn in full sunshine and a moderate breeze carrying full sail. His log entry read: *12 April 1966. 0945 Cape Horn bearing N. one and a half miles.* With a gale on the way he made for a secluded anchorage to sit it out. From there he progressed westward along the full length of the Beagle Channel and into the Strait of Magellan via the Cockburn Channel.

During his passage west along the Strait of Magellan he even climbed 3500 foot Monte Tres Picos near Port Gallant on the western arm of the Strait where he hoped to meet Tilman. Allcard had a particular purpose in mind which was to discover whether certain items left in a bottle at the summit some two hundred years before by Captain Carteret of *HMS Swallow* were still there. He left a note at Punta Arenas for Tilman informing him of his intentions and saying he would leave a white painted arrow on a rock indicating the spot where Tilman would also find another note from him. Tilman observed later that the idea of following arrows painted on rock and picking up notes was 'right up his street' but in fact he had already left for Antarctica. Allcard nevertheless penned a stirring account of his climb to the top of snow-covered Monte Tres Picos where he found, to his profound disappointment, that the items left by the British Navy captain had been discovered and removed 117 years before by a group of Americans. All that was left was their names scratched on a piece of copper plate. Perhaps it was a case of 'to travel hopefully is better than to arrive', but Allcard was rewarded with a 'staggering view... of one of nature's great wonderlands'. Though not in Tilman's class as a mountaineer, he shared Tilman's passion for mountains as well as the sea. It is significant that later when he had retired from the sea and taken up residence in land-locked Andorra, in response to a question about whether he missed the sea, he replied: 'No, it's all nature. Mountains are just waves standing still.'

Once out of the Strait, which presented regular bouts of squalls, driving rain and headwinds, he made passage north through the extensive and tortuous Patagonian channels, past Chiloe Island, and out into the open sea to Valparaiso which he reached in January 1967. He then sailed *Sea Wanderer* to New Zealand. Allcard's capacity to keep moving in the face of contrary conditions at many points in this

N
TIERRA DEL FUEGO
Ushuaia
Harberton
Puerto Williams
Buen Suceso
Le Maire Strait
Staten Island
ATLANTIC OCEAN
ARGENTINA
CHILE
Cape Horn
SEA WANDERER
1966 - 1967

voyage required an almost superhuman mixture of drive and patience which must be given to few. And he was only halfway through his life of voyaging.

* * *

It is worth pausing to consider the pleasures and challenges of single-handing as Allcard experienced them. He was evidently one of a special breed who possessed in equal measure a spirit of independence and a capacity to absorb the pain and stress which this sometimes entailed. An appetite for the sensations associated with the motion of a boat through water, the curve of sails bending to a breeze, the lure of a distant horizon – these are doubtless shared by all who love sailing, but single-handers, for any number of private reasons, push the practical and emotional challenges – and the pleasures – of voyaging to the limit simply by taking them on solo. 'Sails! There's nothing like 'em', reflected Allcard as he crossed the Bay of Biscay in *Sea Wanderer*. 'I never cease to marvel how a few pieces of cloth can drive a heavy hull as fast or faster than a powerful engine.' In recalling his passage around Cape Horn, he reflected on 'what the dickens I was doing there, all alone, facing that infernal weather'. It was partly the freedom to do as he liked when he liked, partly the solitude and the silence, but also the enveloping feeling of being totally alive which, he said, only the sea can provide. A kind of ecstasy drove Allcard on, but the dream of great adventure in isolation from normal comforts and the chance of rescue would be nothing without the practical skills to cope with all eventualities, and Allcard cultivated both with rare enthusiasm.*

* * *

Within a few months of completing his voyage round Cape Horn to New Zealand, Allcard received news from England that his mother was dying. Leaving *Sea Wanderer* in Auckland, he returned to the UK. His arrival was met with a full-page article in the *Sunday Express*. By this stage Allcard was evidently the beneficiary of the new climate of publicity and interest in world-girdling voyages. In the article he

* The subject of single-handing is well covered in Peter Heaton, *The Singlehanders*, Michael Joseph, 1976, and Richard J. King, *Sailing Alone: A History*, Particular Books, 2023.

was asked if he ever got lonely, to which he replied, no but 'it would be ideal to meet a girl with the same idea.' One reader of this article was a twenty-one year old self-described failed actress and nurse called Clare. Being in a dark place in her life, Clare was entranced by Edward's exploits, and wanted such a 'fabulous' life of freedom for herself. The result was the only fan letter she had ever written and somehow her appeal struck a spark in Edward. They met, they talked, and sometime later they married. Asked many years later why he had replied to the letter, he said he liked her honesty.

There followed a hiatus in his voyaging while they took an overland trip in a Land Rover from Britain to Singapore, from where they moved to the Seychelles and bought a palm-thatched hut. With his mind full of sailing and boat-building projects Edward nevertheless decided first to complete the solo circumnavigation begun over a decade before. So it was off to New Zealand where he had left *Sea Wanderer* and onward to Antigua. The family's cruising life together began in earnest once Edward had found the semi-wreck *Johanne Regina* in Antigua and persuaded Clare this was a viable project, indeed his dream ship. Edward's solo voyaging was over, while his new life bore out the advice given to him by the Irish circumnavigator Conor O'Brien: 'If you want a crew, marry one.'

Chapter 5

TO THE LIMIT AND BEYOND

Humphrey Barton: *Vertue XXXV*

The name Humphrey Barton may not resonate in the wider public but for those with a taste for the history of ocean voyaging 'Hum', as he was generally known, is a name to conjure with. Born in 1900, he began sailing early and over the course of a lifetime acquired a formidable reputation as the sailor's sailor. He is best known for his 1950 east-west Atlantic crossing by the direct northern route in the twenty-five foot Laurent Giles designed *Vertue XXXV*, but over a long career he sailed countless craft, showing an almost limitless appetite for taking yet another boat to sea. He cruised frequently with friends and family but was also in demand as skipper and navigator for yacht deliveries as well as ocean racing, not least in the innovative *Gulvain* for the 1950 transatlantic race which he joined only a few days after his epic transatlantic voyage in *Vertue XXXV*.

In the wake of these and other passages he founded the Ocean Cruising Club which, in the words of its current website, is 'a group of people who have said "yes" to adventure.' The qualification for entry was (and is) skippering a boat of seventy feet or less for a continuous passage of 1,000 miles. Barton never sailed round the world but he roved the waters of Europe and the Atlantic with restless energy until very late in life. After retirement he had Jack Laurent Giles design a thirty-five foot boat for him which was essentially an extended Vertue. In this craft, *Rose Rambler*, he crossed and recrossed the Atlantic eighteen times with the seasons like a migratory bird along with his second wife Mary whom he had married in 1970. His first wife Jessie had died in 1959.

With his background as an engineer, Hum's skills as a sailor were buttressed by extensive technical knowledge of boat construction. Alongside his sailing life he worked as a marine surveyor with Laurent Giles and was also frequently in demand for his expertise on a more informal basis among long-distance sailors, including several discussed in this book. In essentials his life was simple. As he wrote in the preface to his first book, published in 1952, 'In the winter I survey yachts and in the summer I go sailing… I would not change jobs with anyone.'

It is easier to list Hum's achievements than to plumb the character which lay behind them, since it was compounded of many elements, some of them seemingly contradictory. He described himself as 'highly strung' with an over-developed imagination and confessed that he hated bad weather, but his sailing career is associated above all with heavy weather and a hard-driving approach to passage-making and ocean racing.* His best known book, *Vertue XXXV*, is littered with what appear to be complaints about the stresses of the Atlantic passage – 'I get bored stiff steering', 'how I shall detest that ghastly awakening at 4am', 'Oh! How I detest these gales', 'this is far too much like hard work' – but he could wax lyrical about his 'wonderful little ship' which 'is standing up to my brutal driving remarkably well'. When conditions really began to get him down and fear threatened to take over, he would think about Worsley and Shackleton's 600-mile voyage in the *James Caird* from Elephant Island to South Georgia which they survived in a far less seaworthy vessel than his own *Vertue XXXV*. 'So what have I got to worry about? Nothing at all.'

In describing the working of his emotions under extreme conditions, Humphrey Barton managed to convey the stresses of an ocean passage with rare immediacy. He was not shy about expressing his fears because he had devised ways of dealing with them, based on his knowledge of boat construction as well as long experience in a variety of craft and conditions. One can also affirm that his determination to reach his destination or to win a race was more than a match for any doubts or fears he may have experienced.

* * *

He took early to sailing in dinghies on Wimbledon Common, graduating soon to a self-built canoe in which he and his brother shot the rapids on the river Wye. At sixteen he managed to persuade his father that the public school he had been sent to wasn't for him and he decamped to a munitions factory where he worked for a year. He joined

* I wish to thank Humphrey Barton's daughter Pat Pocock for supplying valuable information, including unpublished autobiographical notes by her father on which I have drawn extensively.

the Royal Flying Corp in 1917 and gained his wings though it seems the war was over before he was able to see action. He subsequently trained as an electrical engineer, laying cables in a variety of locations in the UK and then in Malaya for three years during the 1920s.

It was during this period that he undertook his first serious sailing ventures in dinghies in the Wash, off the Kent coast, and in Southeast Asia, showing extraordinary self-confidence and resourcefulness at a young age. He joined the firm of naval architects Laurent Giles in 1936 and spent much of the war in Orkney and Shetland with the Royal Engineers followed by a spell as a small boat delivery skipper for the Admiralty. His mastery of boat-handling, whether under sail or power, and his deep understanding of the construction of boats, ballasted this 'highly strung' personality. Throw him into a crisis and he would invariably think his way out of it and take appropriate action. In his writings he could never resist offering lessons on the basis of his experience as both a sailor and a yacht surveyor. He was ever the teacher and fervent advocate for one practice or another.

He also possessed the knack of writing expressively, often under duress, which lends his writings immediacy and charm. On passage he made a point of organising things so that his writing routine was not interrupted, which meant giving much thought to getting the boat to steer herself. Four weeks out of Yarmouth, Isle of Wight, on passage to New York in his Atlantic crossing of 1950 he noted that 'I have such a lot of writing to do before we arrive at New York that I simply cannot afford the time to sit and steer.' The only gap in his record of this passage came with a two-day storm towards the end of the voyage in which the boat was knocked down and sustained serious damage. Typically, he filled the writing gap in short order as soon as repairs had been made and the weather had moderated. To read Humphrey Barton's accounts of his sailing is to gain insight into what it is like to be on the edge, yet it is always done in the spirit, not of heroics, but of what action has to be taken to get out of trouble.

* * *

Most sailors start out in dinghies but few take their dinghy sailing as far as Hum did. One who did was Blondie Hasler who, like Hum, undertook long passages in small open boats. Close to three decades before the 'cockleshell hero' found new fame in the 1960 transatlantic race, he had sailed the three hundred mile round trip from Plymouth to Portsmouth and back in a fourteen foot dinghy. Hum's open boat exploits were equally significant, perhaps more so, and are equally overlooked.

The first chapter of his first book, *The Sea and Me* (1952), records a youthful escapade in the Wash which could easily have ended in disaster. Attempting to beat up the narrow channel to Boston harbour in his twelve foot lug sail dinghy in a rising wind, he soon found he could make no way. With night falling, in desperation he ran off downwind 'in half a gale of wind and a steep breaking sea' in the hope of reaching a pilot boat he knew lay at anchor several miles down the channel. Capsize was a constant threat as steering became more difficult. Bailing furiously, against the odds he managed to prevent her being swamped. As he ruefully conceded, it was more by luck than good judgement that he reached his destination where he was put up for the night by the astonished pilots. He got off with being 'mildly admonished for going to sea in such a boat'. With hindsight he realised he could have lowered sail and mast, rowed to the edge of the channel where the stream was less fierce and after some hard pulling reached the harbour. He reflected that 'as an adventure that short cruise exceeded my wildest expectations; as an example of seamanship the less said about it the better, but, hang it all, everyone has to learn'.

And learn he did because only a few years later he was roaming the Kent coast and beyond in a sixteen-foot half-decked boat which he launched off the beach at Walmer, just south of Deal. He records the thrill of sailing across the Dover Strait to Gravelines, the first time he had set foot outside England, which stoked his appetite for going foreign. He subsequently made numerous trips to other French ports, sometimes alone and sometimes with a companion. With his brother he sailed over to Boulogne then down Channel to Newhaven and on to Lymington via Littlehampton and Bembridge on the Isle of Wight. By any standards this was a substantial coastal cruise. In a small open boat without an engine it was bordering on the heroic.

Perhaps even more striking was his passion for the Goodwin sands which he got to know 'like the back of my hand.' Sailing every minute of every weekend he became so familiar with the four lightships marking the sands that the lightship crews had their mail sent to him. He got to know the swatchway between the North and South Goodwin sands so well that he could find his way through at night. After these ventures he would return to Walmer, sail her on to the beach under full sail with the centre-plate up where he would usually be met by a fisherman who would hook a wire to her stem and winch her up above the high-water mark.

If there was something of the buccaneer in Hum's approach to sailing it was balanced by a severe practicality. After reflecting on the need for adequate buoyancy, ways of keeping bedding and clothes dry, and the problems of navigation in such a craft, Hum concluded his chapter on these exploits on the Kent coast with advice on the best type of boat for this work, and tips on how to establish whether a boat is well-built and sound. The boat should 'have a good flat floor, moderate beam, plenty of depth and be strongly but lightly built... The rig should be bermudan sloop but the sail area should be moderate.' As for testing the strength of a dinghy, 'get a good strong chap to hold the bow firmly. Then get hold of the transom and see if you can twist her. If there is any movement at all, don't buy her.'

Two further open boat cruises catch the eye, the first in Malaya. While working there in 1925 he became part owner of a Dublin Water Wag which bears the distinction of being the oldest one-design class in the world. The original boat, designed in the 1880s, was a thirteen-foot double-ender but by the time Hum joined the newly established sailing club at Port Dickson on the Malacca Strait it had evolved into a fourteen-foot transom dinghy with a modest gunter rig. Hum conceived the idea with a friend of sailing over the fifty mile Malacca Strait to Sumatra and back. The overnight passage to Sumatra took longer than anticipated and since there was a fair breeze for their return they set off back after only an hour ashore. By the time they were within sight of the Malayan coast they had been through another night without sleep, and due to an error by Hum's companion while Hum was resting they found themselves down-wind and down tide from Port Dickson. It took several hours rowing in steamy tropical heat to get back there.

Hum concluded that in retrospect the boat was not really suited for such a voyage but typically reflected that 'all's well that ends well and I do not regret the little adventure for one moment'. At the time of this voyage Hum was twenty-five and by his own admission still had much to learn, at least so far as voyaging over distance was concerned. Characteristically he pushed his craft and himself to the limit.

Similar qualities were shown much later in a particularly hair-raising passage in a thirty foot naval gig which took place during his war service in Shetland. Hum had conceived an ambition to sail to the small island of Foula which lay twenty-six miles west of Scalloway on the main island of Shetland. He found the boat at Lerwick harbour lying neglected and he set to with a group of volunteers from the Royal Engineers to bring her back to sailing condition. She was a yawl with unstayed masts and dipping lug sails which meant considerable business when tacking and gybing, especially when he discovered the masts needed staying. In order to allow the yards to swing free, he fitted only one shroud to each mast which meant shifting it over to the weather side each time he tacked. He spent some weeks training up his crew and after sailing her round Sumburgh Head from Lerwick to Scalloway departed for Foula 'on a perfect Saturday morning and an excellent weather forecast'. After an easy passage they were put up comfortably for the night by the local school mistress and her husband.

The weather next day was not so benign. A hard overnight blow from the southwest had moderated but there was still a heavy sea running. Prudence, he said, demanded that they stay on land but they had brought food for only one day and were expected back on Monday morning. Besides, his enthusiastic crew could see no reason for delay and had faith in their skipper. They set off with a strong breeze behind them and even with a snugged down rig soon found themselves under pressure as waves started breaking aboard, caused by the rising wind meeting a strong weather-going tide. They bailed for their lives for the rest of the passage.

He made the decision to run for Walls which lay to the north of Scalloway and a little closer. He had never been there but knew that it lay behind a small island offering two possible entrances to the harbour, Easter and Wester Sounds, both narrow and difficult to identify from seaward. By the time they were six or seven miles off it was 9pm and he didn't rate their chances if they failed to reach port by dark. All that was visible ahead was a continuous wall of rock, his only known landmark being a small coastguard hut on the cliff top just to the east of Easter Sound. Three miles off he strained to see the hut, thought he saw it, had another look, and decided that must be it. He was committed, and one mile out saw with relief that it definitely was Easter Sound. The narrow passage was a mass of foam as they surfed through on the crest of a huge wave down into the smooth waters of the harbour.

Hum had qualms about telling this story because it was another case, he admitted, of undertaking a passage in an unsuitable boat. I hope, he said, 'that it may be a warning to people who contemplate coastwise cruising in unsuitable craft'. With his surveyor's hat on he noted that 'time and experience, trial and error, have evolved the correct proportions of any boat, yacht or ship', adding that 'an open boat properly handled will survive quite severe conditions, but even if she is correctly proportioned there is a definite limit to what she will stand'. Hum leaves it to the reader's judgement about how close he was to the limit in this venture.

Opinions will differ. Some will say he took an uncalculated risk and was lucky to survive. Others will say that people make their own luck by applying their experience and consistently taking the correct action. At the moment he decided to run for Walls, Hum paid out twenty-five fathoms of the anchor warp astern which had the effect of holding the boat square to the sea and preventing her from broaching. It's a tactic not many open boat sailors would employ but Hum's wide experience served him well here.

What temperament and experience evidently taught him was always to take active measures in meeting dangers. That way, so far as possible, he could retain the initiative and give himself the best possible chance of survival. He was always conscious of the need for a plan B or C and would tuck away information to make use of in an emergency; the pilot boat in the Wash in his early lugsail dinghy venture and the coastguard hut near Walls were good examples. Hum was never one simply to hope things would turn out right.

* * *

Hum had owned several yachts of his own by this time and had plenty of cruising experience. On his return from Malaya in the late 1920s he was granted a year's leave by his company since he had contracted malaria there and was still not fit. His first venture was a modest charter cruise on the Norfolk Broads, to be followed by a passage to Spain and back with his younger brother and sister in the twelve-ton yawl *Temptress*, later to be owned by Edward Allcard. Then came a five-ton gaff cutter called *Jean II* which he kept for five years and cruised extensively in the North Sea, both sides of the Channel and round the British coast. Other ventures included an 850-mile cruise to Brittany in the first of the Vertue class, the gaff-rigged (as she was then) *Andrillot*, and another in the Vertue *Monie* round most of the British coast. In 1939 he skippered Roger Pinckney's Laurent Giles designed *Dyarchy II* from Gothenberg to Lymington via Orkney and the west coast of Britain.

On the outbreak of war in 1939 Hum offered his services to the navy but was considered too old. He then tried the RAF since he already had his wings, having briefly served as a pilot in the First World War. However there was a long waiting list, so he wrote to a relation in the War Office offering his services and only a few days later found himself in Orkney. On the strength of his engineering experience, to his astonishment he was appointed Deputy Commander Royal Engineers with the rank of Major with responsibility for five small islands. Among the benefits of his time there was the availability of a twenty-ton motor yacht complete with a crew of five and a powerful engine which 'was handed over to me and took me from island to island in all weathers'. After three years in Orkney and a fourth in Shetland, during which he made the dramatic trip to Foula and back in the gig described above, he became seriously ill and was invalided out of the army.

Not one to sit and do nothing, when he was fit he offered his services to the Small Vessels Pool, a civilian organization charged with the delivery of little ships from one port to another. Over a period of nine months he delivered nine MFVs of from forty-five to seventy-five feet 'around the mine strewn coasts of the British isles', often in poor weather and in poorly prepared boats. 'I had never handled craft of this size and type before', he reflected, adding laconically that 'I found it very interesting and learnt a lot.' His pay was one pound a day when on the job, the crew got rather less, and they had to buy their own food. It was surely fortunate that austerity was Hum's style.

* * *

Hum's ocean cruising began in earnest after the Second World War, as it did for many of his sailing contemporaries. Despite economic austerity which lasted well into the 1950s, the end of the war stimulated an appetite for new horizons among those such as Hum who had accumulated experience during the interwar years. Besides he was by now a well-established yacht surveyor with a respected and successful company, which gave him a platform for new ventures closely related to his work. And it was a mutually beneficial relationship. Hum's exploits in boats designed by Laurent Giles could only work to the advantage of the company. Furthermore, Laurent Giles's design philosophy, which blended traditionalism and innovation, suited Hum. The Vertue and its later variations were based on traditional concepts but contained some novel details in gear and fittings, including custom-made versions of Highfield levers for running backstays, and ratchet-lever deck winches. In the field of ocean racers Jack Laurent Giles broke decisively with tradition in boats such as *Gulvain* and *Myth of Malham* which combined light displacement with flat or reverse sheer. *Gulvain* had the added novelty of being constructed in aluminium alloy. Both proved highly successful racing boats: *Gulvain* won the Cowes-Dinard race in 1949 and was first home in the transatlantic race of 1950 with Hum as skipper. *Myth of Malham* won the 1947 Fastnet, with Hum in the crew, and again in 1949, but this time Hum was once again aboard *Gulvain* as skipper but was forced to retire when a forestay fitting failed.

There was no doubt, however, that for cruising Hum favoured traditional designs. He famously concluded his account of the 1950 Atlantic crossing with the statement that 'I have sailed in numerous small yachts and have examined many more and I am of the opinion that *Vertue XXXV* is the most perfect small ocean-going yacht that has ever been designed and built.' He certainly gave her a stern test, as we shall see.

The plan was to buy a Vertue class sloop, sail her to America and sell her there for dollars. That way he could combine business with pleasure 'by building her, sailing across and helping the export drive.' Stanley Smith and Charles Violet would seek something like the same end the following year in *Nova Espero* by taking with them var-

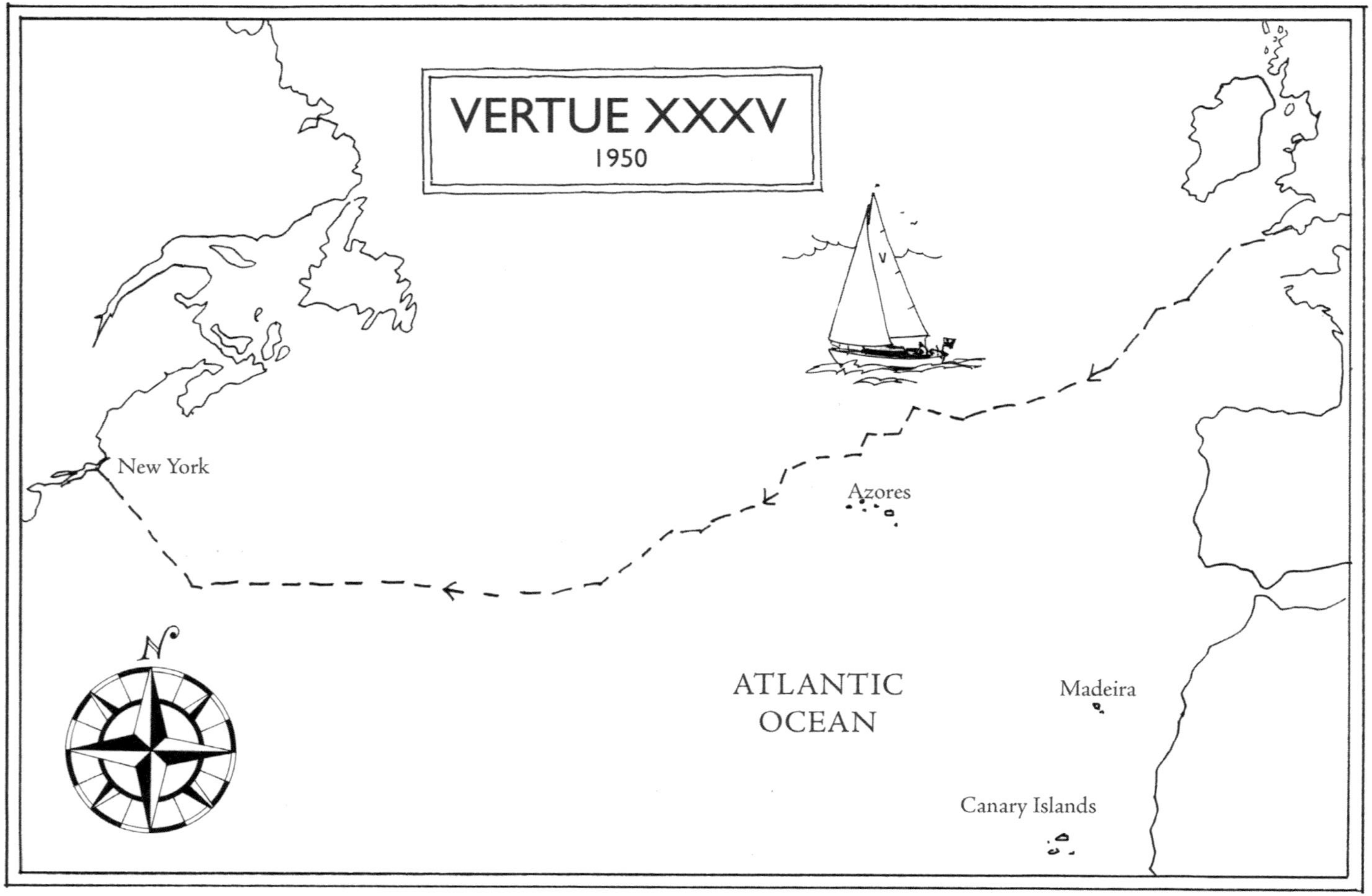
VERTUE XXXV
1950
New York
Azores
ATLANTIC
OCEAN
Madeira
Canary Islands
N

ious products to promote British manufacturing. Marginal as these contributions to Britain's economic performance might have been, they display a consciousness of a Britain striving to re-establish itself after the disruptions of war. The voyages themselves, while in the first instance personal adventures, catch something of the wider spirit of the times.

The decision made, a suitable boat having been found, Hum was both thrilled and appalled at the prospect. He reassured himself that he had a seaworthy and well-prepared boat and that smaller and less able craft than his had made the crossing, not least the Smith brothers' west to east crossing in *Nova Espero* the previous year. Going west by the northern route, however, presented particular challenges. A yacht taking this route could expect a high proportion of headwinds, and that is what Hum and his companion Kevin O'Riordan got. In a shorthand account of the crossing Hum called it 'four gales and a hurricane', and the conditions certainly took their toll. Ten days out Hum realised he had two broken ribs which he put down to having slipped on the varnished cockpit seats a couple of days before when the motion of the boat threw him against a sheet winch. 'What a menace varnished surfaces are,' he reflected: 'scrubbed teak is the answer.' Kevin O' Riordan helped strap him up with 'Elastoplast' and after a few days he was back to strength. By the third week at sea they had experienced their fourth gale in eighteen days, far more than the meteorological predictions for this stage of the season. They had set out in the middle of April.

Hum's account of the voyage in *Vertue XXXV* takes the form of the log he kept day by day and sometimes hour by hour. It conveys a vivid sense of immediacy but includes far more than the kind of jottings cruising sailors often place in the 'remarks' column of the standard logbook. He was meticulous in recording details of his position, weather and sea conditions, gear failure and repairs, and numerous incidental events and crises (of which more later), and much else besides.

Hum's log is also part sailing manual which includes reflections on technical matters derived from his experience as a surveyor. His restless mind roamed not only over problems unfolding in front of his eyes as the boat forced its way westward, but grappled with wider issues. In considering the question of how to make a boat strong enough to deal with severe conditions he railed against excessive scantlings which some builders and owners insisted on, thinking they would make the boat more seaworthy but in fact used so much wood that the amount of ballast that could be carried was not enough to ensure stability. That led to comments on the optimum amount of ballast in a cruising yacht. He described in detail how to rig the boom guy in such a way that in a gybe it could be set up on the other side without leaving the cockpit. (This author found the same system rigged aboard Hum's last boat *Rose Rambler* while on a passage in the late 1980s.) On one occasion, following a crack from the foredeck like a pistol shot Hum realised that the forestay had failed and then proceeded to outline how he had made the boat safe and prevented a dismasting. This prompted a short disquisition on how to keep a bermudan mast straight and all the rigging at the correct tension. 'Very few riggers', he said, 'know how to set up the standing rigging.' He also reflected on various structural problems caused by sailing a boat too fast to windward and opined that the best way to gain ground to windward was to sail on a close reach rather than close-hauled. 'We go half as fast again and the extra distance is negligible.' Summing up his approach to ocean cruising, he recommended that cruising sailors should go offshore racing sometimes to gain knowledge from the racers' attention to detail. Truth to tell, Hum must have been a very exacting skipper to sail with, whether cruising or racing. He missed very little.

Along the way we gain insight into Hum's wider sailing philosophy. Although he had plenty of experience with the gaff rig, he was a strong advocate of the bermudan rig on the grounds of its efficiency to windward, simplicity, reliability and freedom from chafe. He died before the full flowering of the gaffer revival but would doubtless have regarded it with scepticism. Long before the advent of small retro gaffers which lack a forestay to the stemhead, he was highly critical of the practice of having a single forestay to the bowsprit end, leaving the rig vulnerable to collapse in the event of damage to the bobstay or the bowsprit. Again, though he had extensive experience with mainsail roller reefing, not least in *Vertue XXXV* which had Turner ratchet gear, he thought it inferior to points reefing because it was more difficult to maintain the sail shape and was more damaging to

The decisive moment came.... with devastating suddenness: a great fiend of a sea that picked the yacht up, threw her over on her port side and then burst over her.

the fabric of the sail. Above all perhaps, he was an advocate of sailing at optimum speed and never wasting a fair wind – hence his belief in the value of some racing experience. Nursing broken ribs during the Atlantic crossing, he wondered whether he should heave to for a day or two to aid his recovery but could not resist sailing on. 'What a shocking waste of a good breeze it would have been.' 'She really is a wonderful ship', he mused, 'and is standing up to my brutal driving remarkably well.' Hum's general remarks in praise of the Vertue class, quoted above, are well known but on specifics he noted 'her ability to stand up to bad weather, her remarkably high performance under sail and the comfort of her accommodation', which he concluded were 'really quite outstanding'.

During the second week at sea Hum reflected on the risks of voyaging in small yachts, concluding, in light of the fact that very few yachts have disappeared without trace (one being Slocum's *Spray*), that 'they are extremely slight'. As if aware that discussion could not stop there, he then proceeded to offer a long list of possible risks, the greatest of which was falling overboard, and launched into a discussion of the need for lifelines all around the deck of a sea-going yacht, recommending thick-gauge wire and stout galvanized mild steel stanchions through-bolted to the beam shelf. In short, Hum the risk-taker was always balanced by Hum the technician. The romantic, who craved living on the edge, was balanced by the severe realist, the practitioner.

On the question of risk and recovery from near disaster, a good illustration is the response Hum and his crew dealt to the knock-down *Vertue XXXV* experienced on day forty-two of the passage across the Atlantic, only a few hundred miles short of their destination. It was the same storm which hit Adlard Coles's Cohoe and other competitors in the Bermuda race of that year. The decisive moment came, Hum recalled, 'with devastating suddenness: a great fiend of a sea that picked the yacht up, threw her over on her port side and then burst over her'. The doghouse windows on the port side were shattered, leaving her open to the elements. It proved to be a life-saver, however, since the main hatch was jammed and the forehatch sealed with a canvas cover, trapping them below. Hum managed to squeeze out of the doghouse window, suffering only minor cuts from broken glass. He ran the boat off down-wind then together he and Kevin pumped and bailed desperately. A further crisis was triggered by the discovery of a split along the entire length of the cabin coaming on the port side close to the deck. A combination of canvas sail-bags, spare boards, and metal tubing as bracing members was deployed to plug the gap and gradually order and water-tightness were restored. After twenty-four hours the wind moderated to force seven, the barometer rose, and they were able to set a close-reefed mainsail. As it happened the storm had blown them in the direction they wanted to go and the wind remained favourable for the rest of the passage. They arrived in New York after forty-seven days at sea, arriving on 2 June. But it was a close-run thing. Hum spoke of 'those terrible moments when the end seemed so very near'.

* * *

Hum's account of the crossing to New York, besides its value as a manual of seamanship and endurance, was a richly human document revealing much about his attitude to life as well as to sailing. At the core was a mixture of modesty and strong opinions. 'How I detest publicity', he declared in recalling the start of the passage at Lymington when a crowd had gathered to see him off. The truth was he was tired and somewhat depressed at the thought of the magnitude of the task ahead. But this sentiment was also in line with a constitutional resistance to making a fuss or being made a fuss of. Fame with him was most definitely not the spur, and in part for that reason he was and is less visible than some of his contemporary voyagers. Significantly, he wrote only two books about his own voyaging, both discussed above; his only other book, *Atlantic Adventurers* (1953), was a detailed history of small boat Atlantic crossings that contained much information and reflection on a multitude of little-known voyages as well as the better-known ones from the mid-nineteenth century onwards.

As for his strong views on boats and seamanship, these may be matters of opinion but were thoroughly tested by experience in a variety of conditions and types of craft. It is also the case that the debates have moved on, as design concepts, gear, and technology have developed in ways he could scarcely have anticipated. What is not in dispute is Hum's mastery of the techniques available to him. The issue in any case is not whether he was 'right' on details but the way he met the challenges he set himself, and in essence the challenges of small boat voyaging remain constant. What impresses above all is the resourcefulness and integrity of his approach to sailing.

* * *

Hum's influence long outlasted his death in 1980. His wife Mary continued voyaging extensively in the company of fellow Ocean Cruising Club (OCC) members and in 1988 she became Commodore of the club. His daughter Pat married the yacht designer and ocean cruiser Mike Pocock, who also served a term as Commodore of the OCC, and together they undertook numerous long-distance voyages in boats designed by him. Hum's beloved *Rose Rambler* has been well-maintained by successive owners and is still to be seen on the east coast rivers of England. In short, Hum's legacy was secured through the people he knew and the craft he sailed, as well as through the example of the life he led which still has the capacity to lift the spirit. That is surely more than enough to grant him a high place in the pantheon of small boat sailors.

Chapter 6

ON A MISSION

The Smith Brothers and Charles Violet: *Nova Espero*

Among the notable voyages of the postwar years, those of the Smith brothers and Charles Violet in *Nova Espero* stand out not only because of the small size of the boat (a mere twenty feet overall) but for the ambition of the challenges she met. The first was a voyage in 1949 from Dartmouth, Canada to Dartmouth, England by the Smith brothers in what was at the time a half-decked boat with an upturned dinghy serving as a makeshift cabin. The second, two years later, was a return Atlantic crossing to New York against the prevailing wind by Stanley Smith and Charles Violet, with *Nova Espero* now sporting a proper cabin. The third and least known voyage was a single-handed cruise by Charles Violet through the French rivers and canals to the Mediterranean, where *Nova Espero* took a wandering course to Italy, North Africa, back north through France and across the channel to Yarmouth, Isle of Wight, home of her builders. Violet returned to these waters a few years later in a vain attempt to reach Russia. *Nova Espero* then fades from sight having left a fleeting but vivid trace in the annals of ocean voyaging.

The builders of *Nova Espero* were the Smith brothers, Stanley and Colin.* They were brought up in Yarmouth where their father was a boatbuilder and coxswain of the lifeboat – surely an ideal pedigree for aspiring ocean adventurers. During the war they both trained for the RAF Volunteer Reserve at locations in Britain and Canada, serving later as glider pilots in India and Burma. After demobilization, in 1949 they returned to Canada with the dual purpose of establishing a peace colony and setting up a boat-building business, both to be named *Nova Espero*, Esperanto for new hope.

* Robin Somes, a second cousin of the Smith brothers, has brought together a mass of diverse material by and about the Smiths and Charles Violet in *Nova: The History of the Nova Espero* (2020), an indispensable publication for those interested in the Smiths and their time. My account draws heavily on this publication.

The plan for a peace colony was inspired equally by revulsion against the horror of war and the vision of a community which could overcome the impulses which led to war. Stanley penned a poem of around 780 lines which combined his two passions: ships and a utopian vision of the future. In his highly rhetorical verses the ship becomes a metaphor for the human community and the sea a representation of all the forces threatening to overwhelm it. He pictured 'a great new ship of state' which would embody his 'great Design for the future of Man'. In this egalitarian community all would work for the good of the whole. In Smith's vision the ship's passage was strewn with rocks and battered by storms but with the right crew, accurate charts, and a commitment to harmonious living the way could be found. Above all, those who sailed in the ship must work together as a community, banish fear and embrace reason. An interesting feature of the poem is how it deals with the question of power which lies at the root of governance. 'Let us not put a premium on power', he intoned; only those who were capable of 'self-discipline and self-abnegation' should be allowed to drink of power. Those who thirst for power should not be allowed to go near it. In short, paradoxical though it appeared, power should be granted only to those who hated power. It was the Smiths' version of Plato's idea of the 'philosopher-king', though in neither case was it clear how such an idealistic vision could function in the real world of competition for power and advantage.

Stanley Smith had written the poem in the latter months of 1948, in advance of the plan to build a boat. Then in the early months of 1949 the Smiths took passage on a liner to Halifax Nova Scotia, and it was during this time that they sketched out the lines of what was to become the boat *Nova Espero*. By this stage they were also deeply embroiled in plans for the Nova Espero community, and following their first Atlantic crossing from Yarmouth, Nova Scotia to Yarmouth Isle of Wight (described below) they sought to bring the plan to fruition. In early 1950 the brothers issued a manifesto, which was essentially a prose version of the ideas contained in the poem, and called for all those who were interested to join them in Yarmouth, Nova Scotia to establish the community of Nova Espero:

> We built our little boat the "Nova Espero" and made the Atlantic crossing, because we wanted to tell you of plans which we are developing for a world community in miniature which will, we hope, serve as a practical example of the way in which the people of different races, colours and creeds can live and work together in friendship, and achieve a high standard of living.

There followed a lengthy prospectus which set out the idea behind the community: its proposed organization, political arrangements, voting power, laws, education and also the language, which was to be Esperanto on the grounds that it was non-national and supposedly easy to learn. The manifesto was nothing if not comprehensive.

In the event, several hundred applications to join the community flowed in but the brothers were not happy with them. Some expected the Smiths to provide their passage money to Nova Scotia or had different ideas about how such a community should be organized. There was some tension too between the brothers following Colin's marriage in early 1950 and a consequent change in his priorities in the wake of the first Atlantic crossing. In the end the peace colony idea fell by the wayside, but in building a boat together and sailing it across the Atlantic Ocean, the Smith brothers could at least claim to be designing their own future, even if not that of humankind as a whole. In practice the double Atlantic crossing served to establish the seaworthiness of their design and hence their bona fides as boat builders with a view to setting up a boat-building business. What remained of their vision behind the Nova Espero community was a mere echo of the idealism which had driven them to build *Nova Espero* in the first place. It found expression in a forward-looking and positive attitude towards life which carried them through many subsequent adventures but little remained, at least in published form, of the idea of a Utopian community.

* * *

Nova Espero was designed, Stanley Smith wrote, 'as a half-decked sailing boat, measuring twenty feet in overall length, fifteen feet eleven inches on the water-line, with a tonnage of rather less than one.' She had a beam of six feet three inches and draught of two feet ten. She resembled, in fact, nothing so much as a Norfolk Broads half-decker except that she had rather more sheer. She was rigged as a gunter sloop with two hundred square feet of sail. The thrill of seeing their boat afloat for the first time was unsurpassable. 'Given the choice', Stanley recalled, 'I would as soon live those first few hours of *Nova Espero* afloat as have stood back and seen the Venus de Milo completed under my hands.' In short, romance was in the air but practicality soon reared its head. They were running out of money so in a period of three days they built the dinghy which was to serve as their cabin in order that they could move aboard and save money on accommodation costs ashore. Even by the spartan cruising standards of the time, the Smiths were at the primitive end.

By July 1949 she was ready for her first Atlantic crossing (at least as far as the brothers were concerned). They kept their plans secret in order not to worry relatives. This was voyaging on the cheap even by the standards of the time. Colin Smith recalled that they sailed 'without a proper sea-anchor, without a chronometer, without a log, without oil-bags, without oilskins, but not without hope!' They did not even have bunks in their primitive cabin but slept on the floor in sleeping bags. Their limited capacity to carry water meant that they made do with a quarter of a normal daily allowance.

Stanley Smith wrote two accounts of the first voyage, the first being an unpublished draft, completed in 1950, which was the basis for the later much briefer publication, *Smiths at Sea* (1951). Robin Somes, a cousin of the Smith brothers and editor of a collection of material by and about the Smiths, suggests that the first version was regarded by the prospective publisher as too dark, with its emphasis on the dangers and near disasters of the voyage. In draft Stanley Smith admitted to 'terror' on occasion when breaking waves would submerge *Nova Espero* in a 'dashing smother of phosphorescence' while he strove to fit his body into the opening between the upturned dinghy and the floor of the boat. Characteristically, Stanley's prose piled on the metaphors as he described the seas around them: 'big heavy monsters began to climb onto the shoulders of their neighbours like a horde of excited schoolboys crowding out of the school gate; little fellows jostled and squeezed by the big chaps, an occasional hefty bully jamming the caps of the little chaps roughly down over their ears, in fact a real boisterous bedlam.'

By contrast, the published version is as humorous, expressive, and fragmentary as the illustrations which adorn the book, which is to say that it is fun to read but does not dwell on details, least of all the dangers and hardships. When they are described, Stanley Smith makes light of them. A few days out from Nova Scotia they ran into what Stanley described as 'the mother and father of all storms.' 'I have to confess,' he reflected, 'I was a little worried!! But although things were a bit uncomfortable and wet my fears were quite unfounded. Sometimes Nova Espero was completely buried under falling crests, but the head and shoulders of the man at the tiller filled the only opening, so she never became dangerously waterlogged.'*

Approaching Ireland Colin fell overboard trying to grab the mainsheet during an accidental gybe. He lost not only his lunch, just handed to him by his brother, but one of the only two forks they had aboard. Colin later said in an interview on the sixtieth anniversary of the trip that 'I was in the water and all I could see was the boat slowly sailing away from me. I was so cold and unhappy because my meal had gone overboard as well.' Fortunately, Stanley became aware of Colin's disappearance in time and sailed back to get him. In Stanley's account in *Smiths at Sea* the whole incident is encapsulated as follows: 'One day my brother deserted his post… but I soon recaptured him.' The rest of the page is taken up with one of Stanley's inimitable cartoon-like drawings.

The plan for the voyage to remain secret did not survive since a number of passing ships delivered news of their progress, ensuring that their arrival back home in the Isle of Wight would be front page news. Newsreels of the time show the brothers, attired somewhat incongruously in smart suits and ties, being greeted by an armada of small boats and most of the population of the island, including their father in the Yarmouth lifeboat. One assumes this scene was partially staged since they had reached their destination of Dartmouth earlier and had had time to prepare for the Yarmouth welcome. From the evidence of the next voyage, sartorial elegance was not in the Smith genes.

* The incident is engagingly described by Stanley Smith in a British Pathé News interview on their arrival at Dartmouth. www.britishpathe.com/video/brothers-cross-atlantic-in-yacht' (1949). Thanks to Robin Somes for pointing me in this direction. See Bibliography for Chapter 6 for other newsreels.

* * *

Between the Atlantic crossings of 1949 and 1951 a curious interlude took place. In January 1950, the Smith brothers along with their close friend Charles Violet returned to Canada on the liner *Franconia,* accompanied by *Nova Espero,* with the intention of establishing the first Nova Espero community. There followed two hard months of 'frustration and bitterness' as their attempts to get the project going in Canada foundered on the rocks of unreasonable and unrealistic expectations on the part of applicants. It was decided to focus on Britain and in April the Smith brothers returned, leaving Charles with the boat. In July of that same year, Charles confessed, 'I did a rather dreadful thing.' Against Stanley's express request not to attempt a long voyage in their absence, Charles quickly provisioned *Nova Espero* and set off with the idea of sailing her back to England. Only one day out he had an accident with the paraffin stove which left him with his hair on fire, nasty burns on both his hands, and his morale at zero. Unsurprisingly, he records, 'I decided to turn back.' Money was then raised to bring *Nova Espero* back to England and she arrived at Liverpool docks in December 1950 accompanied by Charles. He was met at the dock by Stanley with a grim expression on his face which led Charles to expect the worst. Instead, Stanley said 'Will you sail with me in *Nova Espero* to New York next year?' to which Charles replied without hesitation, 'Yes, Stan, be glad to.'

* * *

The second voyage, which took place in 1951, fulfilled the original plan of a return across the Atlantic but this time with Charles Violet, who shared Stanley's enthusiasm for the project and was equally resourceful. As mentioned, Colin was already married and had other life plans in view. *Nova Espero* herself underwent some changes too. For the return trip she was provided with a cabin and converted to a yawl rig which Stanley regarded as a great improvement: 'We blessed the little mizzen a thousand times for in a moderate gale we could beat offshore under jib and mizzen with the tiller free.' It also, he noted, made lying to a sea anchor much easier. Another key innovation on this trip was the use of a de-salination kit to convert sea-water into fresh. It proved to be highly effective and reliable. In another departure from the first voyage, this time they had a modicum of sponsorship in that they carried samples of British goods from the Festival of Britain to New York. In fact, on occasions they would refer to this as their 'Festival voyage', indicating that the idea of the Nova Espero community had slipped well into the background. An added element of this voyage was that the link with the Festival of Britain gave them a public profile. Its successful completion would make them famous, at least for a while.

The overwhelming impression to be gained from Stanley Smith and Charles Violet's joint account of this voyage, *The Wind Calls the Tune* (1952), is of the morale-sapping toughness of the conditions they encountered and the doggedness and good humour of Smith and Violet in surmounting them. The first voyage had taken a month and a half; this one took three and a half, though it included a ten-day stay in the Azores to mend a broken rudder and a longer stopover in Nova Scotia. They experienced frequent strong headwinds and made regular use of their sea-anchor, a piece of equipment without which this trip would have been much more difficult, if not impossible.

A near ship-wreck on the rocks of Ushant was narrowly averted, accompanied by one of those curious incidents that, as the authors put it, 'sometimes shake the modern sailor into a sympathetic understanding of the superstitions of the sea.' At the height of the storm two bedraggled swallows fluttered into the cabin and were so exhausted they stayed the night, eventually falling asleep. Meanwhile, on a lee shore with the rocks of Ushant only a few miles away, the sailors concluded there was no hope of avoiding disaster and they contemplated inflating their rubber dinghy. And suddenly, we are told, 'a wonderful thing happened. The wind lessened slightly and veered a little north of west', at which point the swallows flew off and made for land. Soon Smith and Violet were able to haul in the sea-anchor, set the foresail and gradually clear the land. There is no heavy-handed attempt in their account to turn the swallows into symbols of anything, just a poignant sense of companionship in adversity.

Ten days later they experienced a knock-down. 'We remember only a fantastic roar and a deafening, stunning bang. Charles was hurled out of his bunk on the port side into the cabin roof opposite... Everything went dark as night and water seemed to fill the cabin.

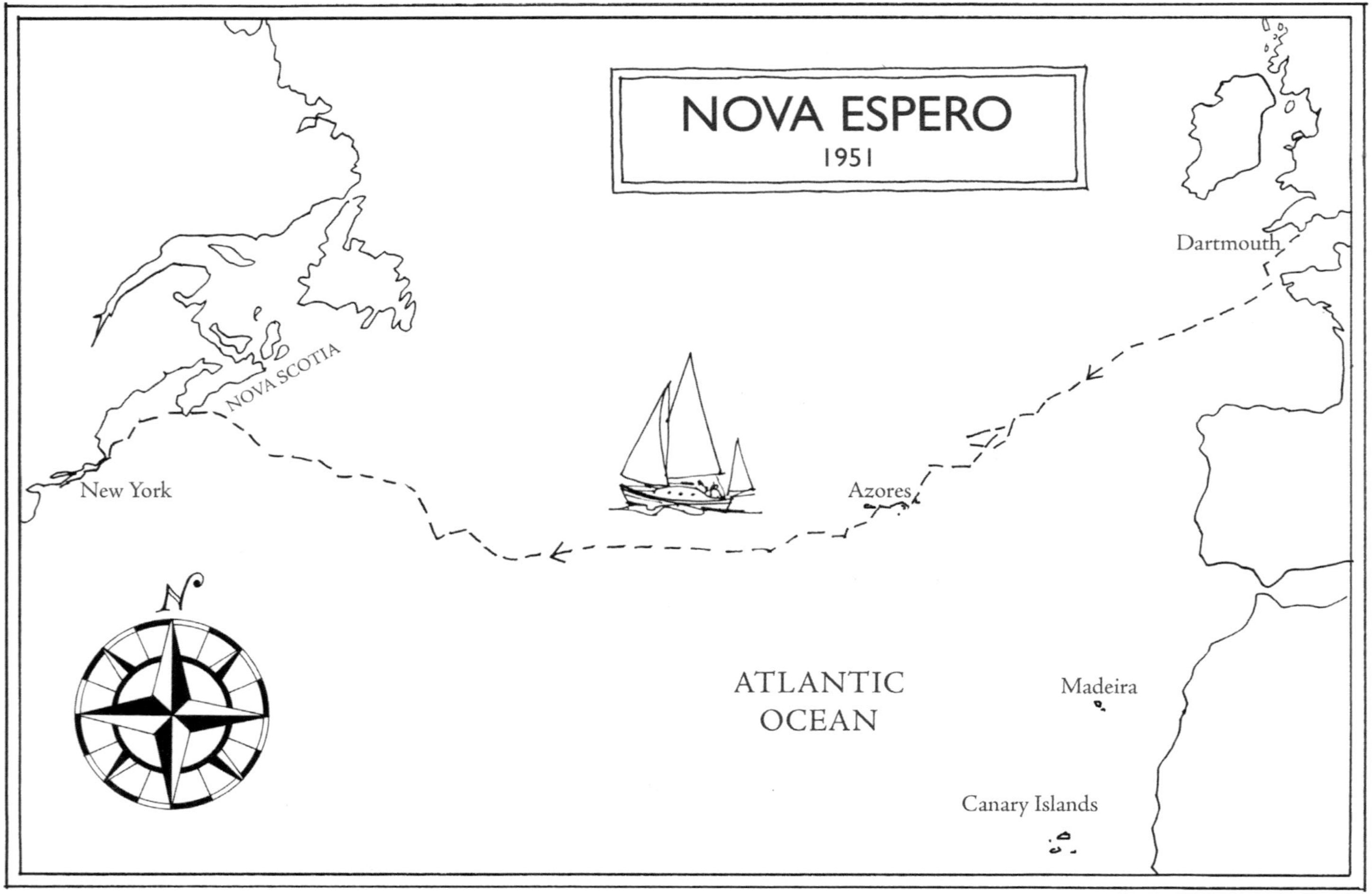
NOVA ESPERO
1951
Dartmouth
NOVA SCOTIA
New York
Azores
ATLANTIC
OCEAN
Madeira
Canary Islands
N

We remember thinking only 'this must be the end... A second later, with a loud sucking noise and another tremendous bang, we saw light again. We watched the water fall down from the cabin roof drenching everything. We heard it swilling about heavily from side to side. The little boat had righted and resumed the old familiar dance on the surface of the sea.' The mast and rigging were still intact but the rudder was damaged beyond repair. After waiting for the storm to subside, they rigged a jury rudder with wood cannibalised from parts of the interior fittings and struggled on to the Azores which they reached after another week's sailing.

Beyond the drama what really appeals in their account is their infectious curiosity about life in all its variety. They make contact with a succession of interesting characters in their periods ashore, reflect movingly, but without self-consciousness, on the deeper things in life, and above all offer a glimpse of what it is to live in a tiny box with another human being under conditions of isolation and stress. In a log entry Stanley describes the sense of being watched over by Joshua Slocum, who himself experienced the phenomenon of another presence close by, in his case the pilot of the *Pinta*, Columbus's flagship. For Smith, such experiences were not delusions but 'as real as the sky and the sea.'

Smith and Violet also discuss how they managed to stay at peace with each other when conditions constantly conspired to generate tension over the most trivial of matters. They developed the practice of systematically examining themselves 'for little mannerisms and habits which might prove unbearably irritating to our neighbour under strain' and through speaking frankly about them were able eventually to eliminate them. Beyond such exercises in crisis management they obviously shared much, without which such intimate negotiations would doubtless have been impossible. 'When we were not reading to each other we would talk of places we had seen, people we knew. We think this is very important and takes a place second only to common interests such as music, literature, love of the sea and sailing.'

The last part of the book describes coasting down from Nova Scotia to New York, a change of rhythm which brings out their talent for observation of people, customs and places. Among the many instances of friendly and often quirky welcomes, in the tiny harbour of

Baccaro in Nova Scotia they fell in with a young man called Obadiah Christy who invited them to supper followed by a revivalist meeting at a Pentecostalist chapel where they were subject to a lively sermon on the wickedness of liquor, smoking and idleness. A few days later, within sight of Cape Cod a seaplane buzzed them and dropped something attached to a parachute. It proved to be a container with a message reading: 'If you are *Nova Espero* clap your hands above your heads as we make a low pass, US Coast Guard PBM 84733.' A big welcome in New York was thus assured, or at least it would have been if they had not been furthered delayed. New York got bored waiting, though the city warmed to the pair once they had arrived.

Unfortunately the promised financial help in return for carrying British goods never materialised. Virtually penniless, they were forced to rely on the kindness of strangers and a loan from the British consulate for their fares back to Britain. Meanwhile, conducting interviews with the press or fielding questions from hundreds of school children all they had to wear was what they stood up in, the rest having become mildewed or worn out: 'Charles wore his old open-necked yellow shirt, and grey trousers slit across one knee and the rear, while Stanley was wearing his usual tee-shirt and rolled up grey bags. Neither of us had socks.'

Stanley's sketches for the book are vividly eloquent of their experiences. They have the same spontaneity as those in *Smiths at Sea* but are representational rather than cartoon-like, yet drawn with impressive freedom and expressiveness. His figures are mobile and alive, his visions of Nova Espero being tossed around in the waves startlingly real. Stanley was as talented an artist as a writer.

* * *

The third voyage was in a new key. Not only was it single-handed but it was a mix of river, canal, coastal and short sea passages – short at least by Atlantic standards, though the total mileage was close to that of an Atlantic crossing. Charles Violet, now joint owner of *Nova Espero*, left Yarmouth in May 1952 and crossed to Le Havre where he headed up the Seine and the Marne, down the Saône and the Rhône to Marseilles. From there he made passage between Corsica and Sardinia to Anzio, south to the Strait of Messina, Malta, and Tunisia, back north to Sardinia and Corsica and thence to the far northern coast of Italy near the French border. For the return leg through France he chose the Canal du Midi, the River Garonne to Bordeaux, and the coast of the Bay of Biscay up to southern Brittany. He entered the river Vilaine at Redon which took him to the Canal du Rance and Saint-Malo. The total distance far exceeded that of an Atlantic crossing and he took a year over it, which included some bone-chilling winter sailing in Southern France. For this trip *Nova Espero* was equipped with an outboard motor, a necessary addition for negotiating rivers and canals.

Charles Violet was a close friend of Stanley Smith and shared his love of sailing and adventure. 'I suppose I am what you would call a rolling stone, for the lure of distant places has a magnetic attraction for me', he wrote. He was flexible about his destinations, and the journey has a distinctly improvised feel. His original idea had been to sail to the Black Sea and explore Russia but on heading east from Southern Italy he was met with continuous headwinds. When after a few days a full gale developed, he became worried about the time he was taking. 'To hell with the Black Sea and the Russians', he thought. He would go and look at Africa, Malta, and Sicily instead. This was a big change but there were plenty of other occasions when he was forced into more local shifts in his plans, either because he was poorly supplied with detailed charts or because he simply chose to follow a whim.

One such example was his decision to follow a boat he had become acquainted with to an island off Corsica to look for treasure. 'For two hours we sailed, and gradually what at first seemed to be a jumble of rocks on the horizon turned into a little green island lying snugly inside the huge granite outcrops.' There followed one of those encounters which has the quality of myth or perhaps wish fulfilment. Exploring the island, he came across two figures coming towards him, 'hand-in-hand and naked, or so I thought'. He reflected that 'human beings in the minimum of clothing are only too rarely attractive... these two were superb', He couldn't help himself being facetious and said 'Good morning Mr Adam; good morning Mrs Eve. I hope I don't intrude.' 'Good Morning, should we say the Archangel Gabriel,' they replied in kind. They turned out to be Belgians who had been exploring for

Roman vases and other artefacts in a wreck. The y lived in a cave and went to Bonifacio in Corsica by kayak when necessary. Violet stayed several days and twice after this initial meeting he ferried Adam and Eve in *Nova Espero* to Bonifacio for supplies. The story had an unfortunate sequel in that the pair had all their finds confiscated by the authorities. The spell of the island was broken for him and he headed for other shores.

His short stay in North Africa was to prove unfortunate in that after being presented by over-generous hosts with a huge plate of goat meat surrounded by 'a wall of grey looking rice' slathered in red-hot sauce he became violently ill. He lay on his bunk for two days until he felt well enough to leave for Sardinia. Some way into the passage, however, he experienced a crisis in which he went blind. Once again, as in the case of *Nova Espero* off Ushant on her second transatlantic passage, 'nature took a hand' and within earshot of waves crashing on nearby rocks, his sight gradually returned. He was able to creep into a sheltered cove where he took four aspirins and slept for twelve hours. He was never able entirely to shake the effects of this illness and it recurred on a number of occasions in milder form, to the extent of giving him difficulties with the authorities in a Sardinian port. It was still with him when he reached France.

Perhaps it is not surprising that Violet's account of this voyage, *Solitary Journey* (1954), is as vividly written as *The Wind Calls the Tune* since he was co-author of the earlier book. Besides the record of resourceful sailing in varied conditions, of particular interest in this third voyage are the glimpses we get of the effects of the Second World War. On more than one occasion Violet falls in with former prisoners of war, not least in Anzio, scene of a desperate wartime battle. Trying to find someone who speaks English he comes across a man who had spent two years in Canada and three in Somerset as a POW and whose accent reflects both sources. In Bastia in northern Corsica he came across a man putting up a poster reading: 'Workers!!!!!! M. Pinay same as the Vichy Government, but instead of selling us to the Germans, is delivering France to the Americans, and consequently the French worker as cannon fodder. GO HOME AMERICANS!!!!!!' In capturing such scenes Violet's book gives us a window into that curious postwar period of transition.

A seaplane buzzed them and dropped something attached to a parachute.
It proved to be a container with a message reading:
'If you are Nova Espero clap your hands above your heads …'

Violet's account has the feel of a personal odyssey and, there are explicit echoes of Homer as he negotiates Scylla and Charybdis in the Strait of Messina, the location of a key scene in The Odyssey. The book ends in typically downbeat fashion which nevertheless completes the circle in perfectly satisfying style: 'When near the entrance to Yarmouth harbour, a row-boat put out to meet me. It was Stan Smith and his father, welcoming me back home.'

In 1954-5 Charles Violet made a second solo voyage through the French canals to the Mediterranean but it gained a much lower profile than the first in part because no book was written about it. The only published account was an article in *Motorboat and Yachting* in 1956.* Furthermore, the original goal of the voyage – which was to sail up the river Don and down the Volga into the Caspian sea – was unachievable since he was not able to gain the necessary permission from the Soviet authorities, despite having been assured by Soviet Consular service in Britain that it would be forthcoming. Thus for a second time Violet's ambition to sail behind the Iron Curtain did not succeed.

Violet's account of this voyage is notable, however, for a stirring description of a gale on passage to the Channel Islands, for the challenges experienced in negotiating the French canal and river systems, and the performance of his ever-reliable Seagull outboard which had already taken him the best part of 2000 miles on his first European cruise. 'Whenever my eye rests on it', he reflected, 'I get a feeling of pride in which there is a touch of awe.' However thwarted were his own goals, the outboard had a 'most successful cruise'. Violet also reflected on the experience of single-handing and tried to explain its attraction, as many solo sailors have before and since. The heightened sensations of nature were part of it: the sunsets, the dawns, a 'quietness that enters the soul'. There was the sense too of access to the world's mysteries, bringing 'the thrill that a curtain of the mind will possibly draw aside and knowledge of the Creator of all worlds will be manifested'. And then, perhaps inevitably comes a 'Clonk! as a block tumbles on its side [and] the mind in a flash returns from its sojourn

* The article in question, 'From the Solent to Corsica with an Outboard Auxiliary,' is reprinted in Robin Somes, *Nova*, pp.127-34

among mysteries unfathomable to human comprehension, and there you are again, alone at sea.'

* * *

There is a danger of underestimating the achievement of the Smith brothers and Charles Violet since they generally recounted their adventures in a laconic fashion and without suggestion of heroics. In truth they were fine sailors, formidably resourceful, and expert boatbuilders. *Nova Espero* was as much a hero of the story as the men who sailed in her and it was they of course, who built their know-how into her, making her the perfect vehicle for their adventures. Despite their lack of resources, the Smiths and Violet prepared meticulously for their voyages, bearing out the adage that the first and most important safety factor is the quality of the boat coupled with the experience of those who sail in her. Significantly, the foreword to *The Wind Calls the Tune* was written by Eric Hiscock, the most professional and one might say sensible of small boat voyagers. Hiscock suggested that Smith and Violet's account of their voyage would win an honoured place alongside those of Joshua Slocum, Conor O'Brien, and William Robinson. Charles Violet's *Solitary Journey* had the benefit of an introduction by legendary yacht designer and offshore racing guru John Illingworth. Higher recommendations could hardly be found.

For the rest, Colin spent his career as a lecturer in yacht design and on retirement moved back to the Isle of Wight where he took over the family firm. He died in 2018 at the age of 96. Charles Violet moved to Lampeter in the 1970s where he had a smallholding and sailed a boat named *Nova Espero 2nd* from Fishguard harbour. He too lived on into his 90s. Stanley went on to design the West Wight Potter, at fourteen feet a good deal smaller than Nova Espero, and a very different design concept, yet still capable of open sea passages. Ever the adventurer, in the mid-1960s he opted to deliver one of these to a customer in Sweden. After riding out three days of force eight to nine in the North Sea he was driven ashore in Denmark and was lucky to survive. Following recovery he continued the voyage inland through Denmark, finally crossing the Kattegat to Sweden. He later married the Danish nurse who had treated him in hospital and settled in Denmark, where he died in 1980.

As for *Nova Espero,* in 1959 Stanley sold his share to Charles, who at some later stage sold her on. It was rumoured that she was destroyed by fire in a boatyard but it was later confirmed that during the 1980s she broke free from her moorings in a storm and was wrecked against the breakwater of Portland Harbour. She lives on in the form of the Siani class yacht of which a few examples remain but her real legacy is contained in the accounts of her voyages and the lives of her three crew members who were forever touched by the experience of sailing her.

Chapter 7

GEORGE AND ISABEL MILLAR

A Tale of Three Boats: *Truant*, *Serica*, *Amokura*

George Millar and his wife Isabel rarely feature in accounts of yachting in the postwar years. They never crossed an ocean, broke no nautical records, nor indeed attempted to, and knew few of the prominent names in the cruising fraternity of that era. Nevertheless, starting almost from scratch as sailors in 1946, they undertook challenging voyages in European waters over the next two decades. George Millar wrote three remarkable books about their exploits: *Isabel and the Sea* (1948), *A White Boat From England* (1951), and *Oyster River* (1963). It is as a writer as much as a sailor that George Millar deserves our attention.

Over the years the Millars, despite George's self-deprecating remarks on the subject, developed the full range of nautical skills to a level of which Eric Hiscock might have approved. In character, however, the Millars were the polar opposite of the Hiscocks. The Hiscocks had an organised and restrained approach to adventure. The Millars, on the other hand, projected an aura of excitement and danger – not as swashbucklers, but with a tendency to aristocratic manners and morals, and seemingly always on the edge of some new and surprising turn of events. They could be spiky and snobbish, especially with customs officials, but were capable of turning on the charm when the occasion demanded it.

There is, however, a Millar backstory. For some, this takes precedence over the sailing exploits, and it is not hard to see why, for Millar was a proper war hero. While serving in 1942 as a second lieutenant in the Western Desert he was captured and moved to a prison camp in Italy. When the Allies landed in Italy, Allied prisoners of war were transported to Germany. Millar and another British soldier escaped from a train some way south of Munich. Proficiency in French and German enabled him to pass for a migrant worker, and he made it to Vichy France, from where he crossed the Pyrenees into Spain and then home, where he volunteered for the recently-established Special

Operations Executive (SOE). In June 1944, a week before D-Day, he was parachuted into France, where he worked with the Maquis on sabotage operations against German forces. Four months of intense and dramatic activity followed, until De Gaulle's Free French forces moved in and SOE withdrew from France. He was awarded the MC for his escape from captivity, the DSO for his resistance work, and the Légion d'Honneur and the Croix de Guerre by France.

His two accounts of his wartime exploits, *Maquis*, on his Resistance work, and *Horned Pigeon*, about his escape from Germany, appeared in 1945 and 1946 respectively. Both were substantial books of around 400 pages, and their fluency and speed of production are a result of his pre-war career as a journalist in Glasgow and, after a short stint as a deckhand on a freighter, in London. He resumed journalism at the end of the war, when he was sent to Germany by the *Daily Express*.*

* * *

In 1946 the Millars set out for Greece via the French rivers and canals in their thirty-ton Looe lugger *Truant*. They had been married that May – a second marriage for both of them – so the voyage was a kind of honeymoon; and they both wanted to escape grim post-war Britain, hardly a climate in which their restless souls could thrive. George financed the voyage by sending reports to the *Daily Express* en route. There is also a suggestion that they were running guns to the monarchist forces in Greece, then in the throes of civil war, but this is both unlikely and currently unprovable, since the relevant documents remain embargoed.

Unlike most other books written by sailors of their generation, which tended to be blithely unpolitical, Millar's sea works give the reader inklings of the political conflicts which beset the postwar world. A native Scot, he had been educated at Loretto and Cambridge, and possessed the manners and some of the attitudes of his class. Where else in the literature of the sea do you find a vivid description of fox-hunting such as is to be found in *A White Boat from*

* Millar's life and writings are well explored by Ben Lowings in *The Chancellor – George Millar: A Life*, Taniwha Press, 2021.

England? Even firm opponents of bloodsports will find this compellingly related interlude a literary tour de force. Here as elsewhere Millar does not explain or justify his actions but simply, or not so simply, relates what he did.

Unsurprisingly Millar was generally in support of the forces of tradition and order but not unquestioningly. He declared in *Isabel and the Sea* that the 'the war had this effect on me personally, it killed most of my political convictions', and said of a French hostess in the Gulf of Morbihan that he liked 'her refusal to admire democracy' – though he was equally dismissive of dyed-in-the wool conservatism. On the Greek civil war he was dismayed as much by the fanaticism of the monarchists as by the Communist-led opposition. Though he was a confirmed patriot, he mentioned in *A White Boat from England* that in conversation with some English people in Gibraltar he condemned as over-simplified and ungenerous the loudly-expressed claim that 'we' had 'won the second German war' and that we had 'stood alone'. In *Oyster River* the bitter war between France and the Algerian independence movement forms a sinister background to the Millars' summer in the Gulf of Morbihan in 1960 (of which more later). The Millars' escape to sea did not mean isolation from the wider world of politics, and indeed the books are rich sources of information about the years of recovery from the war in Britain and the Mediterranean countries.

At the core of these books, however, are Millar's relationships with Isabel and the sea. His first sailing book is an account of his love affair with both. Their marriage proved strong enough to survive many emergencies, and flexible enough to accommodate two remarkably strong wills. George always backed her up – as, for example, when during their summer in the Gulf of Morbihan she reacted to the attempt of a man to feel her up in a restaurant by pinning the fleshy part of his hand between thumb and first finger to the table with a knife. In George's impassive commentary on the incident one senses both that he thought Isabel's reaction was not only appropriate, but also in keeping with the skills he was familiar with from his commando training.

Isabel's relationship with the sea was complicated. She suffered badly from seasickness. Set against this was her extraordinary

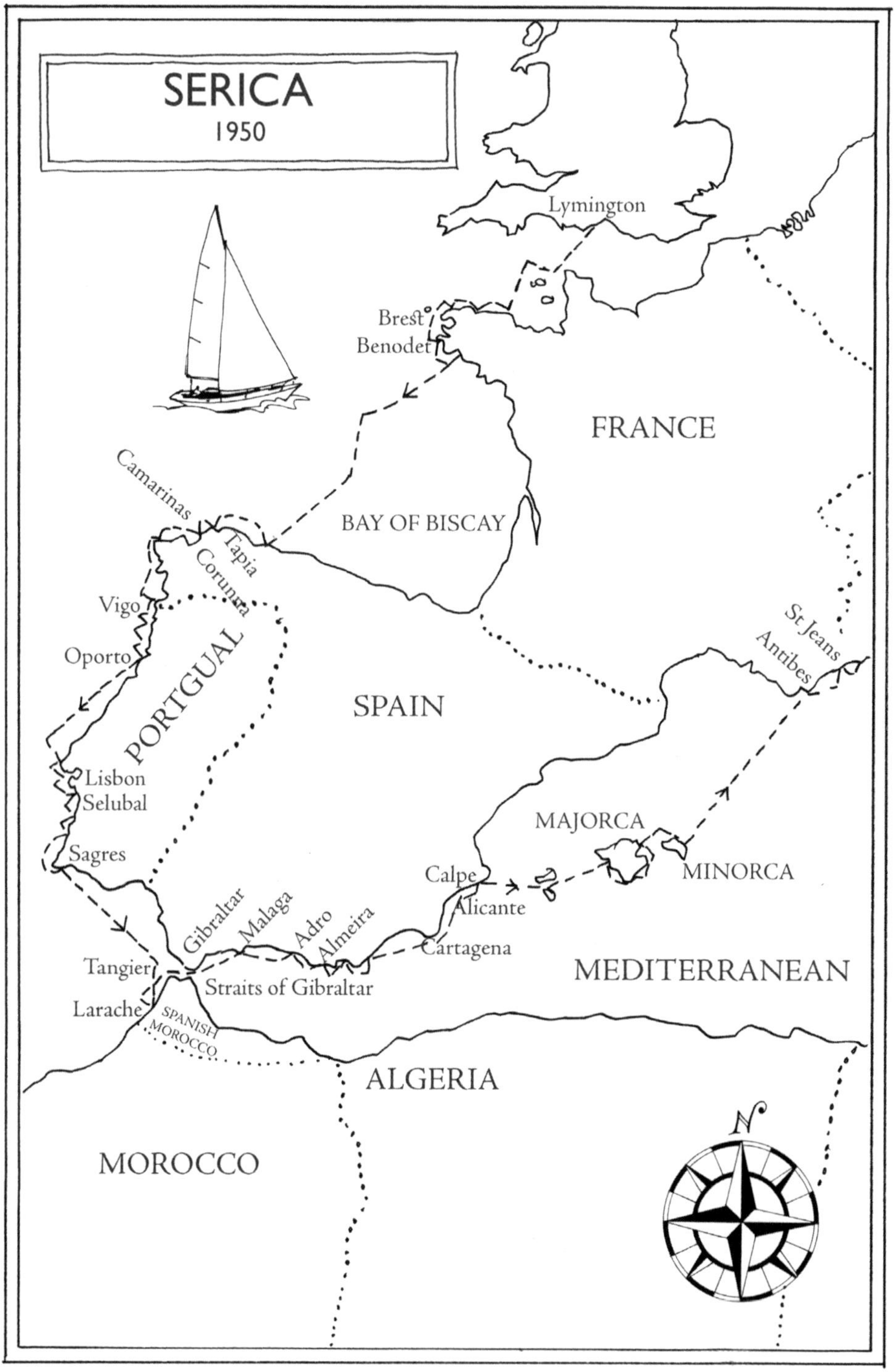

SERICA
1950
Lymington
Brest
Benodet
FRANCE
Camarinas
BAY OF BISCAY
Tapia
Corunna
Vigo
Oporto
PORTUGAL
SPAIN
St Jeans
Antibes
Lisbon
Selubal
Sagres
MAJORCA
MINORCA
Calpe
Alicante
Gibraltar
Malaga
Adro
Almeira
Cartagena
Tangier
MEDITERRANEAN
Straits of Gibraltar
Larache
SPANISH MOROCCO
ALGERIA
MOROCCO
N

strength of will and, despite her diminutive size, of body. She repeatedly proved herself a match for the worst conditions at sea, at which times, Millar reflects, 'she was in strong spirits'. She was also often the decisive one of the pair; her suggestion at the end of their second Mediterranean voyage that they should winter their boat in the small harbour of St Jean near Antibes, a spur-of-the-moment decision which turned out well, was made on the basis of seeing another small cruiser leaving the harbour.

The Millars' voyages (Millar hated the word 'cruise') were coastal and inland explorations, and none the easier for that. Millar imagined sailing the Atlantic but concluded, in a typically deadpan and hard-to-evaluate remark, that 'it would be an anti-climax arriving in America'. As it was, their first voyage took them through the French river and canal system at a time when the French were getting back on their feet and the waterways, still littered with the debris of war, were just resuming operations. George's fluency in French enabled them to negotiate their way through, buy food, spares and fuel for their thirsty engine, and to engage with the many colourful characters they encountered.

Sitting in a bar in Le Havre near the beginning of their first voyage, having ordered a crème de menthe frappé from 'an elderly waiter who trembled from some nervous disease', George listed the people at the neighbouring tables, including a carefully-dressed young French couple who looked like an army cadet and his fiancée, both drunk and clearly angry at something, which turned out to be the sight of eight German prisoners of war drinking in the bar. The prisoners were the guests of five American soldiers, who were far more friendly to them than to the French. Near them at two tables were six prostitutes, and next to them two other women 'in seedy evening dress' who served the establishment as dancing partners. Then a 'tall, cadaverous negro soldier' entered the bar. He paid for a large brandy with a dollar bill, which immediately attracted the attention of the prostitutes, lit a cigarette, and stared blankly through the smoke, unconscious of the people around him. When the band struck up, the French couple got to their feet and danced 'with a piston-like forcefulness' while the smoking American danced alone, with a curious beat in his step 'but portraying all the mannerisms of a man dancing with a woman so faithfully that we did not find his miming at all funny, but rather tragic and terrible'.

The scene reads like a novel or a film script, and there are many like it throughout Millar's writing – indeed, his first published book was a novel. The sailing books are full of dialogue, which must surely be partly invented; but most readers will go with the flow, because the personality the author projects is so intriguing, and the writing managed with such conviction and style.

As they made their way through the French canal and river system, emerged into the Mediterranean, coast-hopped along the French Riviera and down the western side of Italy to the Strait of Messina and on to Greece, their confidence in their nautical skills rose sharply; and it needed to. *Truant* was not an easy boat to manage. She was fifty feet long, thirteen feet in the beam, had two stumpy masts, two engines – which made for complicated manoeuvring – heavy ground tackle and the usual old-boat problems, including leaks in the hull and the deck. And in case Millar's wartime exploits should conjure up the picture of a certified tough guy, Millar described himself as 'a weedy young man of slightly effeminate aspect'. Photos of him do not contradict this description.

Arriving in Piraeus in November 1946 after a five-month voyage, they sold *Truant* to a British general and returned to the UK. Their next boat, *Serica*, was as different from *Truant* as could be. Designed by Robert Clark in 1938 she was forty-five feet long but half the tonnage of *Truant*. Her slender beam, long overhangs and tall bermudan rig made for impressive but often wet performance, especially to windward. In May 1950 they sailed from Lymington over to France, across the Bay of Biscay, through the Strait of Gibraltar to the Balearics, and on to the small port of St Jean on the French Riviera close to the Italian border. Millar said that their aim was not to break any records 'or cover vast watery spaces but merely to move about Europe economically and in comfort, great comfort according to true standards'. They chose this route because 'we had both felt that the easy route [through the inland waterways] was something of a cheat, and we wondered what it was like to sail around the outside'.

It was only typical that in negotiating Finisterre they took the trickiest and most hazardous route – through the Chenal du Four and the Raz de Sein, and in the latter case through the inner channel, following in the wake of a larger craft. In this as in other instances of danger, they seemed to lead a charmed life, though both of them would doubtless have affirmed that fortune favours the brave. Their passage through the Strait of Gibraltar was complicated not merely by the strong Levanter from the east and the powerful tidal streams, but because George was injured when a thrashing jib sheet with wire pennants struck him in the face, leaving bad cuts on the eyelids and the brow. Isabel patched him up, and they went on. What makes his account so compelling is the calm deliberation with which he describes the passage, his injury being merely a significant but incidental part of it.

His account, *A White Boat From England*, contains singing fishermen in northern Spain, and in Mallorca a mysterious man in a wheelchair who had clearly gathered detailed intelligence about the Millars since their arrival, addressed George by name, and because postwar restrictions had ruined his business hated the English. In Alicante there was an angry clash with the police over passports, which perhaps inevitably led to a climbdown by the police. Here Isabel's fluency in the language – she was half Spanish – undoubtedly helped, as did the habits of their aristocratic background, which also showed itself in their taste for the high life, which found them regularly seeking and finding the best restaurants wherever they were.

Lying in St Jean harbour at the very end of their voyage, they were hailed by a man in a rubber dinghy who said his boat had suffered an explosion and that his friend was in a lifebuoy badly injured two miles out to sea. The rescue was achieved at night in very light winds under sail alone, since *Serica*'s engine was not working. Returning to harbour, Millar asked himself a question that contained its own answer: 'had all our meanderings in *Serica* been to some purpose then?' Here, the book ended.

*   *   *

In the light of these two extended voyages to the Mediterranean, the Millars' trip to the Morbihan in the summer of 1960 might seem to be an afterthought. It was intended as a quiet summer following a riding accident which had left George seriously injured. In the event

Making sure that their gun and cartridge belt were ready on the chart table, the Millars eased out of their anchorage under sail.

it provided plenty of interest, starting with manoeuvring a large boat short-handed in shallow, confined waters with powerful tides. They were at home in such waters, and rarely at a loss as to how to escape a difficulty. Isabel regularly fulminated against being 'chartbound', and usually insisted on taking the risky option. In their entire sailing lives they hardly ever lay alongside a quay, and relied on traditional skills and gear; the only exception being the engine, with which both George and Isabel had a love-hate relationship.

The boat that took them to the Morbihan was *Amokura*, a 24-ton yawl designed by Fred Shepherd and built by Moody's in 1939. She was, says Millar, 'bigger and better built than Serica and superior in every way to Truant'. When they had been fitting out *Truant* fourteen years earlier at Moody's yard on the Hamble they had often seen and admired *Amokura*; on the very day the Millars departed for France in 1946 George recorded in *Isabel and the Sea* that 'the smart, blue, ocean-racing yawl *Amokura*, stole past us'. Isabel remarked with unconscious foresight that 'I should like to have a boat with masts as tall as Salisbury spire.'

Oyster River has the same mix of fine writing and nautical adventures as the other books, with the added spice of an intrigue. There is a whiff of *The Riddle of the Sands* in the Millars' fogbound departure from an anchorage at an island in the centre of the Morbihan, out to sea and north to the River Aven. Their object was to escape the attentions of the motor-yacht *Ric-Rac*, whose owner was determined to buy or seize *Amokura*. A local policeman offered an explanation. *Ric-Rac* was crewed by Algerian rebels who coveted *Amokura* because she was a sailing vessel with a reliable engine, and hence far more suitable than their own defective craft for dropping agents in and out of France. George told the policeman that they were not yet ready to leave the Morbihan, and indeed they stayed on for a while longer before becoming convinced that *Ric-Rac* meant business. It was the sound of the Algerians' engine through a thick fog that triggered the decision to leave. Making sure that their gun and cartridge belt were ready on the chart table, the Millars eased out of their anchorage under sail – another escape to add to George's tally.

The Millar's sailing exploits are a window on a time which is not so far in the past but seems utterly unlike our own. The era of mass tourism had not yet arrived. The coast of Spain was undeveloped, Ibiza a place of traditional festivals and fishing ports; the Riviera was more developed, but there were still small harbours to be found, where in the early 1950s smuggling was rife. British goods, not least paints, varnish and paraffin, were a byword for quality, and the reputation of British yachtsmen was second to none. Navigation instruments were simple, an accurate landfall something to be celebrated, weather forecasts relatively imprecise, use of radio transmission rare (and in the case of the Millars non-existent). Adding all that to the Millars' capacity for adventure and their engaging if baffling personalities produces a mixture rich enough to fuel any imagination.

Chapter 8

SOLO ANTI-HERO

Ann Davison and *Felicity Ann*

Ann Davison, the first woman to sail the Atlantic single-handed, was on the face of it an unlikely person to undertake such a project. When she departed Plymouth in May 1952 she had little sailing experience and almost none offshore. Compared to British contemporaries such as the Hiscocks, the Pyes, Adlard Coles, Humphrey Barton, and Edward Allcard who made extensive voyages around the same time, she was a novice. What is more, she regularly downplayed what knowledge she did possess. If she was a hero, it was of the anti-heroic sort. She was inclined to work against the grain, to question the rules of whatever activity she undertook, to defy the stereotypes of both triumph and failure – and she experienced both in her astonishing life. It does not detract from her achievement to say that it is as a human being rather than simply as a sailor that she will be remembered.

Two arresting scenes described in her own writings – one of disaster and one of triumph – tell her story in miniature. The first finds her struggling to stay attached to a cork float at night in a stormy sea near Portland Bill following the wreck of the *Reliance*, a seventy-foot ketch. In the hours since *Reliance* had come to grief on the east side of the Bill, the only other crew member, Ann Davison's husband Frank, the skipper of the vessel, had fallen unconscious, lost his grip on the float and soon after that his life. Ann resigned herself to a similar fate but then a wave that 'thundered down on the float', which should have been the end of her, woke her 'from oblivion to anger'.

Something in her insisted on defying the inevitable. Still clutching the float, she was entirely at the mercy of wind, waves and tides which dragged her far out to sea and then back towards the shore on the west side of the Bill. But in one of those unaccountable miracles of survival a huge wave picked her up and deposited her on a rock by the shore. Crawling to a neighbouring rock as yet another wave broke over her, she then worked towards a cavern she had glimpsed whose floor was above the level of the water. 'Then', she recalled, 'I was standing in the cave.' Some moments of dazed indecision followed until she found a way along the coast to a point where she could scale the cliffs. Her ordeal was over.

That was 4 June 1949. Just over four years later, on 23 November 1953, Ann Davison arrived at night in New York City after a 5000 mile voyage from Plymouth in her twenty-three-foot sloop *Felicity Ann*, amid scenes that were as low-key as the wreck of the *Reliance* had been dramatic. The arrival at her final destination of Pier 9, home of the US Coastguard in the city, was the conclusion of a comic series of manoeuvres and mishaps in New York Harbour which included a hair-raising tow by a fishing-boat, a grounding on a falling tide, the failure to enter her original destination of the 79th Street Yacht Basin which turned out to be closed, the offer of a berth at the fireboat pier, Pier 75, only to be told by the Coastguard that she must follow them to their headquarters. The Coastguard had been anticipating the honour of escorting *Felicity Ann* but had missed her in the darkness. A photograph of her arrival shows a beaming Ann Davison and some equally relieved and happy Coastguard staff. Overnight Ann Davison became famous, her reputation assured in the sailing community and enhanced with the growth of the feminist movement for whom she became an icon.

Different as these scenes are, taken together they illustrate central truths about Ann Davison's life and character. Above all she was a dreamer and risk-taker. 'The only way to live', she wrote in answer to the question of why she had undertaken the Atlantic voyage, 'is to have a dream green and growing in your life; anything else is just existing and a waste of breath.' Her dream, however, was no airy notion but 'largely curiosity, the urge to find out the why, the what, and the how at first hand, without simply taking someone else's word for it'. At its best 'you are rewarded by an insight into living so splendid, so wholly magnificent, you can be satisfied with nothing less than ever after, so that you go on hoping and searching for another glimpse for the rest of your life'. The dream was of doing, not simply being, so to some extent she was driven by a practical imperative. That, however, demanded the mastery of certain skills and the fact was, she wrote, that 'I knew nothing about boats, very little about sailing, and was terrified of the sea'.

The truth is that Ann Davison was so determinedly self-deprecating that you never quite know whether to take her judgements about herself seriously. Was she really such an ignoramus when it came to knowledge about sailing and navigation? On arriving under sail in Casablanca harbour and seeing some people she knew she shouted across to them: 'how do I stop this bloody thing?' If her arithmetic was really so bad as she claims, how did she manage to master celestial navigation sufficiently to make more or less accurate landfalls after lengthy passages? Can we believe her admission that her solo departure from Plymouth to sail the Atlantic was the first time she had sailed a boat on her own, and if so, what does it tell us about her character? Was she brave or reckless, or both? Or just lucky?

* * *

We can get some answers to these questions by looking at how she arrived at the two scenes described above. She did not start out as a sailor. In 1937, when she met Frank, she was a freelance commercial pilot, based near London, one of very few female pilots at the time. Earlier she had worked on a farm in Argentina where she had also learned to fly. Frank too was an adventurer. He had been training as a naval architect when the First World War began but joined up and served in the army throughout the war. He subsequently gained a pilot's licence, became a cowboy in Canada, a lumberjack, a racing driver, bought a boat and sailed single-handed from Labrador up the St Lawrence.

At the time Ann and Frank met, Frank owned a small aerodrome with a fleet of aircraft in Cheshire and needed a new pilot to fly joy-rides over Blackpool. Ann applied and got the job. She also got Frank, who was married at the time but lost little time in divorcing his first wife. Ann and Frank married in 1939 but almost immediately the war changed their lives. The government closed down civilian flying, after which they bought a gravel quarry in North Wales. When that went bust they bought the island of Inchmurrin in Loch Lomond and when the farming business – mainly goats and geese – failed they bought another island, Inchfad, in the loch. The work was just as hard there. Nevertheless, they rose to the challenge and over the next three years managed to make the business pay. They also bought a boat in which, Ann says, 'we had some rip-roaring sails' but, she added, 'I never learned to sail'. She did, though, take up writing, which resulted in several articles and eventually a book, *Home is an Island* (1952), a gritty and often humorous account of their often less than idyllic existence on the island.

They had long shared a dream of buying a boat and sailing the world's oceans, and with the end of the war began a serious search for the right craft. In 1947 they purchased *Reliance* in Fleetwood at a cost of 1450 pounds. At seventy feet long she was very large for a crew of two, besides which huge amounts of work were required. A survey showed that the hull was basically sound but there followed two years of toil and trouble to convert the former fishing boat into a seaworthy cruising vessel which could take them anywhere. The heart-breaking and yet curiously compelling story of these years was the subject of Ann's first book, *Last Voyage* (1952).

The disastrous end of the *Reliance* was in the making long before it actually happened, not least because declining funds meant that there were never enough resources to do the jobs properly. The engine was a huge and antiquated Gardner diesel requiring a complex series of operations to get it going with both of them working flat out. It often failed to respond to their valiant efforts. They never had the chance properly to rig and test the sails. In the end, they left Fleetwood in May 1949, not because she was ready for sea but because of the threat of foreclosure of the mortgage on *Reliance*. Their nominal destination was Cuba but their 'last voyage' of two and a half weeks in fact took them down the Irish Sea, round Land's End, and up the Channel to the pitiless rocks of Portland Bill. Much of the time they had no idea where they were and they faced atrocious weather. On several occasions they were offered help by passing vessels, including the Newlyn lifeboat, but they turned the offers down. They considered putting into Plymouth after Frank had collapsed from exhaustion and Ann was experiencing blackouts, but this option was rejected on the grounds that 'it would have brought on legal miseries which might well, I feared, have put Frank out of his mind for ever'.

As preparation for a solo voyage across the Atlantic, Ann's experience on *Reliance* must surely count as remarkably incongruous. Most people would have concluded that the sea was not for them. It was not merely the devastating loss of her husband but the almost continuous sense of not being in control of a vessel which was clearly unsuitable for them. Yet there are clues to Ann's state of mind at various times before and during her time on *Reliance* which help to explain how, apparently against the odds, she could contemplate the challenge of a solo voyage across the Atlantic.

After establishing themselves on the second island in Loch Lomond, she and Frank realized that they had 'mastered the island'. There were difficulties but they could be dealt with. What couldn't be dealt with so easily was the restlessness that came with the sense of having achieved something. 'I could do with some real gut-stirring', remarked Frank one day. Everything was beginning to work and it was 'too tame'. Both of them were out of sympathy with the socialism of the new Labour government which brought the 'blight of bureaucracy' on to everything and stifled 'individual effort and initiative'. Buying *Reliance* and planning a voyage in her was their ticket to a new life.

The payoff for Ann came in the early stages of their flight from Fleetwood when, despite a gale in the offing and some doubt as to where they were, *Reliance* seemed utterly in tune with the wind and waves. Ann describes her as 'flying like a Pegasus through the night'. The sensation of speed was 'terrific – exhilarating beyond anything I had experienced before', a curious mixture of flying and sailing. It was, she recalled, 'glory and power, an exquisite distillation of life, the span of a lifetime condensed into a few hours'. At that moment Frank came up from below and urged her to slow the boat down: 'do you want to run the guts out of her?' which, she remarks, was 'pretty deflating'. But she had experienced this ecstatic moment and would have many others like it. In short, there was something in Ann Davison which relished, even demanded, pushing against the limits, not for the danger itself but because only there could she experience the sensation of life to the full. Danger, however, always brought fear along with it. Conquering fear proved to be the spur which took Ann Davison forward.

* * *

Ann's memoir of her Atlantic voyage, *My Ship Is So Small* (1956), can be read as a study of fear and how to overcome it. Reflecting on the disaster of the *Reliance*, she says her return to the sea was not out of

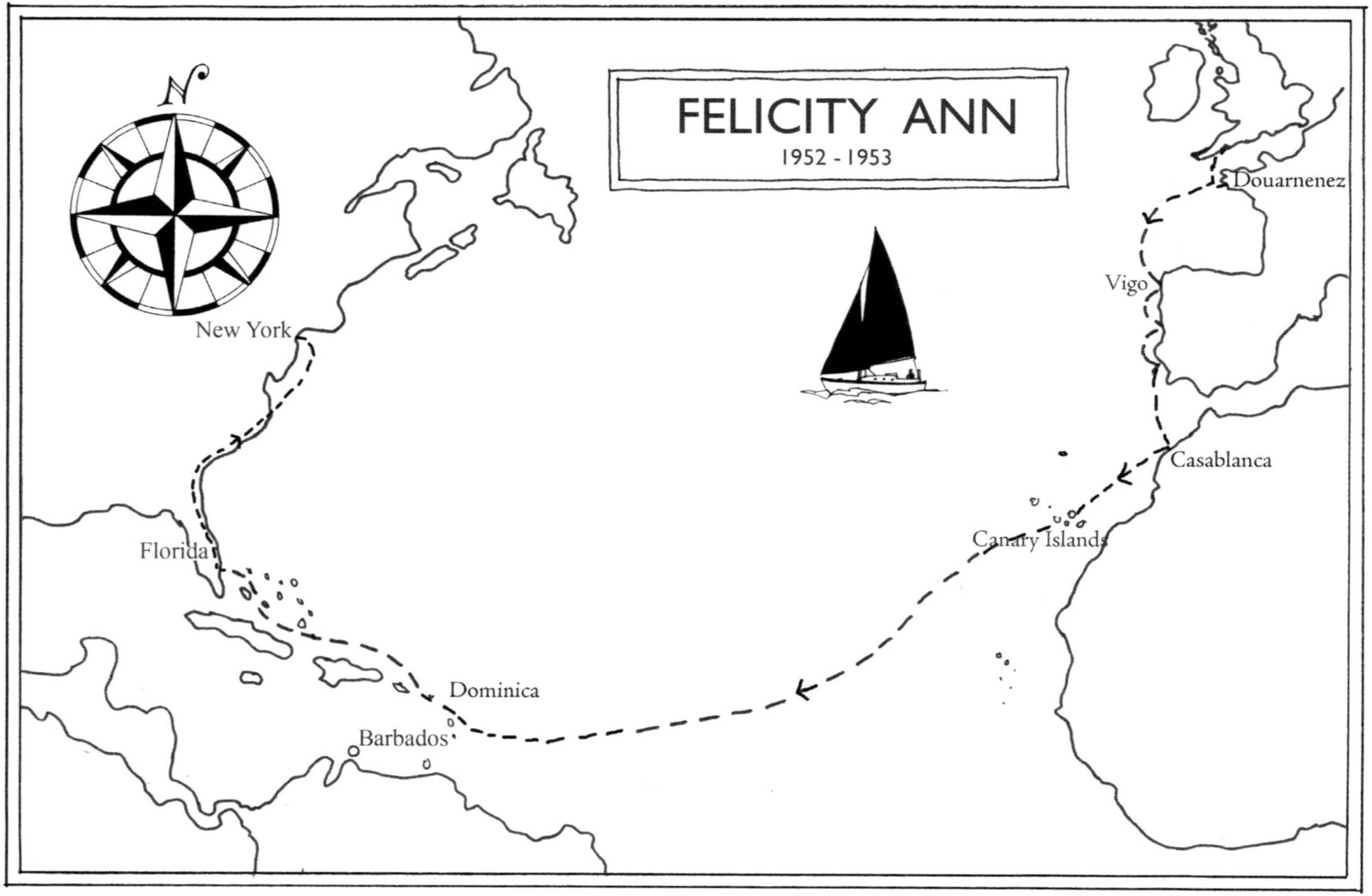
FELICITY ANN
1952 - 1953
N
Douarnenez
Vigo
Casablanca
Canary Islands
Dominica
Barbados
Florida
New York

any spirit of 'defiance, or revenge or expiation, or vindication' but out of a belief that if she could conquer the fear involved in any sea voyage, a fear which had pursued her ever since she had embarked on boats, 'I should find a key to living'. Fear came through ignorance and in her new venture she would try to minimise the areas of ignorance. With knowledge, 'fear would vanish'. Gradually the idea of an Atlantic voyage formed in her mind as the 'essence of life'.

To prepare for the voyage she decided to take as much advice as she could from people of proven expertise. She took sailing and navigation lessons with a Commander Lund, a former Royal Navy instructor, who took her out in his eighteen-foot yawl from Torquay and, as she said, 'taught her the ropes'. It was Commander Lund who found the diminutive *Felicity Ann* and pronounced her the ideal small ship for the Atlantic crossing. Ann had her looked over by legendary Atlantic sailor and yacht surveyor Humphrey Barton, who approved the purchase on condition that several modifications be made to strengthen her. Around the yard where the modifications were carried out perhaps inevitably the boat was affectionately known as 'Sweet FA'.

And so, with considerable trepidation but no serious second thoughts, she went to sea. Ann's account of the Atlantic crossing reads like a picaresque novel – a sequence of adventures and encounters whose protagonist seems constantly surprised by what is happening to her. A born storyteller, she wields the English language with consummate ease, punctuating the narrative with passages of vivid dialogue and reflections on Life writ large. She set out with a broad plan in mind but was open to more or less extensive deviations dictated by weather, whim or, in the case of her entry into Douarnenez six days after leaving Plymouth, emergency. Realising that her ship was waterlogged but too tired to investigate the source of the problem, she had the good fortune to fall in with a French fishing fleet and, following some barely comprehensible exchanges in their respective languages, was towed into Douarnenez.

Her entry into Vigo in northern Spain, this time under her own steam, had some of the same pantomime quality as did the entry into Casablanca. Some of those who encountered her in these ports assumed she would not be sailing further, but running through her narrative is a core of determined, onward-driving energy which never lets her down and makes the reader want to keep her company. Her experiences ashore were often as colourful and exciting as those aboard, the most notable being the Festival of the Lamb in Rabat when she was spirited by someone she met into a reception hosted by the Sultan of Morocco. As the only female in this Muslim setting, she was the focus of intense attention by the press but the Sultan and his entourage apparently took her presence in their stride. When it came to her turn to leave the audience with the Sultan, she recalls, 'I made a real job of a sweeping curtsey, and most graciously the Sultan bowed in return.'

What mattered above all, however, was her progress towards the Canary Islands, her proposed jumping off point for the Atlantic crossing to Barbados. At Las Palmas in the Canaries, *Felicity Ann* was lifted out for bottom cleaning and repainting. There she met Ken Park, a local shipping agent, and his wife Dorothy who showed her the kind of 'unrestricted friendliness and generosity I had found, and continued to find, throughout the voyage'. Ann evidently inspired affection in people she met and confidence in her project. The crossing itself, which she records in the form of her sparkling daily log, took just under eight weeks of slog alternating with visions of 'haunting beauty'. She made landfall at Barbados, proving her navigation was fit for purpose, but was forced by bad weather to divert to Dominica. From there she sailed to Florida and up the intracoastal waterway to New York.

It is clear from her record that, despite being sometimes caught off guard by bad weather, brought down by lack of sleep, concerned about navigation and above all the possibility of being run down by passing ships, her capacity to manage her vessel under all conditions grew exponentially during the voyage. Changing headsails, though always difficult on a heaving platform, became second nature. Deploying the sea anchor on one occasion restored necessary control and when that wore through, she towed warps and rode out the storm for a further two nights. When she needed sleep, as a rule she hove to. During one storm, in a state of extreme fatigue, she had an experience very like that of Joshua Slocum who, when incapacitated by stomach pains, was convinced that his boat was being steered by the pilot of the Columbus's *Pinta*. Ann's dreamlike experience was of two other people aboard: 'one of them sat on the coach-roof and the other came aft holding on to the boom quiescent in its gallows, "OK," he said.

Courage is a fighting quality. It is the ability to make mistakes and profit by them, to fail and start again…

"You kip down. We'll keep watch." Obediently I went below and slept till morning'.

Both these are surely examples of fortune favouring the brave. However, they show that bravery is a matter not of defying the odds but of knowing when to give in gracefully without abandoning hope. They are of a piece with Ann's explicit reflections on courage which she concludes is 'the key to living'. In a striking passage describing her approach to Nassau – the Atlantic crossing behind her and the long passage to New York still ahead – she reflects that courage is not after all a matter of conquering physical fear; criminals can do that. Then what is courage? It is, she says, 'an understanding and acceptance; but an acceptance without resignation, mark you, for courage is a fighting quality. It is the ability to make mistakes and profit by them, to fail and start again…' which is what she did repeatedly.

Perhaps the most telling testimony to the quality of character which enabled Ann Davison to overcome her own self-confessed limitations and rise to the challenges of ocean voyaging came from fellow voyager Peter Pye. In 1954 Pye and his wife were on a return passage from British Columbia to Fowey via the Panama Canal and, having heard and read so much about Ann Davison, they made a detour to visit her in Florida where she was living after her Atlantic crossing. 'There is a quality about men and women who sail the high seas', Pye recalled, 'that is hard to define and even to detect if you meet them ashore, but the moment they come aboard they seem to fit into the atmosphere of the ship as if they belonged; nothing obtrudes, nothing jars. So it was with Ann Davison. "Steadiness" is the word I think I want to describe her presence.'

Significantly, Peter Pye made little of the fact that she was a woman in what was largely a man's world. It was enough that she showed the skills and determination required to complete such an undertaking, which he knew well from years of sailing with his wife Anne that such qualities were not confined to the male sex.* For her part, Ann Davison was well aware that there would be advantages in being the first woman to sail the Atlantic solo, since 'there ought to be a good story in it'. She insisted that this did not influence in the least her de-

* See Chapter 2 on the Pyes.

cision to make the attempt, though it turned out 'to be a useful stick with which to goad enthusiasm in others', and enthusiasm in others was 'a primary necessity when undertaking an enterprise one knows very little about'.

In the end, Ann Davison was one of those rare individuals who met the challenge set by Rudyard Kipling in his poem 'If', which was to 'meet with triumph and disaster/and treat those two imposters just the same'. Kipling, of course, was addressing a boy who, if he could satisfy all the demands set out in the poem, would be 'a man, my son!' Perhaps if Kipling had known Ann Davison he would have included women and daughters.

* * *

After her Atlantic voyage Ann Davison stayed in the United States and continued sailing and writing. She remarried in the mid-1950s and in characteristically spirited fashion wrote up her honeymoon cruise with her new husband for the *Yachting World* Annual for 1957. Her husband was a power-boater but seemingly relished the challenges of a cruise from Florida to the Bahamas in the diminutive *Felicity Ann*, despite being over six feet tall and having no experience in sailing craft. Besides honeymooning there was a particular purpose behind the cruise which was to view a plot of land on the small island of Abaco which they had bought sight unseen. Their plan was to create a hideaway in a remote spot 'untouched by civilization' to which they could 'retreat between ventures'. The idea bore some resemblance to Ann's island ventures in Loch Lomond with her first husband Frank and shows that the dream of freedom and adventure was as alive as ever in her.

The Atlantic crossing, however, soon faded from the headlines. *Felicity Ann* was sold five years after she had reached New York and taken by her new owners to California where she was neglected and forgotten. Ann Davison continued to be interested in boats. In 1960 she and her husband made a trip in a seventeen-foot powerboat through the Everglades taking photographs of wildlife which were featured in the New York Times. That same year they undertook a 5000-mile powerboat cruise up the east coast of the United States from Florida on the Intracoastal Waterway, into the Great Lakes, down the Mississippi, and back to Miami. However, when in 1962 Davison appeared on a television quiz show 'To Tell the Truth', where a panel was asked to guess which of three contestants was the first woman to cross the Atlantic solo, none of the panel had heard of Ann Davison and only of them one chose her out of the three.

Thereafter the trail runs cold. By the standards of the celebrity culture of the second half of the twentieth century the rest of Ann Davison's life was private and unremarkable. At some point she and her husband gave up sailing and moved to a ranch in Florida where they reared exotic cats. She died at her home in Florida in 1992 at the age of seventy-eight.

Then several years later, interest in her revived and new generations of young people were introduced to her achievements for the first time. She would doubtless have had mixed feelings about her elevation to feminist icon but would have welcomed the restoration of *Felicity Ann* which was the trigger for the renewed attention to her life and her voyage. In 2009 *Felicity Ann*, then in private ownership in Alaska, was donated to the Northwest School of Wooden Boatbuilding in Washington State who undertook a restoration in conjunction with a youth charity called the Community Boat Project. The aim was to use the Ann Davison story to empower young people, especially young women, with her example, while the restored *Felicity Ann* provided an 'on the water training platform for women, youth and community'. She was relaunched on 1 May 2018 to local fanfare and considerable interest beyond.

On the other side of the Atlantic in 2017 on the Wirral near Liverpool a blue plaque was unveiled at Mere Brook House where Ann and Frank had lived during the early years of the war, while in the wake of the relaunch of *Felicity Ann*, the Liverpool Museum held an exhibition about her life. The head curator admitted that, until she had attended the unveiling of the plaque to Ann at Mere Brook House, she had never heard of her or her Atlantic crossing. Fittingly, in December 2022 the *New York Times* ran a belated obituary of Ann Davison in their series 'Overlooked No More', devoted to people whose passing had been unnoticed. Ann Davison was news again seventy years on from the voyage that had made her famous, a transformation which she would no doubt have viewed with a mixture of wry humour and deep satisfaction.

Chapter 9

SMALL AND LIGHT

Patrick Ellam, Colin Mudie and *Sopranino*

It is hard not to be in awe of Patrick Ellam, less for the length or scope of his voyaging, which was not remarkable by the standards of some of the sailors of his generation, but rather for the clarity of purpose he brought to it. From the moment he resumed sailing after his war service he had a plan, and a point to prove, which he pursued with extraordinary skill and vigour. His point was that a small and light boat, not much bigger than a dinghy, could be as capable of ocean passages as larger, heavy displacement craft.

In carrying out his plan he proved to be a true virtuoso. Between September 1951 and February 1952 he completed a 5000 mile Atlantic voyage from Falmouth to New York via the Caribbean in the Laurent Giles designed *Sopranino*. For the bulk of the voyage he was accompanied by Colin Mudie, a Laurent Giles employee who had been given the task of producing the detailed drawings of the boat. At just under twenty feet overall, *Sopranino* was not merely small but remarkably light at only half a ton. By comparison, the eighteen-and-a-half-footer in the popular Hillyard range of cruising yachts came in at two and a half tons. Even the Smith brothers' *Nova Espero*, whose length overall was similar to *Sopranino*'s, weighed just under a ton.

In essence, *Sopranino* was a scaled-up dinghy with a beam of only five feet nine inches (to *Nova Espero*'s six feet three inches) and the addition of a bulb keel which was close to half the weight of the unladen boat. Drawing on the innovative strain in Laurent Giles's design philosophy, she also featured reverse sheer which, coupled with short overhangs, allowed for enhanced internal volume for a given length. Central to the concept was unsinkability which was enabled by building watertight compartments at bow and stern which would keep the boat afloat even if the rest of the hull were swamped. *Sopranino* became the prototype for the Barchetta class of cruiser/racers. A larger yawl-rigged version (still only twenty-one feet) with considerably heavier displacement was designed by Giles for British-born John

Guzzwell who built *Trekka* in his adopted country of Canada and between 1955 and 1959 sailed her round the world – then the smallest boat to do so.

It is true, as Eric Hiscock pointed out in his authoritative *Voyaging Under Sail,* that *Nova Espero* and *Sopranino* were by no means the first small boats to have made Atlantic passages. In the last decades of the nineteenth century at least ten boats smaller than 20 feet crossed the North Atlantic. Those voyages and the boats they were made in are described in some detail in Humphrey Barton's *Atlantic Adventurers.* However, each generation, indeed each individual sailor, accepts the challenge according to the state of knowledge of their time and makes a unique contribution to a continuing story. *Sopranino,* as we shall see, looked to the future and her influence on cruising and racing design was considerable, to say nothing of the impact of Patrick Ellam's voyage on the nautical world more generally.

* * *

How did Patrick Ellam arrive at that moment on 6 September 1951 when he recorded in *Sopranino*'s log that the Lizard was abeam and they were 'laying a course for Spain'? As with most of the sailors described in this book, the story begins in childhood. He was born in 1920 and, in common with Edward Allcard and George Millar, into a well-to-do family. He was introduced to sailing at a young age in Chichester harbour. Ellam's father owned a succession of sailing and power boats but crucially ensured that Patrick would learn the rudiments in a small dinghy. For the first year he was given oars only, and the following year a mast and sails. Subsequently during annual three-month summer holidays he explored the creeks and marshes of Chichester Harbour, gaining competence in boat handling as well as a knowledge of winds and tides.

By all accounts, not least his own racy chronicle of his early life called *Things I Remember* (1998), Ellam was an independent and adventurous child given to practical jokes, a born risk-taker who was generally unimpressed with authority. Rather than go to Oxford where he had passed the entrance exam, he opted to travel to France and Germany to learn the languages. The late 1930s were an interesting time to be in Germany, especially in Munich where Ellam was present at a Nazi

The Lizard was abeam and they were laying a course for Spain.

rally addressed by Adolf Hitler, but he was evidently more interested in girls and beer than in politics. His brush with France was equally perfunctory, though he did acquire a fair command of the language. More in keeping with his venturesome spirit was a car journey with his mother and his girlfriend Joan through Norway and Sweden up to the Arctic circle and down through Finland to Estonia, Latvia and Lithuania. They all took turns at the wheel, while Ellam was the trip's mechanic, apparently able to turn his hand to almost anything.

Ellam's character traits seemingly fitted him perfectly for wartime service with the Special Operations Executive (SOE), which he joined after two years in the artillery. His SOE service arose from the appearance of a notice at his camp reading: VOLUNTEERS ARE URGENTLY NEEDED TO DROP ALONE BY PARACHUTE BEHIND THE ENEMY LINES. 'So of course I volunteered', Ellam remarked. After training in a range of skills and skullduggery, he was assigned to a small naval force tasked with picking up agents and downed air force pilots from the French coast under the nose of German shore batteries and German 'R' boats (small minesweepers). Among the other operations he was involved in was getting people out of a French prison which, he says, 'was easy'.

When the war in Europe was over he was posted to Ceylon (now Sri Lanka), preparatory to the proposed re-taking of Singapore from the Japanese. In the hiatus before any military action was due, he borrowed a small open dinghy and sailed her three hundred miles down the eastern coast of Ceylon. Then the atom bombs were dropped on Japan, bringing an end to the war in the Far East, and once again Ellam had time on his hands before being shipped home. This time he built a twenty-four-foot catamaran out of old aeroplane fuel tanks with a wooden platform with enough space for him and his friends 'to eat, drink, and sunbathe'. Sailing and boat design, to say nothing of enjoyment of life, were evidently still very much on his mind.

* * *

One key to Ellam's major achievement – the Atlantic crossing in *Sopranino* – was his laser-like focus on the kind of vessel required to achieve his goal of proving that a very small boat, which could be trailed behind a car and kept at home, could go anywhere on the sea in safety. Most attempts to produce very small yachts relied on 'scaling down the big fellows', he noted, which usually meant poor performance and excessive weight for trailing. His decision was to attack the problem from another angle: 'to produce a boat the size and weight of a dinghy but modified so that it would be really safe at sea in any weather while retaining the dinghy's high speed and manoeuvrability'.

Ellam was by no means the first to proclaim the potential seaworthiness of fast dinghies. In the late 1920s Uffa Fox had designed the International 14 with a planing hull which was capable of sailing at double the speed of any other dinghy of the time. He proved his point in 1928 by sailing *Avenger* the hundred miles from Cowes to a regatta at Le Havre, winning all the races against French boats, then sailing her back to Cowes. Fox, however, never intended to cruise in his dinghy. Racing was his intention, and the channel crossing, besides proving the speed and seaworthiness of his design, was a means of getting to the racing venue.

Ellam showed something of the same drive and self-confidence, with the additional motive that going offshore in a dinghy was a try-out for the ultimate project of an Atlantic crossing. He started with the most extreme design concept he could find, which was the racing sailing canoe. He asked naval architect Kenneth Gibbs to build him a two-man sailing canoe twenty feet long supplied with buoyancy and plenty of lockers, for food, navigation equipment and the like. Then over a series of weekends in the summer of 1949 Ellam gave *Theta*, himself and his crew a severe workout.

The details are astonishing. Starting from Brightlingsea with a friend called John, they sailed *Theta* to Ramsgate where John, who was miserably seasick, was unavailable for the next leg. Jilling around in Ramsgate harbour Ellam came across a student with a rucksack who was 'looking for a lift to France'. 'Can you swim?' asked Ellam. 'Yes.' 'I'll run you over.' In the event, Bob lasted the next three weekends during which they sailed *Theta* to Boulogne, back over the Channel to Folkestone, across again to Boulogne, from there to Newhaven, over to Fécamp, and back across to Chichester harbour where Bob left the boat. In four successive weekends, Ellam observed, 'we had covered 30, 66, 86, and 151 sea miles, regardless of weather and on schedule'.

A couple of weeks later Ellam sailed *Theta* down the Solent to Lymington where the Laurent Giles design office was located. To his surprise he was able to see Jack Giles immediately and put the proposition to him of designing a boat 'the same length as *Theta* but a few inches wider... [with] a small cabin in which the man off watch could sleep in some comfort and a stove on which hot food could be cooked'. Giles eyed him with a quizzical smile and asked a few questions while Ellam 'began to wonder how mad he thought I was'. Whatever the case, Giles offered to design the boat and they soon got down to details of construction and rig. Thus was *Sopranino* conceived.

For construction of the boat he chose a proven builder of racing dinghies as well as traditional river craft, Wootten brothers of Cookham Dean, a company which is still thriving today. They had never built a seagoing vessel before but under the watchful eye of Jack Giles and with regular input from Ellam himself, they applied their skills carefully to the precise brief given to them. The result was a small miracle of grace, strength and economy of space. She was clinker-built in traditional fashion with planking of only three-eighths of an inch thick. The thin oak ribs were closely spaced and in addition there was a series of full-width bulkheads which stiffened and strengthened the whole structure. She had two six foot six inch bunks, space for two stoves and a full-sized chart table plus numerous lockers, making maximum use of the space advantage offered by the reverse sheer design. Among other things this enabled them to carry enough water to last the Atlantic passage, though only with careful rationing. By contrast, Stanley Smith and Charles Violet had relied entirely on a recently produced water purification kit. *Sopranino* carried a mast-head bermudan rig set on hollow spars which was both light and highly efficient. In mid-summer 1950, more or less nine months after conception in Jack Giles's office, *Sopranino* was duly born.

Keen to have a thorough sea trial before setting off across the Atlantic, Ellam asked John Illingworth, Commodore of the Royal Ocean Racing Club (RORC), if they could enter the biennial race to Santander. Illingworth was sympathetic to Ellam's project, having won the Fastnet race in 1947 and 1949 in *Myth of Malham*, also a reverse sheer Laurent Giles design. He readily agreed to let *Sopranino* start with the racing fleet, though not as an official competitor, since she was too small. With barely more than a week to go following launch before the race to Spain, Ellam had a brief trial sail in the Solent with Jack Giles before taking *Sopranino* down channel to Plymouth with a friend as crew for the start of the Santander race. He was immediately impressed by the boat's performance. 'Out in the Channel… she behaved beautifully, dancing lightly over the sunlit waves, making light of the choppy little seas that so often cause small boats to go up and down in the same hole. Not *Sopranino*. She slid gracefully over them, working her way up to windward towards Plymouth.'

An interesting sidelight on the boat and Patrick Ellam's ambitions for her is provided by Humphrey Barton, an Atlantic yachtsman himself and a marine surveyor with Laurent Giles who was well acquainted with the project. As he recalled in his book about Atlantic voyagers, 'I sailed *Sopranino* for a short time once in the Lymington River and I thought her quite an amusing toy, but not a boat that I would care to take across the Solent on a windy day.' He changed his tune once the voyage was achieved, noting that, despite his own experience of her, 'this was the boat that was to come safely through heavy weather in the open Atlantic and arrive in the States none the worse for sailing over 5,000 miles.' Barton had nothing but praise for Ellam and Mudie's cruise 'in an ultra modern boat brilliantly executed by two highly intelligent and experienced yachtsmen.'

That was all to come. Meanwhile, in the face of scepticism from many experts, the race to Santander itself proved everything Ellam had hoped. With strong headwinds down towards Ushant *Sopranino* found herself ahead of two big ocean racers after thirty-two hours of racing, proving, Ellam noted, that 'little boats could go to windward in storms.' After three more days of sailing across the Bay of Biscay the mountains of northern Spain were in sight and *Sopranino* arrived at the finish only a few hours after the last of the official competitors. The example of her performance in the Santander race led the following winter to a meeting of the RORC, chaired by John Illingworth, which resulted in the founding of the Junior Offshore Group (JOG). Even before the Atlantic crossing, Ellam and Sopranino had made an impact on the offshore sailing scene.

* * *

Before she set off across the Atlantic some modifications were made to *Sopranino* in recognition of extra safety requirements for such a voyage. The mast was shortened to make it possible to climb to the top and undertake repairs without tipping the boat over. In the Channel it was possible to lay the boat over on its side and do the repairs while swimming in the water beside her. In the tropics there would be sharks. Shortening the mast also carried the advantage of being able to reduce the weight of the keel and hence carry more stores. Fear of sharks was also partly behind the addition of an aluminium rail round the after deck. It would help prevent them falling off but also discourage them from trailing a hand in the water 'and having it nipped off by a passing shark'. The result, Ellam said, was probably 'the smallest ship in the world' and he meant this in an official sense, in that he managed to persuade the Board of Trade to classify *Sopranino* as a merchant ship. Carrying the same registration papers as an ocean liner would, it was believed, facilitate entry to the world's ports, as indeed seems to have been the case.

Choice of crew was as important as preparing the boat. Colin Mudie had not only done the detailed drawings for *Sopranino* but was an experienced racing skipper, including aboard her, and a capable navigator. Despite the inevitable hardships of such a voyage and living in close quarters they proved to be highly compatible. *Sopranino* was by all accounts a happy ship. Ellam's narrative of the voyage contains passages in italics by Mudie which enliven the text and make it in effect a joint product.

Their route took them south from Falmouth towards Lisbon, then Casablanca and on to the Canary Islands where they picked up the north east trades for their destination of Barbados. The original intention had been to reach Lisbon in one hop but gales in the Bay of Biscay lasting several days led them to put in at La Coruña. During the worst of the gale they lay to under bare poles with the helm lashed down 'and left her wallowing beam-on to the seas.' After a period of anxiety about how she was taking the seas, they realised that she was riding the waves comfortably, absorbing the breaking crests with ease and 'when anything big did catch her unawares she was giving and going with it without any harm'. The ping-pong ball theory of small boat behaviour in big waves appeared to be working.

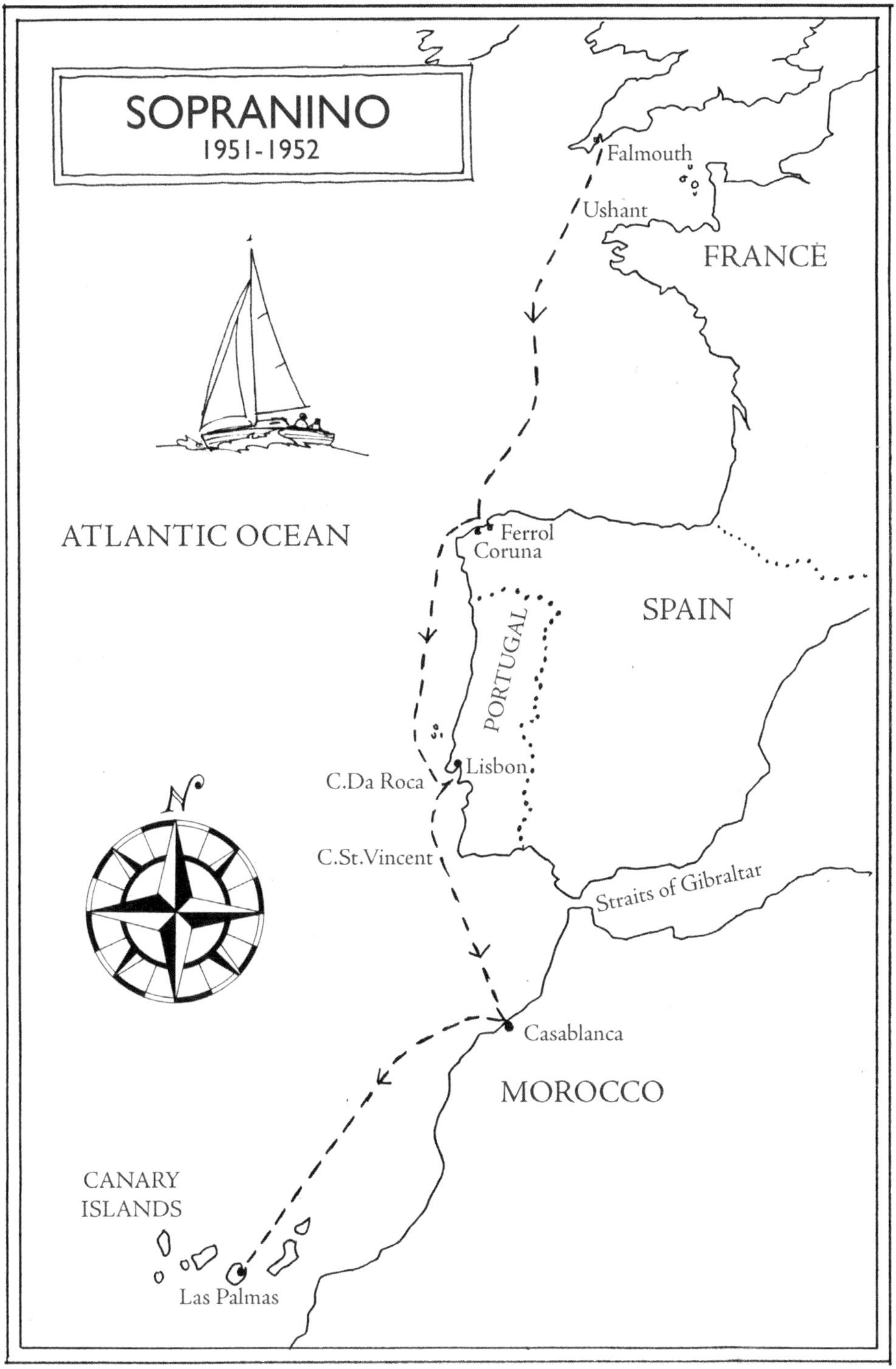
SOPRANINO
1951-1952
Falmouth
Ushant
FRANCE
ATLANTIC OCEAN
Ferrol
Coruna
SPAIN
PORTUGAL
Lisbon
C.Da Roca
C.St.Vincent
Straits of Gibraltar
N
Casablanca
MOROCCO
CANARY
ISLANDS
Las Palmas

One of the interesting features of the Ellam/Mudie narrative of the voyage is the attention given to health and crew morale. Illness was an ever-present possibility and source of anxiety. Mudie had come down badly with food poisoning in La Coruña which had cost them ten days while he recovered. He then suffered a painful allergic reaction to a detergent while at sea on passage from Casablanca to Las Palmas which required hospitalization when they reached port. They later discovered that standard anti-seasickness pills were an effective antidote. They both suffered at various times with stomach problems and seasickness. A Spanish doctor in the Canaries had a good look at their medicine chest, picked out one tube of ointment and a bottle of pills and said 'if anything goes wrong outside, put some of this ointment on it and if anything appears upset inside, take one of these pills'. What these were we are not told. Mudie recorded 'how very well it worked. We were better than new after a month of this treatment.'

As for crew morale, they instituted a regular 'Sports Day' to keep them fit. It involved only one event which was a race around the ship outside everything. Mudie wrote: 'At the word "Go" from the man with the stop-watch you leapt out of the cockpit, ducked under the boom, swung around the rigging, two steps forward to round the jib, back outside the rigging on the other side, and around the stern to your seat again at the tiller. Patrick has the record for the course at thirty-seven seconds...' They also made a point of climbing the local mountain at every port of call, again for the very good reason that passage-making could lead to atrophy of the leg muscles. At sea they kept to a pattern of watches which guaranteed both crew eight hours sleep in twenty-four and, though neither was routine-minded, on the long passage from Las Palmas in the Canaries to Barbados they fell into routines for navigation, meals, drinks, cleaning out the bilges and all manner of chores, as much to break up the monotony as to get the work done. For the same reason they held celebrations every five hundred miles to mark their progress, consisting of a glass of sherry with dinner.

The 2800-mile Atlantic passage was a notable success. They took twenty-nine days which made an average of ninety-six nautical miles a day at an average speed of about four knots – impressive for a boat with a waterline length of only seventeen and a half feet. There were no substantial gear failures or damaging emergencies. Keys to their success were twin headsails, which they had first used on passage from Lisbon to Casablanca, and self-steering gear. With the twin headsails rigged the boat rolled considerably but they reconciled themselves to that. Less easy to get used to was the need to steer all the time which was a great incentive to invention of a self-steering arrangement. Ellam experimented with taking lines from the clews of the two sails through blocks to the tiller, supplemented by 'a damping device and bias control to keep her from over-correcting.' It worked but was subject to periodic failures. Colin then brought his designer's skills to bear and turned it into a robust and practical system of automatic steering gear that was to serve them well across thousands of miles of ocean. They dubbed the system 'Harry', after Harry Lime, the Third Man in the classic film of that name released only two years before. Actually, Ellam reflected, it was worth more than two men 'for it worked steadily, day and night, week after week. And what is more it never fell sick and didn't eat anything.'

Given the success with which these two individualists organised themselves for long sea passages, it is perhaps no surprise that the main emergencies happened on land. On arrival in Casablanca they found rioting against the French colonial authorities stirred up, Ellam observed, by the Communists. There had been a certain amount of shooting 'but rather more stoning and knifing.' They were steered to a mooring close to the French navy for their protection and advised not to go into the city unarmed. 'One evening we were coming home in the dark, when a man came up on a bicycle and asked us for a light... I took my gun out from behind my shopping bag and covered him, while Colin gave him his light. It's just the way you do things in those parts.' On a very different note, Ellam almost lost his life taking a walk on the harbour wall in a gale when two enormous waves piled in on top of each other and he was swept over the edge and crashed onto rocks below. Somehow between waves he managed to scale the wall and run back towards the docks, rendering Colin's prompt rescue effort in a small launch unnecessary.

The Caribbean offered more variety of experiences, good and bad. In Barbados they socialized with actor David Niven, while in Jamaica

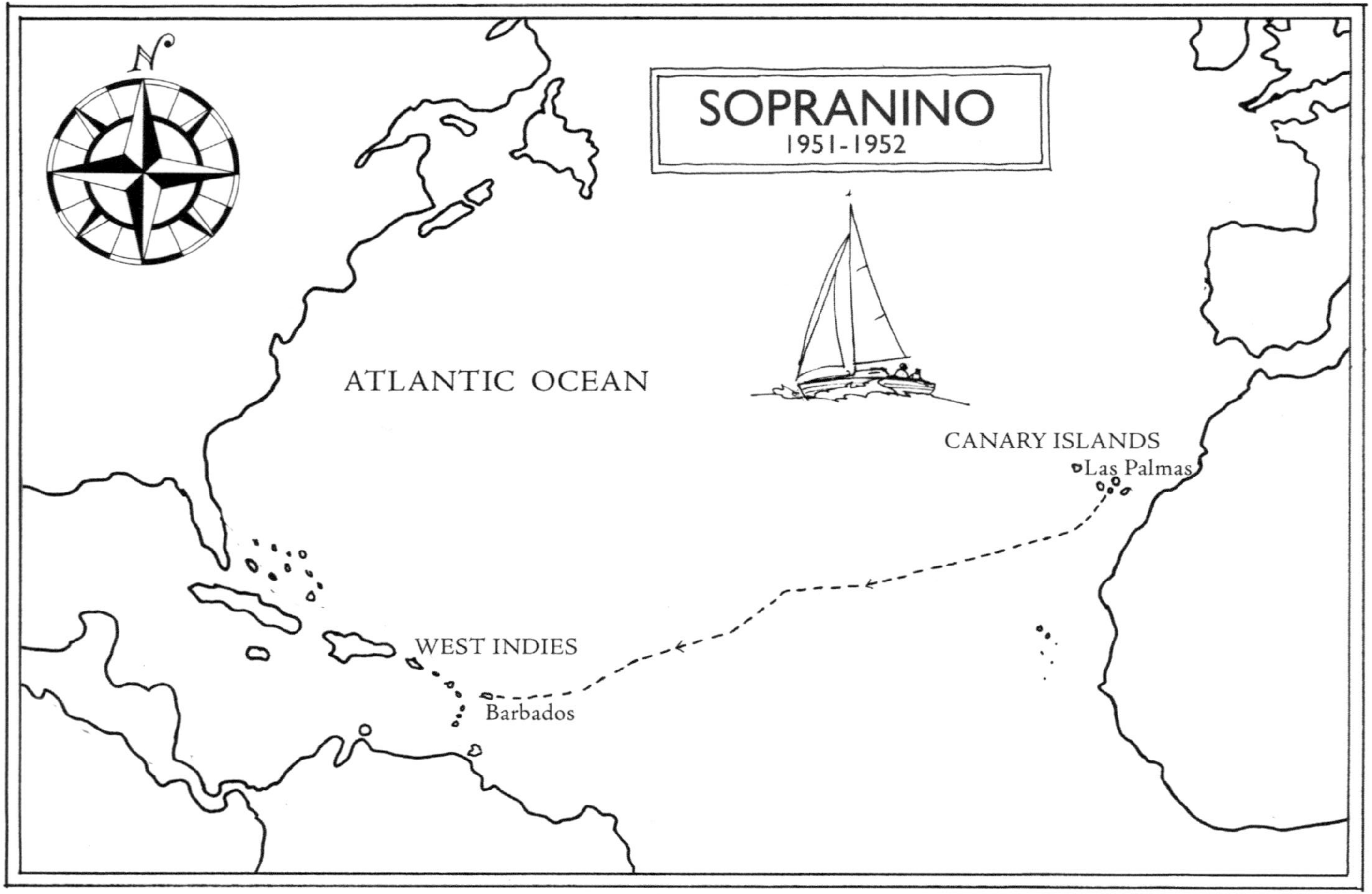

N
SOPRANINO
1951-1952
ATLANTIC OCEAN
CANARY ISLANDS
Las Palmas
WEST INDIES
Barbados

they were hired as crew for a film starring Ray Milland as skipper of a schooner. They were put up at a hotel owned by Errol Flynn, all expenses paid plus 'a few pounds'. Money was always a problem in these straitened postwar times. They had left Falmouth with seventy-five pounds which by the time they reached Lisbon was much depleted. Their finances were then boosted by Colin taking on a job designing a deckhouse for a twelve metre racing yacht being converted to a cruising vessel. But such income went only so far. The Ray Milland film came at an opportune moment.

Like all the postwar voyagers, Ellam and Mudie sailed on a shoestring, the main payoff in financial terms coming long after the fact with the publication of the inevitable account of the voyage. The strains of staying financially afloat, as well as the dangers of unfamiliar places and people, came unpleasantly together in an encounter that took place in Jamaica when Ellam and Mudie were confronted by three knife-wielding muggers. It was soon clear that they had little option but to yield up what valuables they had. Ellam concluded that their responsibility was to finish the voyage, not get into a fight with local mobsters. His coolness in such situations owed much to his wartime experiences, as was the case with George Millar who was equally adept at reading a situation and dealing with it.

With their arrival at Barbados the rhythm of the voyage changed. They island-hopped from Barbados via the Windward islands and Leeward Islands to Puerto Rico and on to Jamaica and then Cuba. At an island near Cuba Mudie left *Sopranino* for a flight to Bermuda where he was to join another boat for the transatlantic race. Ellam took two local boys as crew for the 150-mile passage to Havana which proved to be more challenging than anticipated on account of thunder storms, waterspouts, and a lack of wind. Consolation was provided in Havana by his encounter with a big-game fishing boat which tied up near him at the dock. Its owner, 'a big rugged-looking type', came over to introduce himself. 'My name's Hemingway. Come and have a drink.' After 'a very pleasant and rather alcoholic evening', Ellam concluded next morning that 'the show must go on'. From there he departed solo for Miami, nearly coming to grief off Florida. Leaving the boat there for several weeks, he travelled to Nassau where he sat out the time waiting for an American visa.

The last thousand miles to New York City took Ellam through the recently completed Intracoastal Waterway, much of it under motor power in a forty-seven foot yacht he had agreed to deliver to the Chesapeake Bay. With *Sopranino* in tow he negotiated countless bridges, canals, and creeks in startling contrast to the voyage up to that point. Having delivered the large yacht to a harbour in Chesapeake Bay, Ellam received a tow from a young coastguard officer in his thirty foot power boat via the Delaware Canal and River to Cape May on the Delaware coast. From there Ellam sailed alone to New York Harbour. He records no fanfare on his arrival in New York, simply the satisfaction of the successful realisation of an idea. He concludes that 'we had opened up the possibility, for thousands of young people who cannot afford to buy or to run large seagoing boats, of owning their own little boats in which they can go on out to the wide seas away from the artificial surroundings of modern life, and learn the many things that such an experience has to teach'.

* * *

The various elements of this voyage demonstrated Ellam's supreme adaptability as a sailor, whether under sail or power, in a wide variety of conditions. His experience served him well in the career he chose a few years later which was that of a delivery skipper, about which he wrote an incident-packed book called *Wind Song* (1976). Shortly after arriving in the United States he had met June who became his wife and partner in the delivery business. Settling in the United States, he wrote a number of other books, including one on yacht cruising, but it is *Sopranino* (1954), and above all the voyage it records, for which he will be remembered and celebrated.

As for Colin Mudie, there is a remarkable sequel to the Atlantic voyage. In 1958 he, his wife, a friend and the friend's son set off from the Canaries in the pod of a balloon which was designed for both air and sea. The pod/boat was fifteen feet long, made of foam-plastic, and, when in sailing mode, carried a Lungström rig, a double mainsail made of two boomless sails stitched together at the luff and set on an unstayed rotating mast. It worked best downwind which made it eminently suitable for trade wind sailing. They managed 1200 miles in the air but were then forced to land on the sea and release the balloon.

From there, with Colin taking over from his friend as skipper, they managed the remaining 1500 miles to Barbados in 20 days.

In 2011 Ellam, now ninety, and Mudie, eighty-five, were reunited at the regatta marking the sixtieth anniversary of the founding of the Junior Offshore Group and pictured together alongside the newly restored *Sopranino*, loaned for the occasion by the Classic Boat Museum in Cowes. Neither sailor looked ready to become a museum piece. Ellam had another seven years of what was evidently youthful old age while Mudie had ten. As for Sopranino, she may be in a museum, but she lives on in the record of her epic voyage.

Chapter 10

ONCE WAS NEVER ENOUGH

Miles and Beryl Smeeton and *Tzu Hang*

The forty-six-foot ketch *Tzu Hang* was running before a severe gale about seven hundred miles west of Cape Horn at just over fifty degrees south. It was February 1957. Aboard were Brigadier (Retd) Miles Smeeton, his wife Beryl, and John Guzzwell, a twenty-five-year-old boatbuilder and sailor born in the Channel Islands but now a resident of British Columbia. Beryl was at the helm. She had become accustomed to the sight of enormous waves and breaking seas, which for the most part the ship managed well. As she checked astern to take the measure of the next sea she saw a wall of water which she knew *Tzu Hang* had no chance of riding. She remembers falling out of the cockpit and finding herself in the water, surrounded by mountainous waves, with no sight of Tzu Hang. Then a wave lifted her and she spied her thirty yards away, minus masts and doghouse, lying very low in the water.

Down below, meanwhile, Miles and John took some moments to recover from what they later established was a pitchpoling. The water was waist-high, the cabin filled with soggy debris, and nothing was where it should be. Going on deck they saw Beryl swimming towards them and seizing hold of rigging from the broken mizzen mast, which she used to pull herself towards Tzu Hang. Once she was close enough, Miles and John grabbed her and lifted her aboard.

Five weeks later, after twelve exhausting hours pumping, many more hours of carpentry to fill the gaps in the deck and to construct a jury rig, with a makeshift rudder in the form of a fifteen-foot steering oar, they arrived safe and well in the Chilean port of Coronel. That they should have set off again towards Cape Horn after nine months of repairs, and this time without John Guzzwell, is truly astonishing. That the result should be similar – on this occasion a broach and roll-over, once again with the loss of both masts – almost defies belief. The damage was less severe than before; once again under jury rig, they reached a Chilean port. From Valparaiso they shipped *Tzu Hang* to the UK, where she underwent repairs and a thorough refit at Tucker's yard in Burnham-on-Crouch.

Many people would have taken these events as a sign that they should moderate their ambition or even retreat to the land. This was not the Smeeton way. They continued to roam the world for another twenty years, reaching high latitudes in both hemispheres, exploring inhospitable and often uncharted waters. Perhaps inevitably it is the double dismastings, thrillingly described in Miles's *Once is Enough* (1959), that define their reputation. The truth is, however, that while the Smeetons were past masters at dealing with life-threatening emergencies they were equally adept at the long haul. What drove them on? Who were they?

* * *

The bare facts are these. Born in 1908, Miles became a career soldier who spent the bulk of his prewar service in the Indian army. He loved riding, polo, duck-shooting and pig-sticking, and seized every opportunity to go climbing and exploring. He was six foot six, a natural leader, apparently without fear and direct in manner; his qualities were tailor-made for wartime service. He moved effortlessly from the cavalry to tanks, serving with distinction in North Africa, where he was awarded the MC, and Burma, where he gained a DSO.

Beryl met Miles in 1931 when she was the wife of Miles's commanding officer in Poona whom she had married in 1927. Her marriage to a man more than ten years older than her, though not entirely loveless, was without passion or indeed children. Beryl was drawn to Miles's adventurous spirit and drifted away from her husband, resulting in a more or less amicable divorce. Beryl and Miles were married in 1938.

Beryl's rebellious spirit had shown early. From childhood she 'threw herself into everything with an almost manic energy', the Smeeton's biographer Miles Clark writes.* Regretting always that she had not been born a man, she embraced danger and hardship without reservation.

* Miles Clark, *High Endeavours: The Extraordinary Life and Adventures of Miles and Beryl Smeeton* (1992). This is a compelling biography by Miles Smeeton's godson who was also a sailor and explorer. He died at the age of thirty-two following a sailing trip on the rivers of Russia.

Fiercely independent and scornful of all comforts and conveniences, she amassed during the 1930s an extraordinary record of travel and exploration. This included a 1000-mile trek from Tierra Del Fuego northwards up the Andes, overland journeys from India to the UK and back, mostly solo, and a 500-mile trek through the jungles of Burma and Siam. In 1938 she climbed to within 2000 feet of the summit of Tirich Mir, at 25,460ft the highest mountain outside the Himalayas. On that occasion she was accompanied by Miles, whom she had just married, with Tensing Norgay as their guide. (After Tensing reached the summit of Everest with Edmund Hillary in 1953, Beryl was one of the first people Tensing called.) Her achievements remain almost unknown, because she published little about them and claimed that her writing 'read like a railway timetable'. From the evidence of her one published book, a few articles and her unpublished diaries, this is unfair. She wrote engaging, if unadorned prose, but preferred action to composition. For the most part she left the writing to Miles, who had a fluent pen and the added incentive of financing their nomadic lives. He wrote eight books, five of which were about their life at sea.

That life came about almost accidentally. At the end of the war they had settled on a farm on a small island near Vancouver. There they bought an open sailing boat which they cruised for a few months around the islands, soon moving on to a thirty-six-foot cabin cruiser. This in turn sparked the idea of more extensive voyaging. They returned to England, where they had some financial assets waiting to be released, and as they searched the harbours and creeks of England for the right yacht they formed the idea of sailing back to BC and selling the boat there to pay for the trip.

In February 1951 they found *Tzu Hang* at Dover. Launched in 1938, she was a forty-six-foot double-ender with a bermudan ketch rig, heavily built of teak in Hong Kong and sailed very little by her one previous owner. Apart from a small doghouse she had a flush deck and a small self-draining cockpit. The Smeetons immediately took to her, invested her with almost human qualities, and drove her as hard as they drove themselves. Close to perfect as she was in their eyes, they nevertheless made some modifications to suit their generally short-handed sailing. The rig was reduced by doing away with the bowsprit which made for a more manageable inboard rig and they installed a second forestay to the stemhead, allowing her to carry twin staysails for downwind sailing. At the beginning of 1957 they exchanged the wheel for a tiller enabling easier self-steering which was achieved simply by the use of shock-cord when on the wind and sheets connected to the tiller when sailing downwind. They never felt the need to install bespoke self-steering gear. Following their first dismasting they fitted roller reefing to the mainsail which they found simpler and quicker to operate than points reefing. Though the sail set less well than before, the gain was that they 'never hesitated to adjust the sail to the wind's force.' All in all *Tzu Hang* proved to be a well-balanced boat as well as a comfortable home for the Smeetons, members of their family, and such additional crew members as they took on board over their many years of cruising.

Miles was familiar with the principles of navigation from his wartime service in the desert, but the Smeetons' combined sailing experience was limited to short passages, with virtually no nights at sea. Their first proper passage was across the Thames estuary from Dover, where they bought the boat, to the River Crouch where she was to be refitted. It was a tricky crossing at best; with characteristic bravado the Smeetons undertook it at night and made the Crouch on the morning tide. Once the work on *Tzu Hang* was complete, they gained experience locally before making a trial cruise to Holland armed with Eric Hiscock's recently published *Cruising under Sail*. Their ten-year-old daughter Clio, who over many thousands of miles of voyaging proved to be as tough as her mother, recalls her father's irritation at the regular refrain: 'This is how Hiscock says you do it!'

Even after Miles met Eric Hiscock a few weeks later and they became firm friends, he would fulminate against the standards Hiscock demanded: 'He is like a bluewater Mao.' Many months later, north of the Galapagos Islands at night, Beryl noticed a ship following them. 'Better get our lights up,' said Miles.

'No need,' replied Beryl. 'Eric Hiscock says that we are below the size for which lights are compulsory.'

'Damn Eric Hiscock!' shouted Miles.

After their trial cruises in the North Sea, with Clio aboard they departed for Fowey, where they made preparations for the Atlantic crossing. Outwardly there was nothing remarkable about their maiden ocean voyage. They took a year to reach home, sailing via Spain, Portugal, the Canaries, Barbados, the Panama Canal, and the Galapagos Islands. What stands out in Miles's account of the voyage is the apparent ease with which these relative neophytes coped with the challenges. Crossing the Bay of Biscay they experienced strong headwinds the whole way. 'It was rough and wet, so we were soaked, lying in wet clothes on wet bunks, and wondering whether we were experiencing a gale or not. This is what we imagined ocean passages were like anyway.' (They were later able to determine that it had indeed been a gale).

Typically, on arrival in Tenerife they opted to climb Mount Teide, an active volcano some 12,000 feet high. It could be partly 'climbed' by taxi, still leaving 7000 feet of rocky path requiring a night on the mountain. Fortunately, they were told, a refugio had just been completed not far from the summit but on reaching it they discovered it was not yet finished. Always happy to make do, they shared the only room with a roof with the building workers and put up with mice gnawing at their rucksacks. It is no surprise to find that the Smeetons later became firm friends with sailor and climber Bill Tilman who, besides sharing a similar military background to Miles, was at least as hardy as the Smeetons and like them devoted equally to the sea and mountains.

It was also in Tenerife that they fell in with the Belgian couple Annie and Louis van de Wiele and their steel ketch *Omoo*, which was at an early stage of a circumnavigation, memorably recorded in Annie Van de Wiele's *The West In My Eyes* (1955). Miles later described her account as 'one of the best cruising stories ever written.' The Van de Wieles were just as impressed by the Smeetons. 'Astonishing people, these Smeetons,' recalled Annie. 'It was undoubtedly the most unusual and energetic family I have ever met. They were full of ideas and indomitable spirit... They had found the secret of living life to the full. We found ourselves completely in sympathy with each other.' They met up in Barbados after the Atlantic crossing, then again at Panama in transiting the canal and remained friends until late in their lives. Years later, the Smeetons came across *Omoo* in Mombasa but she was now in different hands and without the Van de Wieles 'she seemed forlorn.' Years later still, the Smeetons visited the Van de Wieles in the castle in southwest France where they had made their home. This connection is good evidence that the community of voyagers in this postwar era knew no national boundaries.

Once through the Panama Canal, they sailed for the Galapagos Islands where, Miles reflected, they could have spent months, so rich in wildlife and eccentric characters were they, but they wanted to be home in the Straits of Juan de Fuca before the summer fogs descended. It was now 30 March 1952. Before departing for home, they left a note in a bottle for Peter and Anne Pye in *Moonraker* which, Miles recorded, 'was picked up by another yacht and delivered to *Moonraker* when she arrived in Balbao [the Pacific end of the Panama Canal]'. From there it was close to five thousand miles to Vancouver, taking them across the doldrums, which called to their minds scenes from Coleridge's *Ancient Mariner*, until the north-east trades set in, giving them swifter progress towards their destination. They reached home in early June two and a half months after leaving the Galapagos Islands.

* * *

The idea of selling *Tzu Hang* on their return to British Columbia soon evaporated. At home, with *Tzu Hang* moored a few hundred yards away, the boat became 'our new love'. But it was no use keeping a yacht like *Tzu Hang* and not planning further cruises. Beryl announced one day: 'Australia in fifty-five' and that was immediately adopted as their next target. They set off from their home at Musgrave Landing in British Columbia in early September 1955, sailing first southwards to San Francisco before heading for Hawaii and from there via tiny Fanning Island to the Samoan islands and on to New Zealand and Sydney. Their aim was a two year cruise in the Pacific.

In the event, as was frequently the case with the Smeetons, plans proved to be highly flexible. While in San Francisco they had met John Guzzwell, also a British resident of British Columbia, who was embarking on a circumnavigation in the twenty-one foot Laurent Giles-designed *Trekka* which he had built himself. The Smeetons and Guzzwell immediately took to each other. Miles described the twenty-five year old Guzwell as 'young, athletic, powerful, and very reserved. He gave us an impression of great reliability; all the strength of his character seemed to flow through his hands which were so skilled and sure in carpentry'. As for *Trekka*, she was 'a little jewel, beautifully

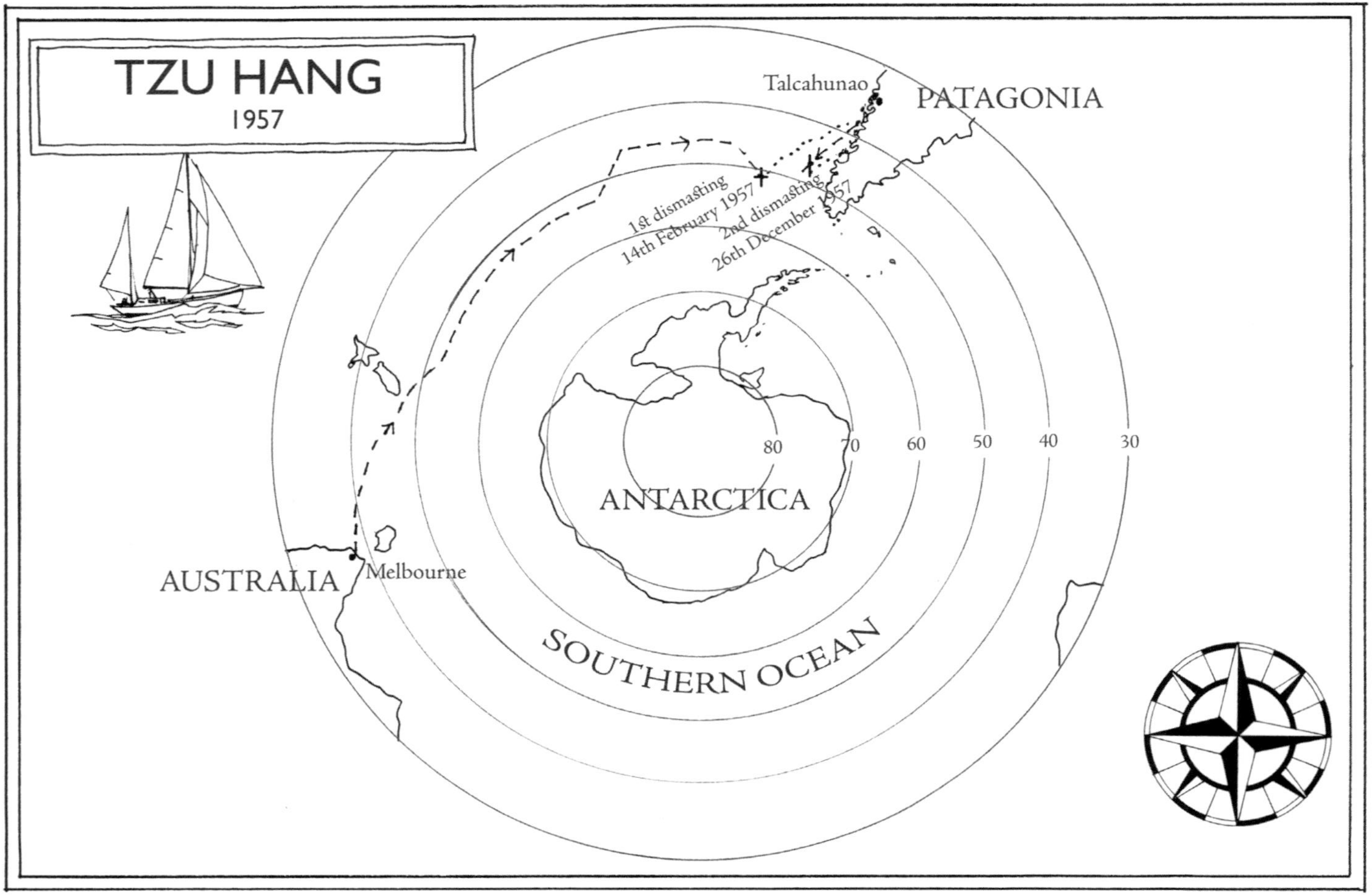

TZU HANG
1957
Talcahunao
PATAGONIA
1st dismasting
14th February 1957
2nd dismasting
26th December 1957
80
70
60
50
40
30
ANTARCTICA
AUSTRALIA
Melbourne
SOUTHERN OCEAN

built and tended, looking frail in comparison to *Tzu Hang* but feeling remarkably robust when one stepped aboard'. They met again in Hawaii, at Fanning Island, in Tonga, and again in New Zealand. The idea of sailing *Tzu Hang* round Cape Horn had come up on several occasions during these encounters and it gradually developed into a firm plan. John said he would love to join them and would leave *Trekka* in New Zealand. Storing her ashore in the Bay of Islands, he joined *Tzu Hang* for the trip to Melbourne, from where, a few days after the close of the 1956 Olympic games, they embarked on their voyage through the Southern Ocean towards their near disastrous encounter with roaring forties described above. Clio, meanwhile, was shipped back to England to boarding school and was told by her parents that she should not expect to hear anything from them for two months.

Inevitably most attention has been focussed on the first dismasting in which *Tzu Hang* effectively somersaulted down a massive breaking wave, with the additional complication of a man (or in this case a woman) overboard. However, the second dismasting was every bit as traumatic and potentially fatal to boat and crew. Miles and Beryl were on their own this time; John Guzzwell had returned to New Zealand to relaunch *Trekka* and continue his circumnavigation. In December 1957 Miles and Beryl set off southwards from Valparaiso, where *Tzu Hang* had been repaired, with the aim of taking the Strait of Magellan into the Atlantic or, if that proved too difficult, going round the Horn. The second dismasting took place at about 48 degrees 30 minutes south, a little further north than the first, but this time they were only 300 miles off the coast of Chile, not the 700 miles of the previous case. In this second instance they were lying a-hull in wind estimated to be above force nine, though one can assume that some of the gusts were storm force. In the initial phase of the storm they had carried a tiny storm jib and *Tzu Hang* careered downwind with the wind on her quarter, the boat sailing much of the time unattended. When they felt it was clearly unsafe to continue like this, they took down the jib, lashed the helm to leeward and let her lie a-hull. Miles and Beryl retired down below and tried to get what rest they could. It was while she was in this position that the broach and roll-over took place.

The results were similar to the first time – both masts broken off, the doghouse severely damaged and a great deal of water and chaos inside the boat. They took four days to get to the point of being able to sail her to safety under jury rig. For the first few days Miles had the sense of a third person aboard. Beryl thought it was simply an echo of the last time when John had been with them, but Miles believed it was in line with numerous stories told by sailors in distress, not least the first solo circumnavigator Joshua Slocum, and as we have seen, Ann Davison in her Atlantic crossing. An attempt to land at a port on Chiloe Island, the closest place where ship repairs might be available, was abandoned as too hazardous. They were forced to settle for Valparaiso, a further six hundred miles north. Helped by a southerly wind they entered Valparaiso bay a month after the initial incident.

It is hardly surprising that such dramatic events should have invited questions about coping with heavy weather. Following Miles's published account of their double dismasting, among the many expressions of admiration for their courage and resourcefulness were some criticisms of the boat and its crew. *Tzu Hang*, it was claimed was a 'wrong 'un' and 'was badly let down by her crew'.* Needless to say, Miles rejected both accusations, as did John Guzzwell in later reflections published as an appendix to his *Trekka Round the World* (1999). The pitchpoling which caused the first dismasting occurred in extreme conditions in which, as oceanographic research has since confirmed, freak waves are not uncommon. *Tzu Hang* was running under bare poles at the time and towing sixty fathoms of three inch warp in an effort to slow her down. It was evidently not enough to prevent disaster. Given a vertical wall of water of great height with a breaking crest, it is doubtful, Guzzwell concluded, whether any craft of *Tzu Hang*'s size and displacement could have survived undamaged.

Miles himself, however, came to the conclusion, with reference to the second dismasting, that lying a-hull in a bad storm was never a good option, since it meant the boat would lie beam on to the seas. He concluded that lying to a good sea anchor could have held her about 45 degrees to the wind rather than beam on which might have enabled her to ride out the wave which rolled them over.

* Smeeton tells this story in *Because The Horn Is There*, pp.6-7, though he does not say who the author was or in which magazine the critical remarks were published.

In the initial phase of the storm they had carried a tiny storm jib and Tzu Hang careered downwind with the wind on her quarter...

Whatever the case, the Smeetons' experience remains a touchstone for discussions of tactics in heavy weather sailing. In the chapter on 'Survival Storms' in *Heavy Weather Sailing*, Adlard Coles concluded, with specific reference to *Tzu Hang*, that 'in weather conditions such as these few yachts would live without sustaining damage, whatever their type and whatever the method of defence adopted. The astonishing things was that she survived at all.' What can be affirmed is that over a further two decades of ocean voyaging, in which the Smeetons encountered extreme conditions on a number of occasions, including, as we shall see, a third encounter with the waters around Cape Horn, their 1957 experiences were not repeated. There may have been an element of luck but equally they evidently learned the ways of the sea to good effect.

* * *

Once the nomadic life had seeped into the Smeetons' bones their roaming instincts knew no bounds. In autumn 1958, following repairs to *Tzu Hang* after the dismastings in the Roaring Forties, they wandered up the east coast of Britain from Tucker's boatyard in Essex and through the Caledonian Canal to Ireland, where they stayed six months. From there they sailed via Shetland to Scandinavia, then back across the North Sea and up the Seine to the heart of Paris where they lay for the winter of 1959-60.

Then began an extraordinary five years cruising, which included lengthy explorations on land, particularly in Africa. Leaving Paris in March 1960, they sailed down to the Straits of Gibraltar and through the Mediterranean, with frequent and often lengthy stops. In March 1961 they embarked on a passage of the Suez Canal and the Red Sea, which brought them in December to Mombasa in Kenya. For the next year they took overland journeys in Kenya, Tanganyika, Northern and Southern Rhodesia, and Bechuanaland. They drove over 10,000 miles in a battered old VW Kombi. Among many notable incidents was a broken fuel pump in Northern Tanganyika which resulted in Beryl hitch-hiking 120 miles to find a replacement, 'returning by means of an Indian fish lorry, the back of an African's bicycle, and, finally, on foot'. It was during their time in Bechuanaland, when they became involved in collecting animals for Gerald

Durrell's Jersey Zoo, that Miles's view of big game hunting underwent a transformation.

In May 1962 the Smeetons returned to *Tzu Hang* and began a hectic criss-crossing of the Indian Ocean, taking in the Maldives, the Seychelles, Madagascar, Ceylon as well as several ports in Mozambique and as far south as Durban. The following year they sailed east to Singapore via the Strait of Malacca, to Sarawak, and on to the Philippines, a phase of their leisurely circumnavigation which, their biographer observes, 'came closest to exploration in the old sense', given the absence of reliable charts in many instances. Miles's account of this voyage in *Sunrise to Windward* (1966) is vintage Smeeton in its rich blend of sailing adventures and close observation of people and places. Their passage through the Strait of Malacca finds them negotiating the complex political tensions between Indonesia and the newly-formed Malaysia as well as dealing with a blown-out mainsail in one of the busiest sea lanes in the world. It was this cruise that gained the Smeetons the Royal Cruising Club's premier award, The Challenge Cup.

Remarkable as this period of voyaging was, the next phase if anything surpassed it. In February 1964 they set out into the Pacific, bound for Japan. Miles had taken the surrender of Japanese forces in Burma, during which he had received the personal sword of the Japanese Chief of Staff there. With help from a historian at the Japanese Defence Department they managed to trace the soldier, and a meeting took place in the saloon of *Tzu Hang* at which the sword was returned to its grateful owner.

Tzu Hang then sailed the full length of Japan, arriving in the autumn of 1964 at Mori in the northern tip of Hokkaido where they planned to spend the winter. With *Tzu Hang* hauled out, they occupied a small square building with bare concrete walls and primitive heating facilities. For three months the temperature barely rose above freezing. There, along with their daughter Clio, they existed on a diet of 'whale meat, fish, cabbage, sheep's heart and liver' while Miles drafted his account of their African and Southeast Asian adventures, *Sunrise to Windward*.

The passage from Japan back to British Columbia via the Aleutian islands, occupying the summer months of 1965, had a truly pioneering quality. Few yachts had ever done it. Navigation and pilotage were difficult because of frequent poor visibility, sudden changes of weather, and often poorly charted waters. Encounters with other human beings were restricted to the occasional fisherman and American Coastguard officer. Encounters with wildlife, on the other hand, were much more frequent and more welcome to the enthusiastic and increasingly knowledgeable members of *Tzu Hang*'s crew.

Sea otters, blue foxes, whales and countless other new species of animals and birds crossed their paths. They even had a sighting of what they believed must be a 'sea monkey', a species observed only once before by a German naturalist accompanying Vitus Bering in the region in 1741. As Miles recalled in *The Misty Islands*: 'It looked to be the size of a sheep and had long pepper-and-salt hair like a cairn terrier, of a reddish-yellow colour.' Much investigation by Miles Clark, the Smeetons' biographer, and others has failed to determine whether such a creature actually existed.

The Smeetons had always been as devoted to domestic animals. Their attachment to their pets was a theme of their voyaging from the start; they became integral parts of the ship's company. In their first ocean voyage it was a hamster, which Miles and Beryl had thought would be a convenient pet for Clio. When the hamster died it was replaced by Cully, a Siamese cat, and Poopah, a Portuguese rabbit hound. The longest-serving pet was the Siamese cat Pwe, which shipped out with them from British Columbia in 1955 and accompanied them for eighteen years and 130,000 miles of voyaging. She featured regularly in Miles's account of their most dramatic moments. During the twin dismasting crises in the Pacific, Miles never failed to record Pwe's frantic efforts to find comfort in the ensuing chaos and conveyed the anxiety of all the crew when it was thought Pwe was lost. When Clio, now 23, joined the boat in northern Japan in 1964 she brought with her a puppy she had found abandoned in Afghanistan. It proved to be a Powinda breed of the Kochi people near Kabul, grew to the size of a golden retriever and turned out to be an excellent traveller.

Clio's attachment to animals resulted in a lifelong commitment to conservation and breeding of endangered species which she still pursues as President of the Cochrane Ecological Institute in Alberta, Canada, founded by her and her parents in 1971. For his part, Miles, who had been bred in a culture where wildlife was routinely exploited for sport, underwent a transformation in his attitude towards the animal world and recalled his earlier practices with some regret.

* * *

It was September 1965 when they reached home. They were now approaching their sixties. Miles's knees were giving way, necessitating an operation to remove the cartilages, but they were not yet ready to give up their nomadic life. In September 1966, having sold their island farm and bought another in the eastern foothills of the Rockies near Calgary, where Clio had just moved, they sailed for England. That voyage, via the Panama Canal, was less noteworthy than the return in the second half of 1968, which took them westabout round Cape Horn.

Miles justifiably called this the sailor's equivalent of the north face of the Eiger. He interwove their own story with the history of the region going back to the Schouten brothers' momentous first recorded doubling of the Horn in 1616, to be followed by Spanish, British, French and other fleets, mostly rounding the Horn from the east. Miles included the pantheon of twentieth century Cape Horners, notably single-handers, whom he singled out for special praise, such as Alfon Hansen, Vito Dumas, Marcel Bardiaux, Bernard Moitessier, Bill Nance, Francis Chichester, Alec Rose, Robin Knox-Johnston, and of course Edward Allcard. Like Allcard, as we have seen in an earlier chapter, Smeeton sailed these waters as if in company with a select band of sailors going back centuries, their historic presences providing both inspiration and guardianship over the Smeetons' own efforts.

Like many before them, the Smeetons found that getting to the Horn from the east, above all making passage through the Le Maire Strait between Staten Island and Tierra del Fuego, was a challenge in itself. Strong tides and a gale force southerly wind almost forced them to divert east round Staten Island which would put them at least sixty miles downwind, once they met the prevailing westerlies south of Staten Island. They hung on and made it through the Strait, only to be met, as was Anson's fleet in 1741, with a westerly gale against which they could make no headway. They hove to for several hours and were then rewarded with a moderate breeze from the northeast which allowed them to head directly for the Horn. On 15 December

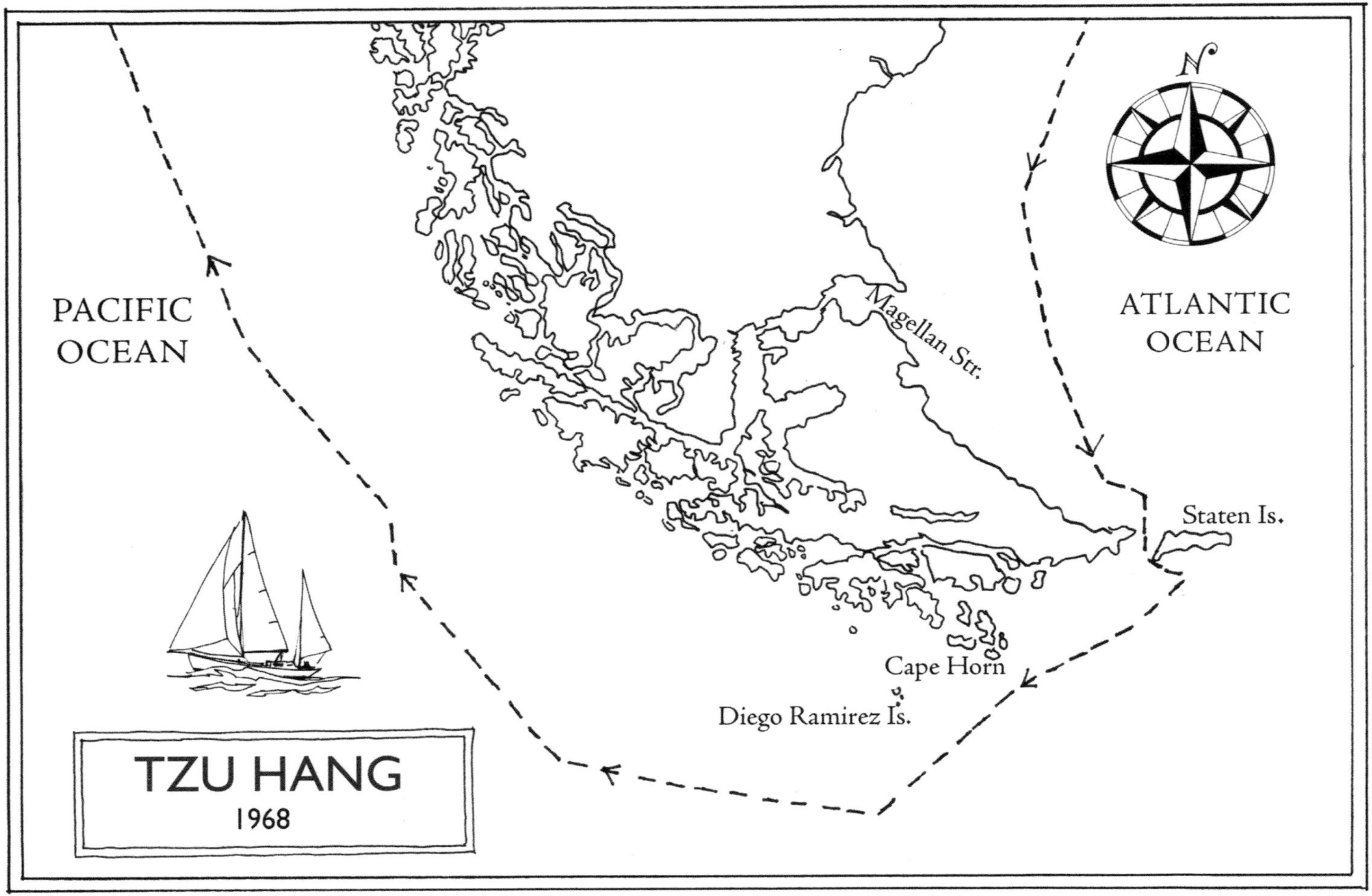
PACIFIC OCEAN
ATLANTIC OCEAN
N
Magellan Str.
Staten Is.
Cape Horn
Diego Ramirez Is.
TZU HANG
1968

they reached the latitude of Cape Horn and enjoyed a rare moment of warmth and calm weather sitting in the cockpit in bright sunshine drinking a glass of Uruguayan wine. The next day Cape Horn bore north five miles. The sun had gone but so had the gales. They fell silent. 'We felt as if we were trespassing in the halls of strange Gods,' reflected Smeeton, 'and that we must go past in silence, lest we awake their wrath.'

The commonly accepted definition of rounding, or 'doubling', Cape Horn is to sail from 50 degrees south in one ocean to the same latitude in the other. It took *Tzu Hang* only fourteen days, a notably quick passage. Smeeton was keen to emphasise that this way of rounding the Horn represented the 'supreme challenge', as compared with sailing out from the channels and islands north of Cape Horn island and then back to an anchorage in the channels and islands, which is the way Marcel Bardiaux and Edward Allcard made their westabout passages. While expressing profound admiration for solo sailors, not only for their skill in handling their boats in testing conditions but 'for their courage and initiative in being there at all', Smeeton insisted that, just as a mountain can be climbed by various routes, 'the most difficult way was the ultimate challenge'. An element of competitiveness, manifesting itself in an urge always to test himself against the most difficult option, was part of Miles Smeeton's make-up.

On this passage the Smeetons were fortunate to have as a third crew member the twenty-six-year-old Australian Bob Nance, who already had considerable ocean experience, including an eastabout rounding of the Horn in a yacht called *Carronade*.* As with John Guzzwell, their choice of crew was inspired. In one of the many touches which enlivens Miles's account, he describes how, during a gale-blown sleepless night, Beryl and Bob entered into deep discussion about bread-making, resulting in 'two bakings which took half the night and ended with eight

* Sailing was in Bob Nance's blood. His brother Bill had circumnavigated solo south of the three Capes (Cape of Good Hope, Cape Leeuwin, and Cape Horn) in his *Cardinal Vertue* between 1962 and 1965, only the second person to do so, an achievement which until recently has been too little celebrated. Justice has now been done to Bill Nance's story by Nicholas Gray in his fine book *Astronauts of Cape Horn* (2018), Chapter 9 of which is based on extensive conversations with Nance.

fresh brown loaves slung in a netting hammock under the deckhead'. In recognition of their entire career of voyaging, with special mention of the rounding of the Horn, the Smeetons received the 1973 Blue Water Medal of the Cruising Club of America.

* * *

The twilight years of Miles and Beryl Smeeton were brighter than those of most normal lives. In 1975, giving way to a passion for the Northwest Passage, on which he hoped to write a book, Miles joined a Canadian icebreaker which managed to steam most (but not all) of the way through. The following year a further opportunity arose and Miles joined the icebreaker Bernier in Victoria, BC, which successfully transited the passage to the North Atlantic.

There was more to come. For many years Beryl had had a lump in her breast, about which she had kept quiet; but by the mid-1970s she could no longer hide it, and was undergoing treatment. When they received an invitation from Bob Nance, to whom they had sold *Tzu Hang*, to cross the Atlantic with him to Europe, they jumped at the chance. Now both over 70, they departed New York in 1979 for Newfoundland and from there to the Faroes and Orkney.

Later that year Beryl died, with, Miles reported, 'still a twinkle in those brave blue eyes'. Devastated as he was by the loss, Miles could not resist adventuring when the opportunity arose. In 1981 he received an invitation from John Guzzwell to join him and his wife on their 'honeymoon cruise' to Hawaii, which, after some qualms about his physical condition, Miles accepted. He survived it well, but his services appear to have been most valuable in keeping the peace between Guzzwell and his bride, who was new to the privations and dramas of ocean sailing. Miles reportedly saved the marriage. Learning to fly a microlight and ice-yachting seized his imagination in the years that followed, and he was stopped only by a stroke when he was eighty-two. Clio recalls that in his last hours 'he was in a great fever to leave, and seemed to be looking forward to death with the same sense of excitement with which he looked forward to a hard climb or an ocean crossing'. Death for Miles was evidently just one more adventure.

Chapter 11

SMALLEST ROUND THE WORLD

John Guzzwell and *Trekka*

John Guzzwell is hardly a household name, even among many who take an interest in the history of bluewater sailing, yet he was the first British-born sailor to circumnavigate the world solo. He set out in 1955 and returned in 1959, taking sixteen months out in 1956-7 to accompany the Smeetons aboard *Tzu Hang* for their fateful first attempt to round Cape Horn. The more famous voyages of Francis Chichester and Robin Knox-Johnston took place a decade later and represented momentous and more eye-catching achievements. Chichester's solo circumnavigation of 1966-7, taking the route of the tea clippers, was the fastest to date by a sailor from any country, included only one stop, and contained the longest continuous solo voyage in recorded history. Knox-Johnston's epoch-making win in the 1968-9 Golden Globe single-handed race represented the first non-stop solo circumnavigation of the world. If Guzzwell deserves special attention it is not only because he was the first British solo circumnavigator but because his *Trekka*, at just under twenty-one feet, was the smallest boat to do so. His 'record' stood for close to twenty-five years, though Guzzwell had no thought of records when he started out. The rage for records in this field with its associated publicity was some years away.

Guzzwell was out of the limelight in part because he had no interest in courting publicity and told few people about his venture. He also had a complicated past which all but obscured his connection to the British Isles. He was born in England in 1930, brought up in the Channel Islands, spent two of his teenage years in South Africa where his mother was born, and emigrated to Canada in his early twenties. Just to add to the patchwork, he spent two of the wartime years as an internee in Germany, following the Nazi occupation of the Channel Islands. Though still a British passport holder during his circumnavigation, by this stage he had little connection with the country of his birth.

Unlike most of the sailors portrayed in this book, Guzzwell was still a boy when the war began, but he had already sailed thousands of miles with his parents. His father was a restless adventuring type who had gone to sea as a marine engineer at a young age. When John was only three, his father had a fifty-foot ketch built in which the family sailed to South Africa. On their return to Britain (John and his mother coming by steamer) his father sold the boat but replaced it with an eighteen-foot cutter called *Try Me* in which John learned the basics. By the time the war began the association between sailing and freedom was well established in him. They had even tried to escape from Jersey in *Try Me* when the Germans invaded but were thwarted by the weather.

On their release from the German internment camp in 1945 Guzzwell's father insisted he should learn a trade, and at fifteen years old John was apprenticed to a joiner. Following his father's death in 1948, the family moved to South Africa where John continued his apprenticeship. There was no thought of boatbuilding at this stage but the skills he learned stood him in good stead later. It was on his return to England after two years in South Africa that he became fired by the ambition of sailing over the horizon. On a visit to Jersey he felt he did not fit in there anymore and, recalling stories his father had told him of British Columbia during his youthful years wandering the world, John was inspired to emigrate. The attraction was not only the wide-open spaces and the association with his father's life of adventure, but British Columbia's copious supply of lumber for boatbuilding, for he had already decided that the long voyage he intended to make would be in a boat built by his own hand.

Guzzwell approached the building of his boat with great deliberation, inspired by the example of other circumnavigators in self-built boats – Joshua Slocum, Harry Pidgeon, and Marcel Bardiaux. With limited funds, he would have to build small but he sought out the best in design, choosing the Lymington firm of Laurent Giles on the strength of *Sopranino*'s successful Atlantic crossing of 1951-2 and lengthy voyages in other Laurent Giles designs. For a fee of fifty pounds Jack Giles drew him a boat similar in concept to *Sopranino* with reverse sheer, short overhangs, and diminutive size, though *Trekka* was a foot longer, more heavily built, and carried a yawl rig.

Guzzwell soon found his feet in British Columbia working as a joiner, which enabled him to accumulate the funds to start building. With practised wood-working skills but no background in boat-building he had much to learn but evidently did so quickly. His first step was to buy a book on the subject. He found lofting initially daunting but successfully negotiated this and the many other challenges involved in working with curved surfaces. In the small sash window and door factory where he worked he learned to use power tools, a development in which the north Americans were far ahead of the British, but, lacking access to these at his private workshop, he built the boat with hand tools. Drilling for fastenings was with a traditional 'egg-beater' drill. All the planking was cut out with a hand saw and finished with a hand plane. The design called for edge-glued carvel planking copper-fastened to closely spaced timbers, producing an immensely strong structure. His was a project in which the term 'hand-made' had real meaning. He later reflected that 'there is something almost sacred about building a boat... almost like creating a living being'.

A notable feature of the building phase was Guzzwell's ability to attract support from people in his surroundings, including four weightlifters who helped him turn the boat over once the planking was complete and a workmate who helped him rivet the three thousand fastenings required to secure the planking. He was clearly an engaging and sympathetic personality with a talent for friendship, which was surely not unconnected with the fact that he was tall, ruggedly good-looking, and, despite being a man of few words, self-confident and unassuming.

The result of his labours was a boat which took him thousands of miles in often inhospitable waters without major structural or gear failures, testimony to Laurent Giles's design and Guzzwell's building skills as well as his capacity to handle the boat in the most difficult conditions. He carried an outboard motor which served its purpose in anchorages or harbours when the wind died, though with only four gallons of fuel aboard the engine was unused for long stretches of time. *Trekka* was first and foremost a sailing craft. A bermudan-rigged yawl, she carried a large wardrobe of headsails ranging from a big genoa to a tiny storm-jib and a spinnaker in addition. The small cockpit was little more than a footwell without coamings, so helming meant sitting on the side-deck in dinghy-sailing fashion. Halfway through his circumnavigation Guzzwell build a small plywood dinghy with removable transom, and carried it inverted over the cabin top. For a large man this was a small space to live in for extended periods but he proved more than equal to the challenge, having from the outset conceived of *Trekka* as a vehicle for his own specific needs. In the right conditions she was capable of regular daily runs of over 125 nautical miles, representing an impressive average speed of over five knots on a nineteen-foot waterline.

* * *

Guzzwell left Victoria on the tenth of September 1955 and had a slow start trying to get through the Strait of Juan de Fuca but after a windless first night the breeze picked up and *Trekka* was on her way. As he emerged onto the open sea he was hailed by a voice from a passing trawler in a thick Norwegian accent: 'Vere de hell you tink you are going in dat bloody little pisspot?' In reply to Guzzwell's shout of 'Honolulu' the voice roared back, 'Vell you're bloody crazee, put goot luck!' *Trekka* experienced her first gale the next day, which he sat out lying beam on to the seas after experimenting with a sea anchor, a seemingly risky move, as he acknowledged, but it worked. Coming through unscathed did him some good since, he recorded, 'I now had confidence in my boat and a little more in myself too.' It was timely preparation for the next gale which came only two days later and was much more severe, with thirty-foot waves and winds he estimated touched over sixty knots. In this case the wind was from the north and he ran before it through most of a day and the next night, towing warps and hand-steering. It was the worst gale he experienced on the entire circumnavigation.

He had not intended to stop in San Francisco but the prospect of a rest was attractive and he closed the coast some miles north of the Golden Gate. The voyage almost came to a premature end when he mistook some black buoys for channel markers and ended up aground in a small bay on a falling tide. In future, he reflected, he would never make the mistake of approaching a coastline without adequate charts. He was lucky to have been observed by a vessel at anchor in the bay which pulled him into deep water, allowing him to proceed to San Francisco.

It was a fateful move since it was there he met Miles and Beryl Smeeton and their daughter Clio, who, like Guzzwell, had left British Columbia for passage across the Pacific some weeks before. It marked the beginning of his long association with the family and with *Tzu Hang*. They agreed to meet up again in Hawaii, where the idea of rounding Cape Horn in *Tzu Hang* was first mooted. After a four-month stopover in Hawaii, in March 1956 the two boats continued their leisurely transit of the Pacific via tiny Fanning Island – one of a chain of cable stations across the Pacific Ocean, the Samoan Islands, Tonga and finally New Zealand. Characteristically, along the way the crews of both boats took every opportunity to explore the islands on foot, under sail, and also by swimming in the case of the Mariner's Cave in the Tongan Islands, which could be reached only under water. Ten year old Clio proved as keen and adept as the adults in making the dive.

By the time they reached the Bay of Islands in New Zealand's North Island, the Cape Horn plan had firmed up. Guzzwell would come with them as crew while *Trekka* would be stored ashore. They stayed at their base in Russell in the Bay of Islands for four months preparing *Tzu Hang* for the passage to the Horn. The end of November 1956 saw them in Melbourne where they attended the Olympic Games, until on 23 December, minus Clio, who had been dispatched to school in Britain, they left Melbourne 'bound for Port Stanley in the Falkland Islands'.

Miles Smeeton's account of *Tzu Hang*'s pitchpoling and dismasting on the first attempt to reach Cape Horn was described in such detail and so vividly in *Once is Enough* that it might be thought there was little to add. Guzzwell himself said he could not match Smeeton's narrative but his account in his *Trekka Round the World* has its own qualities. Among other things, the severity of Beryl's injuries after being thrown from the boat – a blow to the head, a broken arm, an injured foot – come over more strongly than ever. Reduced as she was, she nevertheless helped with the bailing and clean-up throughout the crisis, though it was two weeks before she was able to come on deck and take a hand at steering. Guzzwell's description of plugging the

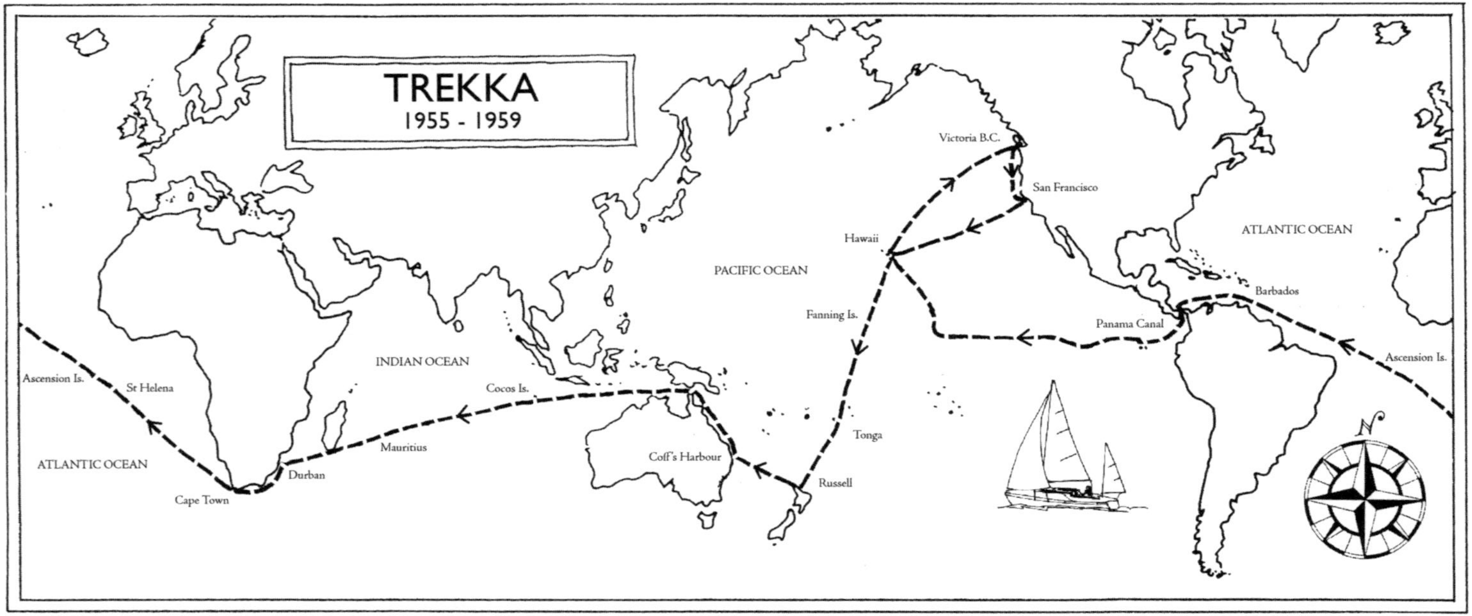
TREKKA
1955 - 1959
Victoria B.C.
San Francisco
ATLANTIC OCEAN
Hawaii
PACIFIC OCEAN
Barbados
Fanning Is.
Panama Canal
INDIAN OCEAN
Ascension Is.
Ascension Is.
St Helena
Cocos Is.
Tonga
Mauritius
ATLANTIC OCEAN
Coff's Harbour
Durban
Russell
Cape Town

gaps in *Tzu Hang*'s deck, fashioning the jury rig, the steering oar, and all the other repairs which enabled them to make the boat seaworthy again come over with particular clarity and force. With a great deal of trial and error and no little struggle they even managed to get *Tzu Hang* to go to windward.

However, Guzzwell made a special contribution in the form of photos and an extraordinary five minute 16mm film which was later broadcast on ITN. Unsurprisingly there is no footage of the pitch-poling itself, since he was below at the time, though he confessed that on first sight of Beryl struggling back to the ship covered in blood for 'a crazy moment I thought, "oh what a shot for color film"'. It was impossible at the time but his filming of the Southern Ocean in the days and hours before the dismasting gives a powerful impression of the conditions faced by *Tzu Hang* and her crew. On quieter days he would film from the dinghy towed astern. The last minute of the film, taken from *Tzu Hang*'s cockpit, shows much more severe conditions of the type experienced in the pitchpoling, with huge waves awash with the foam of breaking crests. Guzzwell's still photography was similarly graphic in its own way. Together they constitute a rare and valuable record of sailing in the Southern Ocean during this era.

Thirty-four days after the dismasting they reach the Chilean port of Coronel. The experience deepened the bond between Guzzwell and the Smeetons. 'There was a wonderful feeling of comradeship between the three of us,' he recalled, 'we all realised that without the other two we would never have survived.' Guzzwell affirmed that the time he spent with the Smeetons was largely responsible for the conclusion of *Trekka*'s successful circumnavigation. As a training course in coping with extreme conditions his experience on *Tzu Hang* would be hard to match. As it was, with still two-thirds of his own circumnavigation to go, full of challenges as it proved to be, he was spared anything on the scale of the drama on *Tzu Hang* in the Southern Ocean.

* * *

Guzzwell's route from North Island, New Zealand took him across the Tasman Sea to Australia; north up the coast to the Barrier Reef in the wake, like so many others, of Captain Cook; through the Torres Strait; across the Indian Ocean to South Africa; over the Atlantic to Panama and into the Pacific. Rather than head directly north for British Columbia, which meant facing contrary winds and currents, he sailed once again to Hawaii and from there on a slant to British Columbia. Departing New Zealand in April 1958, he took a year to reach the Panama Canal, crossed his outward track near Hawaii in July 1959 and reached home two months later.

The story of this voyage is of wildly varied conditions which, at one extreme, found him taking five days against light headwinds to cover thirty miles towards Coff's Harbour on the Australian coast. At the other extreme was his experience of a cyclone some way north of Coff's Harbour. His response to news of the impending storm showed how practised he had become at dealing with bad weather, however low his morale went – and plummet it certainly did when the wind went round into the northeast, putting him on a lee shore. He clawed his way offshore to ride it out as far from danger as possible and took active measures to increase the distance between him and the shore, setting the storm jib when he could and devising a makeshift sea anchor to slow his drift towards shore when no sail could be set. The cyclone lasted four full days during which time he learned he had been reported missing and aircraft had been out looking for him. Another sailing boat was also missing and later found wrecked ashore some way north of *Trekka*'s position.

Conditions were not always so extreme. In the Indian ocean with following winds *Trekka* achieved successive daily runs of over 120 miles, leading him to talk of the 'kindly Indian Ocean', in notable contrast to the experience of Eric and Susan Hiscock who spent much of their crossing of this ocean during their first circumnavigation under a trysail of fifty square feet. By this stage Guzzwell had perfected a self-steering system which allowed him to leave the tiller for extended periods for rest or to attend to the many tasks involved in keeping the boat sound and seaworthy.

In common with all sailors who arrived in Durban after the Indian Ocean crossing, the prospect of the 900-mile passage round the 'cape of storms' to Cape Town was daunting. The problem was the swift Agulhas Current which flowed down the African coast and kicked up fearsome seas in the face of a strong south-westerly. The record was littered with tales of trouble and strife, as Guzzwell put it, but on closer inspection it turned out that most of the horror stories were the consequence of poor preparation. He took the opportunity in Durban to prepare *Trekka* thoroughly for the challenge. Besides re-painting and re-varnishing, he reduced weight by taking only enough stores to get him to Cape Town, since when she was light she took the seas more comfortably than when laden. A new suit of sails completed the preparations. In the event the passage proved to be a mixed picture. He had to seek shelter in Port Elizabeth half-way through the passage, met with strong winds off Cape Agulhas, and was hit by fearsome gusts on the approach to Cape Town, but he and *Trekka* arrived in a good state of repair.

The rest of the voyage proceeded according to plan but not without incident and colour. Guzzwell left Cape Town on 14 February 1959, two years to the day after *Tzu Hang*'s dismasting, bound for the Caribbean, making brief stops at St Helena and Ascension Island, another isolated island which housed a cable station. There he was invited on to the United States Airforce Base where the mascot was a donkey called 'Hardaway' that had learned to drink beer straight from the can and 'would spend his days bumming drinks from the men'. At the high point of the Island he made a wish by a tiny lily pond where, it was said, if you held the old piece of chain that lay nearby, your wish would come true. 'I know it works,' Guzzwell said, 'because my wish came true on day in September six months later.'

He meant, of course, his safe return to Victoria, British Columbia. He was generally fortunate in the Atlantic weather on passage to the Caribbean and was able to relax much of the time. He was entertained for days on end by the drama around him of dorado catching flying fish. The dorado accompanied him for 1200 miles during which he tried but failed to catch any. Some days out of Ascension Island a record was played for him on the BBC programme 'Listeners Choice', his choice being 'The Breeze and I' by Caterina Valente which for those with long enough memories perfectly recalls the mid-1950s non-rock and roll element of the hit parade. After a brief stopover in Barbados his most notable experience on the way to Panama was a waterspout which roared by fifty feet away but left him unscathed. Any anxiety he had about transiting the Panama Canal disappeared when an experienced canal hand he had met at the Cristobal Yacht Club volunteered to help him on the way through. Best of all, his Canal dues, calculated at 79 cents a ton, came to 2 dollars and 16 cents – 'good value' he thought compared with going round Cape Horn.

Between the Pacific end of the Canal and Hawaii he achieved the best daily run of the whole trip of 175 miles, which included forty-three miles due to a favourable current. In one week *Trekka* covered 1101 miles. For much of this passage he sat in the cockpit reading 'without a stitch of clothing on, as my shorts had the seat worn out of them from constant rubbing on the fibre-glass deck.' Half-way between Hawaii and home he celebrated his twenty-ninth birthday with a meal of canned steak followed by a canned Australian Christmas pudding with custard, while sitting on deck viewing a 'wonderful tropical sunset that would have measured force 8 on the Richter scale'. It was one of those moments, he noted, which he would return to in memory when he was away from sea and caught up in the rush of everyday life.

There remained, however, a sting in the tail on this final leg. In yet another storm he reflected that it was not possible to get used to riding out a gale in a small boat because each one was different, and he even had the sense in one frozen moment as a monster wave advanced towards him that 'it was going to be *Tzu Hang* all over again'. The moment passed but the storm continued for forty-two hours. He arrived home in Victoria to a tumultuous welcome but perhaps predictably he reflected that, although he wanted to get back to Canada, 'part of me wanted to delay the homecoming' since it would be his last passage in *Trekka* for a long time. He had been away for four years and was now faced with making a life ashore.

* * *

An important theme of Guzzwell's circumnavigation was the people he met. He was evidently happy in his own company, revelling in the small space he had created in *Trekka* where he felt supremely at home, but he was no hermit. Though not, he admitted, a great conversationalist, he was a social animal who rarely missed an opportunity to link up with like-minded people. Meeting the Smeetons was the most important and long-lasting example but there were numerous others. In the Bay of Islands in New Zealand he met 'Batch' Carr

His most notable experience on the way to Panama was a waterspout which roared by fifty feet away but left him unscathed.

and his wife Ann who owned a seventy-ton ketch called *Havfruen III*, also on a round the world voyage. They were to meet many times over the coming months before going their separate ways in the West Indies. In New Zealand Guzzwell formed a close bond with Francis and Mille Arlidge who offered him a shed to store *Trekka* in the Bay of Islands while he was away on Tzu Hang. When over a year later he left New Zealand to complete his own circumnavigation, he found that the Arlidges were the hardest to leave, since they 'had looked after me as one of their own sons, never complaining or asking for anything in return'.

At Cooktown on the Great Barrier Reef he fell in with sixty-five-year-old retired British civil servant Norman Young who had left Britain with two other men well over sixty and crossed the Atlantic to the West Indies in his Falmouth Quay Punt. Young had since crossed the Pacific and acquired some younger crew members for the passage up the Australian coast. *Diana* and *Trekka* sailed virtually in company up the Great Barrier Reef. Guzzwell was intrigued by the sight of an elderly bachelor living a life of adventure and speaking the accents of the Queen's English, but he had more in common with Norman's young crew Gary. Gary was a nineteen-year-old from Queensland who was delighted to find in Guzzwell a kindred spirit who was much closer to him in age than his skipper.

The boats parted company in northern Australia, *Trekka* heading directly for the Indian Ocean and *Diana* for Darwin to pick up new crew before making her own crossing. Some months later they encountered each other again in Durban. If proof were needed, Guzzwell's experience shows that there were many others like himself undertaking great adventures whose stories remain largely unknown simply because they did not write about them.

* * *

With the publication in 1963 of *Trekka Round the World* Guzzwell achieved modest fame in the wider world to add to his status as a celebrity in his home town. On arrival in Victoria he was given a hero's welcome by the Royal Canadian Navy and crowds ashore. The city honoured him with a plaque and the local sailing club presented him with a burgee. Not yet thirty, Guzzwell had put his name in the record books but had also left himself with the challenge of finding a way of life which suited his roaming instincts. He soon 'met a young lady', married, got a job 'and pretended to be a normal human being'. After the voyage, he reflected, 'this was not an easy role and I was often caught with a far-away look in my eyes'. The roaming instinct never left him.

The upshot was more voyaging, this time with his wife Maureen, and then, when children came along, the whole family, which required a larger boat. In 1965 he moved to England and built a forty-five-foot boat he named *Treasure*, again to a Laurent Giles design, which he and his wife sailed to New Zealand where they settled with the children for several years. The offer of a yacht delivery job took him to Hawaii where the family stayed for six years before returning in the mid-1970s to the Pacific Northwest. There they found a secluded property on Orcas Island, lying between Vancouver Island and the mainland. Along the way he was building boats to commissions but with the isolation and the burden of work his marriage failed and a new chapter in his life began when at the age of fifty he met and married Dorothy Saunders.

It was a happy marriage but not plain sailing. A honeymoon voyage to the South Pacific, in which the ageing Miles Smeeton accompanied them as crew, led to a period of roving in the Pacific, interspersed with trips back to British Columbia to earn money. The life evidently did not suit Dorothy and she opted to train as a flight attendant which entailed her moving to Chicago, then San Francisco and subsequently Seattle. John, meanwhile, ever eager to go down to the sea again, entered a race to Japan in *Treasure* and some years later at the age of sixty-eight the Transpac Race from San Francisco to Hawaii in a thirty foot boat called *Endangered Species* which he built himself. He came in ninth on handicap. Until late in life he remained an inveterate rover, bearing out his caution to readers in a new edition of *Trekka Round the World* (1999): 'beware, dear reader, the sea has an enchantment that may captivate you and make you a bit of a misfit on land'.

In later years, after a lifetime of voyaging and boatbuilding to the highest level of skill, Guzzwell was in demand for talks about *Trekka*'s circumnavigation. As Honorary Commodore of the Classic Boat Festival of British Columbia he spearheaded the revival of interest in classic boats and maritime traditions, yet crucially his achievement also represented an embrace of the new in design and building techniques.

As for *Trekka,* she circumnavigated the world a second time in different hands in the late 1960s and in 1980 entered the Maritime Museum of British Columbia where she remains a prize exhibit, looking in as fine a condition as when she left John Guzzwell's workshop in 1955. On his death at the age of 94 in August 2024 one could be forgiven for thinking that in spirit he, like *Trekka,* lives on.

ACKNOWLEDGEMENTS

My first debt is to Sam Llewellyn, editor of the *Marine Quarterly* where versions of most of these chapters were first published. His skill as an editor has been matched by unstinting encouragement and support for this project. I am grateful to him for permission to use material previously published in the *Marine Quarterly*. Warm thanks are due to Julia Crockatt for listening to many pages of this book with her usual appreciative but critical ear.

I have received much help and encouragement from relations of some of the sailors portrayed in these pages and I am grateful to them for the time they have taken in reading and commenting on my draft chapters. These include Janice Aslin, niece of Eric Hiscock; Clare Allcard, wife of Edward Allcard; Clio Smeeton, daughter of Miles and Beryl Smeeton; and Pat Pocock, daughter of Humphrey Barton. Pat Pocock also sent me unpublished autobiographical writings by her father which proved invaluable in understanding his complex character. Besides reading a draft chapter, Robin Somes made available to me a mass of material by and about his cousins, the Smith brothers, and Charles Violet, which he subsequently published in book form as *Nova* (2020), an indispensable source on *Nova Espero* and her crew. These contacts have helped to bring alive this generation of sailors for me in a peculiarly direct way.

I would like to acknowledge that the original versions of the maps of Edward Allcard's voyage round South America in Chapter 4 were drawn by the late Kate Krabel, daughter of Edward and Clare Allcard. Thanks are due to Clare Allcard for permission to make use of these maps.

Dick Wynne of Lodestar books has been an exemplary editor both on the technical side and in providing the kind of support which all authors need. I could not have wished for better. I am grateful to Claudia Myatt for undertaking the cover and the illustrations (including the maps) which convey so skilfully the feel as well as the look of these ocean adventures.

Comments on various drafts by my brothers Philip and Ian, with whom sailing experiences and talk about sailing goes back decades, have been important to the completion of the book. Jim Sumberg's input is similarly underpinned by many years of shared interest in sailing and writing about sailing. Thanks are due also to Jim's brothers Jack and Dick for their supportive emails. I am grateful to Julia Jones for helpful comments on the Edward Allcard chapter.

I have learned much from all those mentioned above but the responsibility for any errors or shortcomings in the text is mine alone.

The book is dedicated to the memory of my father, John L. Crockatt (1920-2022), who got me and the whole family started in sailing, and whose bookshelves from the 1950s onwards introduced me to the wider world of voyaging which led ultimately to this book.

BIBLIOGRAPHY

The dates are of the editions referred to in this book, with dates of original publication, where necessary, in square brackets

Chapter 1 Eric and Susan Hiscock

Hiscock, Eric C. *Wandering Under Sail*. Oxford University Press, 2nd edition, 1948 [1939].

——. *I left the Navy*. Edward Arnold, 1945.

——. *Cruising Under Sail*. Oxford University Press, 1965 [1950]

——. *Around the World in Wanderer III*. Oxford University Press, 1956.

——.'If I did it again…', *Yachting World Annual 1957*. Iliffe.

——.'On the West Coast of Ireland'. *Yachting World Annual 1958*. Iliffe.

——. *Voyaging Under Sail*. Oxford University Press, 1970 [1959]

——. *Beyond the West Horizon*. Oxford University Press, 1963.

——. *Beyond the West Horizon*. BBC film available on thesailingchannel.tv.

——. *Atlantic Cruise in Wanderer III*. Oxford University Press, 1968.

——. *Sou'west in Wanderer IV*. Oxford University Press, 1973.

——. *Come Aboard*, Oxford University Press, 1978.

——. *Two Yachts, Two Voyages*. W W Norton, 1984.

—— (ed). *The Yachting Year, Volume 1: 1946-7*. Eric C Hiscock

—— (ed). *The Yachting Year, Volume 2: 1947-8*. Eric C Hiscock

Chapter 2 Peter and Anne Pye

Barton, Humphrey. *Atlantic Adventurers: Voyages in Small Craft*. Adlard Coles, 1962 [1953].

Pye, Peter.'Moonraker to Southwest Ireland: Summer 1946'. *The Yachting Year, Volume 1, 1946-7*. Eric C. Hiscock.

——.'Moonraker Sails to Ensanada de San Simon'. *The Royal Cruising Club: Season 1947*.

——. *Red Mains'l*. Herbert Jenkins, 1952.

——. *The Sea is for Sailing*, Rupert Hart-Davis, 1957.

——.'Moonraker in the Hebrides'. *Royal Cruising Club: Season 1960*.

——.'Hazards of the Sea'. *Yachting World Annual 1960*, Iliffe.

——. *The Peter Pye Omnibus* (containing *Red Mains'l, The Sea is for Sailing, Sail in a Forest, Backdoor to Brazil*). Ashford Publishing, 1986.

Chapter 3 Adlard Coles

Coles, Adlard. *In Broken Water*, Adlard Coles, 1956 [1925]
——. *Close Hauled*. Seeley, Service, 1926.
——. *Sailing Days*. Robert Ross, 1945.
——. *More Sailing Days*. Robert Ross, 1947.
——. *Sailing and Cruising*. Batsford, 1949 [1937].
——. *North Atlantic*. Robert Ross, 1951 [1950].
——. 'Ten Yachts'. *Yachting World Annual 1959*. Iliffe.
——. *Heavy Weather Sailing*. Adlard Coles, 1967 and later editions.
——. *Sailing Years: An Autobiography*, Granada, 1981.
Spinlove, Jane.'Adlard Coles', *The Marine Quarterly*, 35 (Autumn 2019).

Chapter 4 Edward Allcard

Allcard, Edward. *Single-Handed Passage*, Putnam, 1950.
——. *Temptress Returns*. Putnam, 1952.
——. *Voyage Alone*. Robert Hale, 1967.
——. *Solo Around Cape Horn and Beyond....* Imperator, 2016.
Allcard, Clare. *A Gypsy Life*. Ashford, Buchan, and Enright, 1994.
Barton, Humphrey. *Atlantic Adventurers: Voyages in Small Craft*. Adlard Coles, 1962 [1953].
Gray, Nicholas.'Edward Allcard'. *The Marine Quarterly*, 25 (Spring 2017).
——. *Astronauts of Cape Horn*. Conrad Press, 2018.
——.'Thomas Thor Tangvald'. *The Marine Quarterly*, 55 (Autumn 2024).
Schinas, Jill.'From 57 degrees to 57 degrees in '66', yachtmollymawk.com March 2017 (accessed 3 March, 2024).
Tilman, H W. *Mischief Goes South*. Hollis & Carter, 1968.

Chapter 5 Humphrey Barton

Barton, Humphrey. *The Sea and Me*. Robert Ross, 1952.
——. *Vertue XXXV*. Rupert Hart-Davis, 1955 [1950]
——. *Atlantic Adventurers: Voyages in Small Craft*. Adlard Coles. 1962 [1953]
MS Autobiographical notes supplied by Patricia Pocock, daughter of Humphrey Barton.

Chapter 6 Stanley and Colin Smith, Charles Violet

Barton, Humphrey. *Atlantic Adventurers: Voyages in Small Craft*. Adlard Coles, 1962 [1953].

Smith, Stanley. *The Smiths at Sea: The True Story of the Smith Brothers Adventurous Atlantic Crossing*. Robin Somes, 2006.

Smith, Stanley and Violet, Charles. *The Wind Calls the Tune*. Robert Ross, 1952.

Smith, Stanley. *October Potter*, Robin Somes, 2020.

Somes, Robin. *Nova: The History of Nova Espero*. Robin Somes, 2020.

Violet, Charles. *Solitary Journey: Nova Espero's Third Voyage*. Adlard Coles, 1954.

www.britishpathe.com/video/brothers-cross-atlantic-in-yacht

www.britishpathe.com/smith-brothers-cross-atlantic-in-yacht

www.britishpathe.com/smth-brothers-go-home

www.britishpathe.com/london-goes-all-festive

Chapter 7 George and Isabel Millar

Lowings, Ben. *The Chancellor, George Millar: A Life*. Taniwha Press, 2021.

Millar, George. *Isabel and the Sea*. William Heinemann, 1948.

——. *A White Boat from England*. William Heinemann, 1951.

——. *Oyster River: One Summer on an Inland Sea*. The Bodley Head, 1963.

——. *Road to Resistance: An Autobiography*. The Bodley Head, 1979.

Chapter 8 Ann Davison

Barton, Humphrey. *Atlantic Adventurers: Voyages in Small Craft*. Adlard Coles, 1962 [1953].

Davison, Ann. *Home Was an Island*. Peter Davies, 1952.

——. *Last Voyage*. William Heinemann, 1953.

——. *My Ship is So Small*. Peter Davies, 1956.

——. 'Honeymoon Cruise'. *Yachting World Annual 1957*. Iliffe.

King, Richard J. *Sailing Alone: A History*. Particular Books, 2023.

Moffat, Ellie. 'Ann Davison – the first woman to sail the Atlantic single-handed'. liverpoolmuseums.org.uk (accessed 3 March 2024).

New York Times Obituary, December 3, 2022 (accessed 16 September 2024)

Stickland, Katy. 'Ann Davison: transatlantic first'. Practical Boat Owner, November 15, 2023. pbo.co.uk (accessed 3 March, 2024)

Chapter 9 Patrick Ellam and Colin Mudie

Barton, Humphrey. *Atlantic Adventurers: Voyages in Small Craft*. Adlard Coles, 1953

Ellam, Patrick and Mudie, Colin. *Sopranino*. Rupert Hart-Davis, 1954.

Ellam, Patrick. *Things I Remember*. iUniverse, 2010.

——. *Wind Song*, iUniverse, 2010.

Junior Offshore Group, 'Patrick Ellam Obituary', jog.org.uk (accessed 3 March 2024)

Chapter 10 Miles and Beryl Smeeton

Clark, Miles. *High Endeavours: The Extraordinary Life and Adventures of Miles and Beryl Smeeton*. Grafton Books, 1991.

Gray, Nicholas. *Astronauts of Cape Horn*. Conrad Press, 2018.

Guzzwell, John. *Trekka Round the World*. Adlard Coles, 1963.

Smeeton, Miles. *Once is Enough*. Rupert Hart-Davis, 1959.

——. *Sunrise to Windward*. Rupert Hart-Davis, 1966.

——. *The Misty Islands*. Grafton Books, 1989 [1969].

——. *Because the Horn is There*. Grafton Books, 1987 [1970].

——. *The Sea Was Our Village*. Grafton Books, 1986 [1973]

Smeeton, Beryl. *Winter Shoes in Springtime*. Rupert Hart-Davis, 1961.

Chapter 11 John Guzzwell

Cox, Graham. 'The Small Boat That Casts a Long Shadow' southernwoodenboatsailing.com 26 August 2024 (accessed 15 October 2024)

Guzzwell, John. *Trekka Round the World*. Adlard Coles, 1963.

——. 16mm Footage of Tzu Hang www.gettyimages.co.nz/detail/video/cape-horn-sailing-round-the-horn-at-sea-news-footage/827433294 (accessed 15 October 2024).

Maritime Museum of British Columbia, 'John Guzzwell and Trekka' Obituary, 12 September 2024, mmbc.bc.ca (accessed 15 October 2024).

Smeeton, Miles. *Once is Enough*. Rupert Hart-Davis, 1959.

Additional Material

Barton, Humphrey. *Atlantic Adventurers: Voyages in Small Craft*. Adlard Coles, 1953

Bender, Mike. *A New History of Yachting*. The Boydell Press, 2017.

Chichester, Francis. *Atlantic Adventure*. George Allen and Unwin, 1962.

Chichester, Francis. *Gypsy Moth Circles the World*. Hodder and Stoughton, 1967.
Fox, Uffa. *Sailing Boats*. Newnes, 1959.
Gray, Nicholas. *Hillyard: The Man, His Boats, and their Sailors*. Lodestar Books, 2021.
Heaton, Peter. *The Singlehanders*. Michael Joseph, 1976.
Heikell, Rodney. *The Gift of a Sea: A Short History of Yachting in the Mediterranean*. Taniwha Press, 2019.
Hiscock, Eric C (ed). *The Yachting Year, Volume 1: 1946-7*. Eric C Hiscock
—— (ed). *The Yachting Year, Volume 2: 1947-8*. Eric C Hiscock
Jones, Julia. *Uncommon Courage: The Yachtsman Volunteers of World War II*. Adlard Coles, 2022.
Knox-Johnston, Robin. *A World of My Own*. Cassell, 1969.
King, Richard J. *Sailing Alone: A History*. Particular Books, 2023.
Kynaston, David. *Austerity Britain: 1945-51*. Bloomsbury, 2007.
Rose, Alec. *My Lively Lady*. Nautical Publishing Company, 1968.
Royal Cruising Club *Journal* (*Roving Commissions* from 1960), 1947, 1948, 1949, 1950, 1952, 1953, 1955, 1956, 1957, 1958, 1959, 1960, 1961, 1963, 1964, 1965, 1967, 1968, 1969, 1970.
Van de Wiele, Annie. *The West in My Eyes*. Rupert Hart-Davis, 1955.